KABBALAH
Key to Your Inner Power

MYSTICAL PATHS OF THE WORLD'S RELIGIONS

KABBALAH
Key to Your Inner Power

ELIZABETH
CLARE PROPHET

WITH PATRICIA R. SPADARO AND MURRAY L. STEINMAN

SUMMIT UNIVERSITY  PRESS®

I dedicate this book to the
magnanimous hearts of East and West
who have come together in the joy of Kabbalah

KABBALAH: *Key to Your Inner Power*
by Elizabeth Clare Prophet with Patricia R. Spadaro and Murray L. Steinman
Copyright © 1997 by Summit University Press. All rights reserved

Frontispiece: The Tetragrammaton, the most sacred name of God
in the Old Testament, from a Bible in Sefardi hand, 1385.

We are grateful to the publishers listed in the acknowledgment section
for permission to reproduce excerpts from copyrighted material
in their publications.

Library of Congress Catalog Card Number: 97-68656
ISBN: 0-922729-35-2

SUMMIT UNIVERSITY ☙ PRESS

This book is set in Baskerville.
Printed in the United States of America

08   07   06   05   04   8   7   6   5   4

CONTENTS

ILLUSTRATIONS

Figures

INTRODUCTION

There was light in my heart like lightning.... The world
changed into purity around me, and my heart felt as if I had
entered a new world.

MERKABAH SHELEMAH

If there is common ground
among the world's religions, it is to be found in mysticism.
Adventurers of the spirit, the mystics have dared to push
beyond the boundaries of orthodox tradition to pursue a
common goal: the direct experience of God. Mystics long to
see God, to know God, to be one with God—not in the hereafter, but in the here and now. And they teach that while you
may seek him in temple or mosque or church, you must ultimately find him in your own heart.

In *Kabbalah: Key to Your Inner Power,* I bring you a unique
interpretation of the Jewish mystical tradition known as
Kabbalah. Through the inspiration of mystics who have gone
before, I would remind you of your birthright as a son or

The Whirlwind: Ezekiel's Vision of the Cherubim and the Eyed
Wheels *by William Blake, c. 1805.*

daughter of God. That birthright, which is your unique portion of God himself, is right inside of you. Only you can unlock it.

What is Kabbalah? It is a subject so mysterious that for centuries only married men over the age of forty were allowed to study it.[1] That view is no longer universally held, and today both men and women of any age study the basic principles of Kabbalah. As one Kabbalist wrote, "From 1540 onward, the most important commandment will be for all to study [Kabbalah] in public, both old and young."[2]

The term *Kabbalah* refers to the mystical tradition of Judaism. No one knows exactly when Kabbalah first began. As a body of knowledge it sprang from mysticism but was not a continuation of any known mystical tradition. Jewish mystical practices can be traced back to around the first century B.C., and the movement known as Kabbalah first emerged around 1200 in Provence, France. But some Kabbalists say the first Kabbalistic revelations dated back to the time of Adam.

Although the teachings of Kabbalah are highly mystical, they are also highly practical. Jewish mystics received revelations about the creation of the universe that are strikingly similar to modern science's big bang theory. They came up with a language and a symbology to describe the qualities of God, our relationship to God, our spiritual purpose in life and the origins of evil.

Most importantly, Kabbalists developed an understanding of the mysteries of God that can help us unlock our spiritual power—the power that God endowed us with from the beginning. The power that launched the big bang.

How can we use the keys of Kabbalah to access that power? By becoming mystics ourselves. Yes, we have the right to become mystics in our own time, using the map that Kabbalists have left us.

The hallmark of Kabbalah is its diagram of the ten *sefirot* (divine emanations or aspects of God), which Kabbalists call

the Tree of Life. It is a blueprint not only for the inner workings of God but for the inner workings of the soul, for Kabbalah teaches that the Tree of Life is inside of you. It is the
link between you and God.

You can reconnect with the Tree of Life of the *sefirot*
through specific prayers, meditations and spiritual practices.
This book outlines some of these techniques. It also shares the
insights of the enlightened spiritual beings of East and West
known as the ascended masters, especially the insights of the
Ascended Master El Morya.

Through the centuries, El Morya has been illuminating
the inner path to God. He is truly one of the world's spiritual
giants. In one of his past lives he was the patriarch Abraham.
According to Kabbalistic tradition, the priest Melchizedek revealed to Abraham the teachings recorded in the *Sefer Yetzirah,*
an early mystical text that had enormous influence on Kabbalah. Abraham is the acclaimed father of Jew, Christian and
Muslim, and he still guides students of Kabbalah today.

In 1875 El Morya, then a renowned Eastern mahatma,
sponsored the Theosophical Society through Helena Blavat-
sky. In the 1920s and 1930s, as the Ascended Master El Morya,
he worked with Nicholas and Helena Roerich and the Agni
Yoga Society. He also played a role in the "I AM" Activity,
which was founded in the 1930s. Since 1952 he has worked
with my late husband, Mark L. Prophet, and myself to teach
seekers how to apply the truths of the world's mystical traditions to their own spiritual journeys.

El Morya has seen to it that the tradition of Kabbalah has
been preserved for all who have come to the place on their
spiritual path where they are ready for it. And he has looked
to the day when students of theosophy and mysticism would
receive the full interpretation of its mysteries.

In exploring mystical Judaism with the help of El Morya,
I discovered a core truth that I believe can help resolve the
central conflict between Jew and Christian, which is their

disagreement about who and what is Jesus Christ. The key is to be found in Kabbalah's teaching on *Tiferet,* one of the ten *sefirot.*

Kabbalah is filled with many profound and liberating concepts. Like each of the mystical paths of the world's religions, it gives us a unique perspective on how to contact the presence of God within and how to sustain a strong connection with that inner source of power. This is a sacred adventure, personal to each one of us. Yet we can learn from the great mystics of all time who have gone before.

My goal in *Kabbalah: Key to Your Inner Power* is to bring to life the path of the Jewish mystics—to share with you their joys and ecstasies, their sacred visions and their practical techniques for experiencing the sacred in everyday life. Together, let us explore the quest of these mystics and find out how we can apply what they learned to our own adventures in self-discovery.

Elizabeth Clare Prophet

Note: Because gender-neutral language can be cumbersome and at times confusing, we have used the pronouns *he* and *him* to refer to God or to the individual and *man* or *mankind* to refer to people in general. We have used these terms for readability and consistency, and they are not intended to exclude women or the feminine aspect of the Godhead. God is both masculine and feminine. We do, however, use the pronouns *she* and *her* to refer to the soul because each soul, whether housed in a male or a female body, is the feminine counterpart of the masculine Spirit.

How good it is to look upon
the face of the Divine Presence!

THE ZOHAR

CHAPTER ONE

THE BIG BANG
AND JEWISH MYSTICISM

The "Beginning" extended itself and made a palace for itself,
for glory and praise. There it sowed the holy seed....
  As soon as [the seed] entered, the palace filled up with light.
From that light are poured forth other lights, sparks flying
through the gates and giving life to all.

THE ZOHAR

In the beginning, there was a
seed of energy infinitely smaller than a proton, surrounded by
nothingness. In a fraction of a second, that seed exploded into
a blazing inferno of matter and energy that cooled and eventually formed galaxies, stars and planets.

That is the big bang theory—the creation myth of today's
cosmologists. Scientists first proposed the theory in the 1920s.
It fell from favor for a time, but in 1965 scientists discovered
microwave radiation that appeared to be from the big bang.
With that discovery, they were close to proving the theory, but

The big bang theory of modern scientists is strikingly similar to the
way some Jewish mystics described the Creation.

they needed more evidence of ripples in the seemingly uniform microwaves that surround everything in space. Then in 1989, NASA launched the Cosmic Background Explorer satellite (COBE) to look at the microwaves. The satellite enabled scientists to see how the universe was evolving when it was only 300,000 years old. What they saw were the imprints of tiny ripples in space that were caused by the big bang.

When the findings were announced on April 23, 1992, excitement in the scientific community could hardly have been higher. George Smoot, head of the research team that made the discovery, said that looking at radiation patterns just after the big bang was "like looking at God."[1] Celebrated physicist Stephen Hawking called it "the discovery of the century—if not of all time."[2]

These findings are a great breakthrough, not only for science but also for religion. For if the big bang theory is accurate, scientists may be confirming the creation myths of Jewish and Hindu mystics.

In the Beginning, There Was "Nothing"

Like modern scientists, Jewish mystics of the thirteenth century said that in the beginning there was nothing—nothing, that is, except the "divine nothingness," the hidden, transcendent God. The God of Genesis who "created the heaven and the earth" was not even manifest. The term the mystics used to describe God before creation was *Ein Sof.** *Ein Sof* means "without end," or "the Infinite." *Ein Sof* is the First Cause. It is ultimate reality—unmanifest, incomprehensible and indescribable.

The major text of the Jewish mystical tradition, the *Sefer ha-Zohar* (Book of Splendor), or Zohar, reveals a process of creation that started deep within the hidden recesses of the

---

*Hebrew terms can be transliterated a number of different ways. Their spelling and style have been standardized throughout this book. For pronunciations of key terms, see p. 251–52.

formless *Ein Sof* and unfolded as a series of emanations. Central to this drama was a single point that gave forth light and sowed "the holy seed," creating a cosmic conception that is depicted as an explosion of light. The Zohar says:

> As the will of the King *[Ein Sof]* began to come forth, He engraved signs in the uppermost pure light. Within the most hidden recesses a flame of darkness issued from the mysterious *Ein Sof,* a mist within formlessness, ringed about, neither white nor black nor red nor green, of no color at all. Only when measured did it bring forth light-giving colors. From deep within the flame there flowed a spring, out of which the colors were drawn below, hidden in the mysterious concealment of *Ein Sof.*
>
> It broke through and yet did not break through the ether surrounding it. It was not knowable at all until, by force of its breaking through, one hidden sublime point gave forth light. Beyond that point nothing is known. Therefore it is called "Beginning"—the first utterance of all.[3]. . .
>
> The "Beginning" extended itself and made a palace for itself, for glory and praise. There it sowed the holy seed in order to beget offspring for the benefit of the world.[4]. . .
>
> As soon as [the seed] entered, the palace filled up with light. From that light are poured forth other lights, sparks flying through the gates and giving life to all.[5]

The sixteenth-century Kabbalist Rabbi Isaac Luria came up with a different theory of the Creation. While other Kabbalists said the Creation began with an act of expansion, Luria started with the concept of contraction, or *tzimtzum.* According to Luria, *Ein Sof,* the Infinite, contracted itself to its centermost point and then withdrew to the sides of the circle surrounding that point in order to create a vacuum. The reason for *Ein Sof's* contraction was this: For the creation of the finite world to occur, the Infinite needed to define an empty space where its finite creation could exist separately from itself.

From the edge of the vacuum, *Ein Sof* issued a ray of light that launched all of creation. The sequence of events is complicated but, in essence, *Ein Sof's* light manifested ten divine emanations. Each emanation was to be preserved in a special vessel. Some of these vessels, however, were unable to hold that light and consequently shattered. As a result sparks of divine light, along with shards of the vessels, scattered, giving birth to the material world. You could say that what happened was Luria's own version of the big bang.

Like the cosmologies of scientists and Jewish mystics, one ancient Hindu creation myth begins with "nothing." The Creation Hymn of the Rig-Veda says:

> The non-existent was not,
> > the existent was not:
> > there was no realm of air,
> > no sky beyond it. . . .
> Death was not then,
> > nor was there aught immortal:
> > no sign was there,
> > the day's and night's divider.
> That One Thing, breathless,
> > breathed by its own nature:
> > apart from it was nothing whatsoever.
> Darkness there was:
> > at first concealed in darkness
> > this All was indiscriminated chaos.
> All that existed then was void and formless:
> > by the great power of Warmth was born
> > that Unit.
> Thereafter rose Desire in the beginning—
> Desire, the primal seed and germ of Spirit.
> Sages who searched with their heart's thought
> > discovered the existent's kinship
> > in the non-existent.[6]

The hymn sounds similar to the opening words of Genesis, the first book of the Old Testament. The Zohar, in fact, teaches that these verses symbolically describe the mystery of emanation from *Ein Sof.*

> In the beginning God created the heaven and the earth. And the earth was without form, and void; and darkness was upon the face of the deep. And the Spirit of God moved upon the face of the waters.
>
> And God said, "Let there be light": and there was light.
>
> And God saw the light, that it was good: and God divided the light from the darkness.
>
> And God called the light Day, and the darkness he called Night. And the evening and the morning were the first day.[7]

The dividing of the light from the darkness could also be compared to Luria's idea of contraction. At first, there was only darkness, nothingness. Then came the light, which launched the process of creation.

Just as science has confirmed the ideas behind Jewish and Hindu creation myths, so it has lent credibility to other statements Jewish mystics have made about the universe. Although scientists are still refining their calculations, they believe that the universe is somewhere between nine billion and sixteen billion years old. About seven hundred years ago, the mystic Rabbi Isaac of Acco reached the same conclusion. He said the universe was over fifteen billion years old, but he didn't base his conclusion on precise scientific measurement. In his book *The Treasury of Life,* he said he based it on the hidden oral tradition.[8]

If this mystical tradition can tell us something about the age of the universe, then perhaps it can solve other mysteries of the universe that scientists have not yet cracked.

Merkabah Mysticism: Visions of God's Throne-Chariot

Before we delve into the revelations of the Jewish mystical tradition known as Kabbalah, let us briefly explore the roots of Jewish mysticism that formed a prototype for the mystic quest.

A mystic is someone who seeks the direct experience of God and union with God. The first identifiable Jewish mystics practiced what is called *Merkabah* mysticism. It was based on the prophet Ezekiel's vision of the *Merkabah,* or throne-chariot, of God. For centuries, mystics have tried to reproduce his experience, recorded in Ezekiel 1:

> I looked and, behold, a whirlwind came out of the north, a great cloud, and a fire infolding itself, and a brightness was about it, and out of the midst thereof, as the colour of amber, . . .came the likeness of four living creatures. And this was their appearance; they had the likeness of a man. And every one had four faces, and every one had four wings.[9]

Within the cloud Ezekiel saw the chariot of God, a glowing object with huge wheels that appeared to be made of a stone like topaz. Beside each wheel was one of the four-winged creatures. Above the creatures was a vault of the heavens that gleamed like crystal.[10]

Ezekiel 1:26–28 records:

> And above [the vault of the heavens] that was over their heads was the likeness of a throne as the appearance of a sapphire stone: and upon the likeness of the throne was the likeness . . .of a man. . . .
>
> And I saw as the colour of amber, as the appearance of fire round about within it, from the appearance of [the man's] loins even upward, and from the appearance of his loins even downward, I saw as it were the appearance of fire, and it had brightness round about.
>
> As the appearance of the bow that is in the cloud in the day of rain, so was the appearance of the brightness round about. This was the appearance of the likeness of the glory of the LORD.

The vision of Ezekiel brings to mind Moses' encounter with the bush that burned but was not consumed.[11] For when Ezekiel looked up, he beheld a whirlwind that came out of the

north. He called it "a great cloud and a fire infolding itself."
He said that a brightness was about it and that out of the midst
of it was the color of amber.

God uses his sacred fire, as he did with Moses and Ezekiel,
to establish a rapprochement with his sons and daughters

The vision of the Merkabah *(the divine throne-chariot) that Ezekiel
saw by the river Chebar was the theme and goal of* Merkabah *mysticism, the earliest form of Jewish mysticism. (The vision of Ezekiel
from the Bear Bible, 1569.)*

whom he would call and anoint to fulfill his holy purposes. Through his inner walk with God, Ezekiel made himself ready, and the quality of his readiness was acceptable in the sight of the LORD. He was a mystic among mystics, a prophet to his people, one among a handful of those whom God called to be his messengers at critical junctures in history.

Imagine yourself as Ezekiel, a priest and captive in Babylon, settled with his fellow Judahites by the river Chebar. One day you look up and to your amazement the heavens are opened to you. The LORD allows you to see the seven planes of heaven and even himself. Imagine yourself in that exalted state before the LORD. The LORD speaks directly and expressly to you and he places his hand upon you.

This interchange happened to a son of man who walked the earth like you and me. What set him apart was the rightness of his heart, the integrity of his soul and the brilliance of his spirit. These are the qualities that all great mystics work to develop lifetime after lifetime.

Scholars are uncertain as to when *Merkabah* mysticism first emerged. Some say that the oldest evidence of this throne mysticism is in the First Book of Enoch, which may have been written as early as the third century B.C. It portrays Enoch's ascent to heaven and his vision of an exalted throne and the Glorious One who sat upon it.[12] A hymn-fragment in the Dead Sea Scrolls discovered at Qumran, dating back to about the first century B.C., describes cherubim blessing the "image of the throne-chariot."[13] Some have deduced from this that the Qumran community embraced some kind of *Merkabah* mysticism.

Merkabah mysticism began to flourish in the first century in Palestine. Some scholars claim that threads of *Merkabah* mysticism are even woven into Jesus' teachings and New Testament writings of the first century. They say, for instance, that Paul's account of being "caught up into paradise" in

II Corinthians 12 and John's vision recorded in Revelation 4 of the heavenly throne and him who sat upon it are *Merkabah* visions. Gnostic texts, which claim to record Jesus' secret teachings, also describe mystic ascents.[14]

Gershom Scholem (1897–1982), the leading modern authority on Jewish mysticism, says that the literary records of *Merkabah* mysticism can be traced through the tenth century. Scholem writes:

> The *Merkabah* mystics occupy themselves with all the details of the upper world, which extends throughout the seven palaces in the firmament of *aravot* (the uppermost of the seven firmaments), with the angelic hosts which fill the palaces, the rivers of fire which flow down in front of the Chariot, and the bridges which cross them. . . . But the main purpose of the ascent is the vision of the One Who sits on the Throne, "a likeness as the appearance of a man upon it above."[15]

Some *Merkabah* mystics who tried to replicate the vision and experience of Ezekiel had the sensation of going on a journey. Rabbi Akiba, a second-century sage and mystic, saw himself rising through the seven heavens and the seven palaces until he found himself standing before the throne of God. Hai Gaon, an eleventh-century Jewish religious leader, said the experience was a journey to the "innermost recesses of the heart."[16] The mystical journey to the innermost recesses of the heart is the treasure in common of every mystic who has sought and found the God within.

Some mystics wrote poems called *Merkabah* hymns. In these, they try to express their inexpressible experience. One hymn reads:

> O wreathed in splendor, crowned with crowns,
> O chorister of Him on high,
> Extol the Lord enthroned in flames
> For in the presence of the Presence,
> In the inmost glory

Of the inmost chambers
You set up your posts.
Your name He distinguished
    from His servant's name,
From the Chariot's servants He set you apart.
Him who the name of one of you mentions
The flame surrounds, a leaping fire,
Around him burning, glowing coals.[17]

The Jewish mystic who wrote this probed the presence of God and perhaps, like Ezekiel, was chosen to enter the higher walk with God step by step. Yet some in authority have tried, and still try, to prevent this intimate contact with God. They try to convince us that personal communication with him is not possible in the modern era.

Your Right to the Mystical Experience

Every religion has factions that are "antimystical," and Judaism is no exception. "The rabbinic tradition was always superstitious and fearful of any mystical movement that arose in Judaism," says Rabbi Devorah Jacobson. "From very early on, the rabbis went to extremes to put hedges and fences around mystical practice and belief."[18]

The rabbis claimed that *Merkabah* mysticism was dangerous. Jewish law warned against trying to replicate Ezekiel's experience. The public reading of Ezekiel's vision was banned except on the festival of Shavuot. Scholem says the rabbis sought to conceal the Book of Ezekiel by withdrawing it from general circulation and from the biblical canon.[19] But Jewish mystics kept practicing *Merkabah* mysticism, usually in secret, for a thousand years or so.

In the early rabbinic period (A.D. 70–200), the rabbis did acknowledge that in times past men had had direct, intimate contact with God. They believed that at the time of Adam and Eve, man communicated directly and easily with God and that

Abraham and Moses also had an intimate relationship with God. But the rabbis said that God had gradually stopped communicating directly with man and that an abyss now separated them, says David Ariel, an authority on Jewish mysticism.[20]

This was the rabbis' explanation for the abyss: The Jewish nation had less need of direct intercourse with God because God had provided them with the laws and teachings necessary to guide them. Also, man's sin had increased the distance between him and God.

"By the time of the early rabbinic period, the Jewish people [had] no expectations of having a direct, unmediated relationship with God," says Ariel.[21] Judaism became a legalistic religion that substituted the observance of the law, ritual and morality for direct mystical experience. Rabbinic Judaism, which developed into modern Judaism, has been suspicious of or even hostile to mysticism ever since.

Ariel notes that the rabbis did allow that in rare cases individuals could communicate directly with God. They believed in miracles and even recorded cases where people had mystical experiences. But the rabbis claimed that personal mystical experiences could not be used as a basis for legal decisions. "They rejected the legal admissibility of the individual religious experience, direct contact with God, or prophecy in favor of the indirect relationship with God that is possible through the fulfillment of the Torah,*" writes Ariel.[22]

While rabbis of the first and second centuries were organizing against mysticism, the early Christian Church was attacking the Christian Gnostics and others for their mystical teachings. "Just as the...principle of continuous revelation posed a serious threat to the Christian establishment, so too the *Merkabah* mystics, by resorting to ecstatic experience,

---

*The literal translation of the word *Torah* is "teaching," but it refers to Jewish law. In the narrow sense Torah refers to the Written Law (the Pentateuch, or the first five books of the Bible). In the broader sense Torah encompasses all the teachings of Judaism, including its written and oral laws, doctrines, philosophy, ethics, customs and ceremonies.

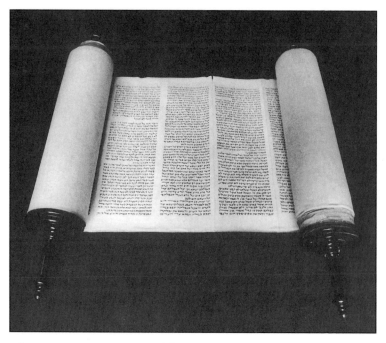

The esoteric interpretation of the written Torah, or Law, reveals the meaning of the hidden mysteries of God, according to Kabbalah. (Chinese Torah scroll from the seventeenth century.)

could have threatened the stability of rabbinic Judaism with its commitment to the sufficiency of Torah," writes scholar Philip Alexander.[23]

Direct and ongoing communion with God is what Abraham, Moses, the prophets, Jesus Christ, Gautama Buddha and all mystics were—and are—all about. Many were persecuted for the gifts and graces that God had bestowed upon them, but they persevered.

They showed us that God's revelations did not stop with the parting advice of the Buddha, with the last book of the Old Testament or with the final words of the New Testament. If our hearts and our spirits are receptive, we can discern the spiritual keys that will lead us to the direct experience of God.

One key is to follow in the footsteps of the adepts of every religion. We can touch the heart and soul of Judaism by learning from the patriarchs, the prophets and the Jewish mystics. They talked with God or his emissaries face to face. By using them as guides, we can unlock the door to the Tree of Life that is Kabbalah and access the power that is ours to use today as modern mystics.

The Origins of Kabbalah

The mystical movement known as Kabbalah emerged in about 1200 in Provence, France. Until the fourteenth century, Kabbalists used a variety of names for themselves and Kabbalah. The Kabbalists of Spain and Provence called Kabbalah "inner wisdom" and Kabbalists "the understanding ones."

Others called Kabbalists "the masters of knowledge," "those who know grace" and "masters of service," meaning those who know the true, inner way to the service of God. By the fourteenth century, Kabbalists called their teaching and movement almost exclusively Kabbalah.

Kabbalah means literally "tradition." It can also be translated as "receiving" or "transmitted teachings," for the Jewish mystics insisted that their doctrines had been transmitted orally, from generation to generation, for millennia.

The question of exactly when Kabbalah originated, writes Scholem, is "indisputably one of the most difficult in the history of the Jewish religion."[24] Jewish mystics have asserted that Kabbalah dates back to Adam. Scholem writes:

> Many Kabbalists denied the existence of any kind of historical development in the Kabbalah. They saw it as a kind of primordial revelation that was accorded to Adam or the early generations and that endured, although new revelations were made from time to time, particularly when the tradition had been either forgotten or interrupted. . . .It became widely accepted that the Kabbalah was the esoteric part of the Oral Law given to Moses at Sinai.[25]

Some scholars have rejected this point of view and have come up with two alternate theories. One holds that Kabbalah is a new creation of the twelfth or thirteenth century that emerged in reaction to the rationalism of Jewish philosophy. The other says that Kabbalah probably originated centuries earlier in the Greco-Roman world; it was passed on orally but it did not surface in Jewish literature until the Middle Ages.

Even the early Kabbalists were ambiguous about the source of their tradition. Rabbi Arthur Green writes: "The early Kabbalists in fact made a dual truth-claim for their esoteric readings of Scripture and their boldly new speculative ideas: they claimed both that they were ancient, the secret wisdom passed down by countless generations, only now given to public reading, and also that they were new, freshly revealed by heavenly voices to the sages of immediately preceding generations."[26] Some rabbis of the twelfth and thirteenth centuries, including the first identifiable Kabbalistic author, Isaac the Blind, even claimed that Elijah had revealed mystical secrets to them.

Kabbalah built on *Merkabah* mysticism and other forms of Jewish and non-Jewish mysticism, but it was not a mere continuation of these traditions. Certain of their ideas were quite novel. For example, Kabbalists adopted a new way of looking at God, creation, man and the purpose of life. One of the most important Kabbalistic innovations was to give the Torah an esoteric interpretation.

Kabbalists believe that it is through the words of the Torah that God reveals truths about himself and the universe. Green says:

> Because the majority of people would not be able to bear the great light that comes with knowing God, . . .divinity is revealed in the Torah in hidden form. Scripture is strewn with hints as to the true nature of "that which is above" and the mysterious process within divinity that led to the creation of this

Kabbalists teach that God revealed Kabbalah to Moses on Mount Sinai. Some claim that Kabbalah dates back even further, to the time of Adam, and that it has been transmitted orally for thousands of years. (Moses delivering the tablets of the Law to the Israelites, from a fourteenth-century Spanish Haggadah. National Museum, Sarajevo.)

world. Only in the exoteric, public sense is revelation primarily a matter of divine *will*, teaching the commandments man is to follow in order to lead the good life. The inner, esoteric revelation is rather one of divine *truth*, a network of secrets about the innermost workings of God's universe.[27]

The orthodox rabbis concentrated on man's relationship with God and how man could fulfill the commandments set forth in scripture. They did not attempt to explore the nature of the Godhead or the divine realm—the very mysteries that Kabbalists sought to penetrate through an active and practical mysticism.

"The Zohar knows no bounds in its extravagant praise of mysticism; at every opportunity it reverts to an expression of its great worth," writes Isaiah Tishby in his definitive anthology *The Wisdom of the Zohar*. Kabbalists believe that the goal of the soul living in this world is to realize "that supreme perception which it enjoyed when it resided in the heights of Heaven." To the Kabbalist, says Tishby, "knowledge of the science of mysticism is the main bridge leading to the attachment of the soul to God."[28]

Let us, then, meet the masters who codified the secrets of Kabbalah.

Moses de León and Isaac Luria: Mystic Geniuses of Kabbalah

It gives me great pleasure to introduce you to Rabbi Moses de León (1240–1305), of León, Spain. He is the mystic genius who wrote the Zohar, the first book to clearly delineate Kabbalistic thought. Scholars agree that de León was one of the most important figures in the development of Kabbalah.

Rabbi Moses de León, wherever you are, I bow to the light of *Ein Sof* within your heart!

"The Zohar must be viewed as a great compendium of all the kabbalistic thought that had come before it, reworked and integrated into the author's own all-embracing poetic imagination," writes Green. "Ideas contained in bare hints or clumsy expressions in the generations before him now spring forth, full-blown as it were, as a part of the ancient wisdom."[29]

Many traditional Kabbalists attribute the Zohar to Rabbi Simeon ben Yohai, a second-century mystic. But through painstaking literary investigation, Gershom Scholem showed that the Zohar was written by Moses de León in the thirteenth century. While scholars are almost certain that de León wrote the Zohar, many of them have pondered whether he had help from higher and more ancient sources.

"One could reasonably believe the author had felt himself possessed by a spirit other than his own as he was writing it," writes Green. "Could de León have felt that Rabbi Simeon was speaking *through* him, that he was the mere vessel the ancient sage had chosen for the revelation of his secrets?"[30] Green also wonders whether de León saw himself as the reincarnation of Rabbi Simeon. Daniel Matt, professor of Jewish studies at the Graduate Theological Union, says, "Parts of the Zohar may have been composed by automatic writing. . . . Certain passages in the Zohar are anonymous and appear as utterances of a heavenly voice."[31]

The Zohar was once accepted in the canon of orthodox texts. The Zohar "succeeded in establishing itself for three centuries, from about 1500 to 1800, as a source of doctrine and revelation equal in authority to the Bible and Talmud,*" says Scholem. "This is a prerogative that can be claimed by no other work of Jewish literature."[32]

It also gives me great pleasure to introduce you to the second mystic genius of Kabbalah, Rabbi Isaac Luria. He was born in Jerusalem in 1534. Luria was known as the *Ari,* an acronym that stands for "the divine Rabbi Isaac."

Rabbi Luria, wherever you are, I bow to the light of *Ein Sof* within your heart!

According to legend, the prophet Elijah appeared to

---

*The Talmud is the authoritative body of written Jewish tradition.

Luria's father and prophesied the birth of a son who would reveal the teaching of Kabbalah. Luria was just eight when his father died, and the boy moved to Cairo with his mother. He was quickly recognized as a prodigy in the study of the Talmud. While he was a young man, Luria began an eight-year study of the Zohar. In order to penetrate its deepest mysteries, he became an ascetic, living in seclusion in a small cottage near the Nile. There he meditated and continued to study the Zohar five days a week, returning to the city to see his family only for the Sabbath. Legend has it that after Luria spent two years in study, prayer and fasting, Elijah appeared to him and initiated him.

Elijah commanded Luria to go to the Holy Land, and Luria arrived in the Palestinian city of Safed in 1570. At that time Safed was the home of a thriving spiritual community. Author Perle Epstein writes, "Safed is a natural mystic's retreat, . . . an ethereal town that could just as well have been a tiny Tibetan enclave or the setting for an isolated monastery in the Himalayan foothills, a Jewish Shangri-La."[33]

The leading Kabbalists of the time were living in Safed. They quickly recognized Luria as their teacher. He taught in Safed for a little less than two years and then died suddenly in 1572 at the age of thirty-eight. He wrote down little of his own teachings, but the writings of his disciples that summarize his work consist of thousands of pages.

Aside from his intricate teachings on Kabbalistic theology, prayer and meditation, Luria taught a pragmatic mysticism. He instructed his followers that it was essential for them to cultivate specific spiritual qualities, especially joy. He also admonished his students to avoid the sin of anger. Luria said that while other sins harm the "limbs" of the soul, the sin of anger harms the entire soul. Anger, he said, also causes the highest level of the soul to leave a person, and an angry person is filled with a "strange god."[34]

The consequences of anger in anyone are indeed grave. Those who unleash unbridled anger can actually lose a fragment or fragments of their soul on the spot.

If day upon day you do not allow vortices of anger to erupt from within and overtake the citadel of your being, you can become a vessel of Divine Love. And when you are able to emerge from encounters with your karma or your psychology without erupting in waves of anger, you will be ready for the ultimate encounter, the one all mystics seek: the encounter with your Higher Self.

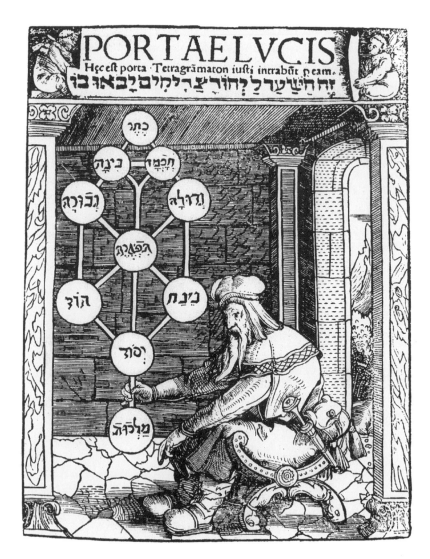

THE INNER FACES
OF GOD

*Ten sefirot out of Nothingness. Ten and not nine, ten and
not eleven. Understand with wisdom, and be wise with
understanding. Test them and explore them.*

THE SEFER YETZIRAH

Remember *Ein Sof,* the un-
manifest, the indescribable, the Infinite? If *Ein Sof* is indescribable and unknowable, then we have to describe and know
God in some other form. Kabbalists say that *Ein Sof* reveals
itself through ten aspects of God's being called *sefirot.* (The
singular form of *sefirot* is *sefirah.*)

The *sefirot* are the spheres that emanated from *Ein Sof's*
big bang. They form a pattern for both divine and human
action and interaction. Kabbalists diagram this pattern as it

*Jewish mystics diagrammed the ten aspects of God as a network
of ten spheres and called it the Tree of Life (left). The Tree of Life is
a blueprint for the inner workings of God, the universe and the soul.
(Engraving by Paulus Ricius, from* Portae Lucis *by Rabbi Joseph
Gikatilla, 1516.)*

extends downward from *Ein Sof* and call it the Tree of Life. They also depict the *sefirot* in the form of a man, the archetype of God's creation that is called *Adam Kadmon.* I will start by exploring the Tree of Life, beginning with *Ein Sof.*

Ein Sof: The Cause above All Causes

A fourteenth-century Kabbalistic text tells us that *"Ein Sof . . . is not hinted at in the Torah, the Prophets, the Writings, or the words of our Rabbis, may their memory be a blessing; but the Masters of Service [the Kabbalists] have received a little hint of It."*[1]

Kabbalists say that *Ein Sof* is beyond description or comprehension because the finite mind cannot contain the Infinite. We can only approximate or gain an equivalency of the Divine Mind. Kabbalists call *Ein Sof* the "Cause above all causes" and the "root of all roots," but, the Zohar says, "no trace may be found, nor can thought by any means or method reach it."[2]

The concept of an indefinable, limitless God that is at the root of all existence has its parallel in other world religions. In Taoism the transcendental First Cause is called the Tao (literally "Way"). Like *Ein Sof,* the Tao is undefinable and unknowable, eternal and nameless. The Tao Te Ching, the most sacred text of Taoism, says, "The Nameless is the origin of Heaven and Earth.[3] . . . As for the nature of the Way [the Tao]—it is shapeless and formless. . . . The Way is Great but has no name."[4]

In Hinduism, the Kena Upanishad says of Brahman, the Absolute, "Neither mind nor eye, neither ear nor speech, can tell us anything about Him, because neither the eye nor the ear nor the mind can reach Him, but He alone is the agent operative through all these organs. . . . But He, in his own nature, cannot be grasped by any one of these."[5]

Likewise, the Christian mystic Pseudo-Dionysius writes: "The pre-eminent cause of all that is perceived by the intelligence is not anything perceived by the intelligence. . . . He is

. . . not word, not intellection, . . . not definable, not nameable, not knowable."[6]

Even though *Ein Sof* is unknowable, Kabbalists have a lot to say about it. Some call it the "Primal Will" or the "will of all wills." Others say it is "pure Thought" or "the Thought which has no end or finality." So ineffable is *Ein Sof* that it first had to create levels or stages of itself before the creation of our world could begin. Here is where the *sefirot* come in.

The Sefirot: Divine Emanations

Why did God create the *sefirot*? Isaiah Tishby says Kabbalists teach that "*Ein Sof,* the hidden God, dwelling in the depths of His own being, seeks to reveal Himself, and to unleash His hidden powers. His will realizes itself through the emanation of rays from His light, which break out of their concealment and are arrayed in the order of the *sefirot,* the world of divine emanation."[7]

The Jewish mystics developed around *Ein Sof* and the *sefirot* a religious language rich in symbols and imagery. Kabbalists have used many synonyms for the *sefirot,* including lights, names, stages, crowns, mirrors, pillars, powers, garments, gates, sources and inner faces of God. Each name describes another aspect of the nature and function of the *sefirot.* Rabbi Moses Cordovero, one of the great Kabbalists of the sixteenth century, says that before *Ein Sof* emanated the *sefirot,* it knew them as "inner lights."[8]

Some Kabbalists say the word *sefirot* comes from the Hebrew *sappir* ("sapphire" or "sparkling lights") because the *sefirot* illumine us about God. Others say *sefirot* derives from the Hebrew *saper* ("to tell"), meaning that they tell us about God.

Rabbi Aryeh Kaplan explains that the word *saper,* and thus the word *sefirot,* has three basic connotations: (1) to declare or express, (2) to record or decree, and (3) to delineate or count. He writes:

The first function of the *sefirot* is to express God's greatness. Through them we can meditate on God and speak of Him.

Secondly, it is through the *sefirot* that God expresses His providence over creation, issuing decrees and recording events. It is in this context that the *sefirot* are God's "Book.". . .

Finally, the *sefirot* delineate God's glory, bringing it into the finite realm of number. Although God is infinite, and in potential encompasses an infinite number of basic concepts, the *sefirot* limit these to ten.[9]

The term *sefirot* first appeared in the *Sefer Yetzirah* (the "Book of Formation" or the "Book of Creation"), the oldest known Hebrew text on cosmology. "Many Kabbalists," writes author Charles Poncé, "consider that [the *Sefer Yetzirah*] is the foundation stone of their study and that without it the mysteries of Kabbalism may not be understood."[10]

Tradition says that the priest Melchizedek revealed the teachings recorded in the *Sefer Yetzirah* to the patriarch Abraham, who either recorded them himself or transmitted them orally to his sons. Author Z'ev ben Shimon Halevi writes:

> According to tradition, Melchizedek, the King of Righteousness and of Salem, and priest of the Most High God, initiated Abraham into the knowledge of the esoteric Teaching which concerns man, the universe and God. Melchizedek . . . is traditionally called a son of God abiding for ever. . . . Out of this encounter between a celestial and a terrestrial man came the spiritual line known later as Kabbalah.[11]

Read the description of the *sefirot* as it is taught in the *Sefer Yetzirah:*

> Ten is the number of the ineffable *sefirot.* . . . The beginnings of the *sefirot* have no ending and a boundless origin; they are each vast distances. . . . The Lord the only God, the Faithful King, rules all these from his holy seat, for ever and ever. Their countenance is like the scintillating flame flashing in lightning, invisible and boundless. . . . Their ending is as their

The priest Melchizedek revealed the teachings of an early mystical text, the Sefer Yetzirah, *to Abraham, according to Kabbalistic tradition. The* Sefer Yetzirah *("Book of Creation") describes the ten* sefirot *(divine emanations of the Godhead), a concept that was later developed by Kabbalists. (Abraham paying tithes to Melchizedek, enamel plaque by Nicholas de Verdun, from altarpiece, Klosterneuburg, Austria, twelfth century.)*

beginning. They are as brilliant flame flowing upwards from the surface of a roaring coal.[12]

The *Sefer Yetzirah* depicts the *sefirot* as divine emanations, and the Zohar describes them as attributes of God or agencies through which God reveals himself. In other words, each part of God has a specific name with a specific vibration that we can access through the universal 'computer' of the Mind of God. Each *sefirah* is a different way of perceiving and receiving God.

Rabbi Moses Luzzatto, an eighteenth-century Kabbalist, depicts the *sefirot* as transformers that decrease the intensity of the light of *Ein Sof.* He writes:

> The ten *sefirot* (emanations) act as "veils"—ten stages, vessels or degrees which the Creator issued to serve as channels through which His bounty might be transmitted to man: restraining that bounty to the extent that the worlds shall not disappear because of the too great abundance of Light, yet providing a sufficient amount of it to ensure their continued existence. He therefore made ten vessels in order that the bounty, in traversing them, would become so densified that the lower creations could bear it.[13]

The *sefirot* represent not only the inner workings of God but the ongoing workings of his universe—and the relationship between the two. Poncé describes the *sefirot* as "vehicles through which change and transformation take place. . . . The *sefirot* are a bridge connecting the finite universe with the infinite God."[14]

One God or Many?

Kabbalists disagree about the relationship between the *sefirot* and *Ein Sof.* Some say the *sefirot* are the vessels or instruments that *Ein Sof* created to accomplish its work. Others describe the *sefirot* as the essence of *Ein Sof.* They say that the *sefirot* and *Ein Sof* are identical and cannot be separated. In an attempt to reconcile the dispute, Cordovero teaches that the *sefirot* are

God's essence and God's instruments at the same time, the pre-eminent view of later Kabbalists.

Some have charged the Kabbalists with embracing a dualism bordering on polytheism and challenged them to explain how the ten *sefirot* fit into the Jewish mandate of monotheism. "The Oneness of God was a vital issue," writes Daniel Matt. "The traditional Jewish declaration of God's unity is the Shema, Deuteronomy 6:4: 'Hear O Israel! *YHVH* [the LORD], our God, *YHVH* [the LORD] is one.'"[15]

The Zohar defends the unity of *Ein Sof* and its emanations and says that the *sefirot* are the essence of the Godhead, inseparable from him in any way: "It is they, and they are It, like a flame attached to a burning coal, and there is no division there."[16] The Zohar also describes the relationship between *Ein Sof* and the *sefirot* as being "like a lamp from which lights spread out on every side, but when we draw near to examine these lights, we find that only the lamp itself exists."[17] "The *sefirot*," writes Gershom Scholem, "emanate from *Ein Sof* in succession—'as if one candle were lit from another without the Emanator being diminished in any way.'"[18]

Luzzatto also makes the case for the oneness of *Ein Sof* and the *sefirot*. "All the *sefirot* are nothing but the Light of the Infinite Himself," he says. "There is no difference between Him and the *sefirot*—only He is the Cause and they are the effect, or the result. The expression 'He clothes them' means that His will perpetually animates the *sefirot* in order to maintain them as channels, through which He controls and governs the world."[19]

The Kabbalistic conception of the oneness of the *sefirot* is similar to the Christian concept of the Trinity. Matt writes:

> The Trinity consists of three persons of God, all coequal, co-eternal, and indivisible. It is considered a profound mystery of faith. The *sefirot* are ten manifestations of the Infinite, ten aspects of the divine personality. . . . They are called "the mystery

of faith." [Thirteenth-century Kabbalist Abraham] Abulafia offers this revealing criticism: "The masters of the *kabbalah* of *sefirot* intended to unify the Name and flee from the Trinity, but they have made it ten! As the gentiles say, 'He is three and the three are one,' so certain kabbalists believe and say that Divinity is ten *sefirot* and the ten are one."[20]

The Creation of the Tree of Life

How did the One, *Ein Sof,* become the ten *sefirot?* Luzzatto says that *Ein Sof* limited its own infinity to create the *sefirot:*

> When there arose in the Creator's most pure and simple will the desire to manifest creation (which was to receive His Light in measured and limited proportion), He Emanated His Light in a successive pattern of descending degrees until the present creation came into being. He did this . . . by both concealing His infinite, immeasurable Light and concurrently extending it and sending it forth. By this process of extension, which signifies delimitation, the *sefirot* came into being.[21]

One thirteenth-century Kabbalistic text says that the first *sefirah, Keter,* "receives from the root *[Ein Sof]* without any interruption in a subtle whisper. It emanates and pours forth from its reservoir upon the other crowns *[sefirot]* which are always close to its emanation."[22]

The Zohar describes a complex pattern of emanation.[23] First, out of the mystery of *Ein Sof* issues a spark or flame of darkness. It is described as darkened because it is concealed. From this spark a fountain bursts forth that is surrounded by what is translated as "air" or an "ethereal aura," which is *Keter.* The fountain is not knowable until, by the force of its breaking through the aura *[Keter]* that surrounds it, a single, hidden point shines. This point is the second *sefirah, Hokhmah.*

After *Keter* emanates *Hokhmah, Hokhmah* yearns to cleave to its source, *Keter,* and to be illuminated by it. But a curtain is drawn between them. Tishby says the partition is erected "so that the essential being of *[Hokhmah]* should not suffer any damage and the process of emanation be interrupted."[24]

As I see it, the barrier between these two *sefirot* is like the veil in the Tabernacle that hung between the Holy of Holies (which only the high priest could enter) and the holy place (where the other priests were allowed). *Hokhmah* is of a lower vibration than *Keter,* and thus *Hokhmah* cannot pierce the veil and reenter *Keter.* But the strength of *Hokhmah's* desire magnetizes a ray of light through the curtain and causes *Hokhmah* to shine with a secret illumination.

Hokhmah then extends itself and makes a "palace," which is the third *sefirah, Binah.* *Hokhmah's* light, or seed, enters *Binah's* palace, or womb. A cosmic conception follows, which the Zohar depicts as an explosion of light, as I cited in chapter 1: "As soon as [the seed] entered, the palace filled up with light. From that light are poured forth other lights, sparks flying through the gates and giving life to all."[25] The big bang theory of creation could not have better paralleled the teaching of the Zohar.

The Zohar depicts *Binah* as a "river that wells up and flows out."[26] Tishby says the seven remaining *sefirot* "are represented as being within *Binah* like an embryo in a mother's womb, and, as the process of emanation continues, they are emanated through the mystery of birth as seven children."[27]

These are the names of the ten *sefirot* that emanate from *Ein Sof* and make up the Tree of Life: *Keter* (Crown); *Hokhmah* (Wisdom), *Binah* (Understanding), *Hesed* (Love/Mercy), *Gevurah* (Justice/Judgment), *Tiferet* (Beauty/Compassion), *Netzah* (Victory), *Hod* (Splendor/Majesty), *Yesod* (Foundation) and *Malkhut* (Kingdom). *Malkhut* is also known as *Shekhinah* (Divine Presence), the feminine aspect of God. (fig. 1)

The *sefirot* form a dynamic chain through which the hidden forces of God flow. *Malkhut/Shekhinah,* as the last *sefirah* in that chain, channels the divine energy downward to our

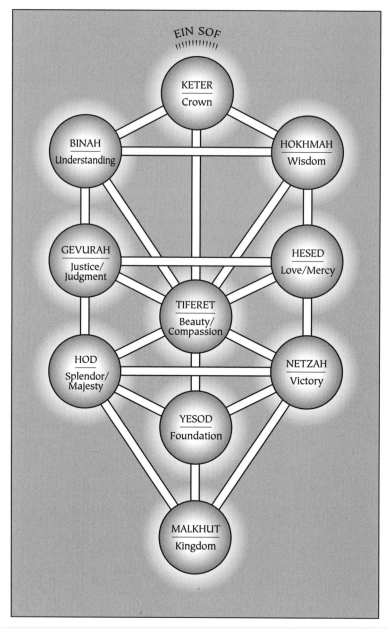

FIGURE 1. *The Tree of Life*

world, and it is this energy source that sustains and nurtures us. *Malkhut* is also the gateway we must pass through as we begin our ascent up the ladder of the *sefirot* back to *Ein Sof.* It is through her that we can begin to access the power of God in the Tree of Life.

Was Jesus showing John the Revelator the Kabbalistic Tree of Life in Revelation 22? When Jesus dictated that chapter to his disciple and scribe, he showed him "a pure river of water of life, clear as crystal, proceeding out of the throne of God and of the Lamb. In the midst of the street of it, and on either side of the river, was there the tree of life, which bare twelve manner of fruits, and yielded her fruit every month: and the leaves of the tree were for the healing of the nations."[28]

In chapter 3, I explore some of Jesus' statements recorded in scripture that seem to allude to the mystical teachings of Kabbalah. For now, I will say that I believe Jesus knew the principles of Kabbalah and that he taught them to his innermost circle.

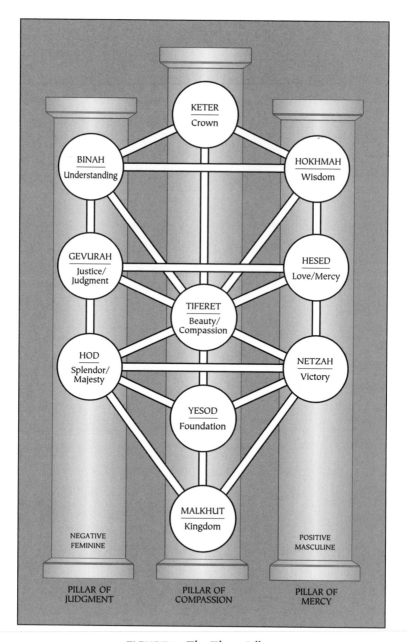

FIGURE 2. *The Three Pillars*

CHAPTER THREE

THE TREE OF LIFE:
THE SEFIROT UNVEILED

*What is this Tree that you speak of? All the Powers of the
Blessed Holy One are arranged in a series of layers like a Tree,
and as a tree brings forth fruit when watered so do the Divine
Powers when charged with the water of the Blessed Holy One.
    What is the water of the Blessed Holy One? It is wisdom.
It is the souls of the righteous.*

THE BAHIR

Kabbalists accomplished an
amazing feat. They devised a way of understanding the vast
personality of God, of which you and I are a part, by breaking
it down into ten aspects, the *sefirot*. Then they grouped these
aspects together in different combinations and assigned qualities to those groupings.

We can learn how to access the power of the *sefirot* by
becoming acquainted with these facets of God's personality
and by understanding what they meant to the mystics who
tapped into their power and charted them on the Tree of Life.

Kabbalists group the *sefirot* into three columns, or pillars,
within the Tree of Life. (fig. 2) The right-hand column of the

tree is made up of *Hokhmah, Hesed* and *Netzah*. The *sefirot* in this column have a masculine and positive polarity. The left-hand column is made up of *Binah, Gevurah* and *Hod*. The *sefirot* in this column have a feminine and negative polarity. The central column is made up of *Keter* at the top, *Tiferet* at the center, then *Yesod* and *Malkhut* at the bottom.

The three columns take on qualities of their own. Kabbalists call the column on the right the Pillar of Mercy. They call the column on the left the Pillar of Judgment or the Pillar of Severity. These two columns are associated with the opposing forces in the universe. Kabbalists teach that the right pillar embodies the force of expansion and the left pillar embodies the force of constraint. These extremes are balanced by the attribute of Compassion, which is embodied by the *sefirot* in the center column, called the Pillar of Compassion or the Pillar of Equilibrium. The balancing and harmonizing of the extremes of Mercy and Judgment through Compassion is what sustains our world.

These opposite but complementary forces of expansion and constraint are intended to be in equilibrium, like the *yin* and *yang* of the Great Tao. "There is not a Light emitted by the Emanator," writes Moses Luzzatto, "which is not inclusive of Mercy, Judgment and Compassion. These Lights issue neither separately, nor individually; instead, they emerge from the three pillars already intermingled. It is this fusion of the principles of Judgment, Mercy and Compassion that supervises the governing of the world."[1]

The First Triad: Keter, Hokhmah and Binah

Another way Kabbalists group the *sefirot* on the Tree of Life is to divide them into three triads, each of which expresses a unique element of the personality of God. The first triad is made up of *Keter, Hokhmah* and *Binah* and represents the realm of the intellect. (fig. 3)

The first triad "symbolizes the dynamic function of a thought process anterior to the world and [is] therefore an archetypal model," writes Charles Poncé. "It represents, in other words, the thought process of God."[2] God has a thought process and *he is thinking through you now.* This teaching reminds me of the admonishment of the apostle Paul: "Let this mind be in you which was also in Christ Jesus."[3] In other words, let the mind that is *Keter, Hokhmah* and *Binah* be God's mind thinking through you and realizing the object of his thought in you.

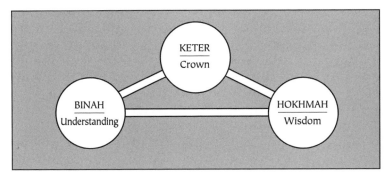

FIGURE 3. *The First Triad*

Keter (Crown) is the highest *sefirah* on the Tree of Life. *Keter* and *Ein Sof* are coeternal and identical or nearly identical. Like *Ein Sof, Keter* was conceived of as "Nothing," even as it was conceived of as "Will." In the Zohar, the manifestation of "the infinite will" in *Keter* is called "the Holy Ancient One."

Some Kabbalists say that because of its proximity to *Ein Sof, Keter* cannot be known. A thirteenth-century Kabbalistic text says, "Supernal *Keter* is a world hidden unto itself."[4] The Zohar calls *Keter* "the will that cannot ever be known or grasped, the most recondite head in the world above."[5]

While some Kabbalists say *Keter* cannot be known, others give it names and qualities and debate its relationship to *Ein*

Sof. Arthur Green says: "Kabbalistic history is filled with ongoing debate as to the nature of *Keter* and its relationship to *Ein Sof*, a debate in some ways reminiscent of the arguments about the eternity of the Second Person in early Christianity. This seems to be the Zohar's position: *Keter* is eternally present within *Ein Sof*, but is not to be identified with it."[6]

The Kabbalists, says Green, describe *Keter* as "the catalyst of all being, but not yet a thing in itself."[7] The Zohar says *Keter* "includes everything" and is "the sum of all, . . . a generality with no particular."[8] A thirteenth-century hymn to *Keter* reads:

> Everything is in it, for the internal powers
> of the *sefirot* are in it. . . .
> The constitution of everything is in *Keter*.
> There is no front or back,
> right or left in this *sefirah*.
> It is called 'Indifferent Unity'.[9]

'Indifferent Unity' is like the Buddhist concept of Undifferentiated Suchness. In Buddhism, the term *Suchness (Tathatā)* is used to convey a reality that is beyond description. This reality is the Absolute—the ultimate, unconditioned and true nature of all things. The Absolute, however named or defined, is present as the seed truth in all religions.

Hokhmah (Wisdom) is the second *sefirah*. It is the highest *sefirah* on the Pillar of Mercy, the right-hand column of the Tree of Life. (fig. 2) *Hokhmah* is the first, or primal, point of creation. It came into manifestation through an act of will by *Ein Sof* and *Keter*.

Although *Hokhmah* is the second *sefirah*, Daniel Matt says Kabbalists call it "Beginning" because "*Keter* is eternal and has no beginning" and because *Hokhmah* "is the first ray of divine light to appear outside of *Keter*."[10] The Zohar says *Hokhmah* is the divine Thought and, like *Keter*, it is unknowable: "Thought is the beginning of all; and in that it is thought, it is internal, secret and unknowable."[11]

Hokhmah contains the blueprint and all the archetypes of creation. "When the most secret of secrets *[Ein Sof* or *Keter]* sought to be revealed," says the Zohar, "He made, first of all, a single point *[Hokhmah],* and this became thought. He made all the designs there; He did all the engravings there."[12] In other words, says Green, "Everything that is ever to be already exists in that infinitesimal point as it emerges within God; as the first defined Being, . . . *[Hokhmah]* becomes the source of all further being."[13]

Scientists talk about that single point of energy just before the big bang. We could suppose that, as Kabbalah says, everything that was to come into being existed in that single point, *Hokhmah,* just before the explosion of light took place.

Hokhmah is the archetype of masculine, generative activity and is often called *Abba,* or Father. Thus *Hokhmah,* or Wisdom, is the Father of all creation.

Author Z'ev ben Shimon Halevi sees *Hokhmah* in the divine mind and human mind as the "inner intellect." He says *Hokhmah* is "experienced by human beings as the flash of genius, inspiration or revelation.[14] . . . From this potent area the most profound ideas and observations come. . . . Originality is its hallmark."[15]

Binah (Understanding) is the third member of the first triad. *Binah* is the upper *sefirah* on the Pillar of Judgment or Severity, the left-hand column of the Tree of Life. (fig. 2) This *sefirah* holds in check the expansive nature of *Hokhmah.*

Like some Hebrew words, *Binah* does not translate easily into English. In addition to "Understanding," *Binah* can be translated as "Intelligence," "Insight" or "Discernment." The real meaning of the Hebrew word *Binah* lies within that cluster of English words.

While *Hokhmah* is masculine and active, *Binah* is feminine and receptive. As *Hokhmah* is called *Abba,* or Father, *Binah* is called *Imma,* or Mother. She is the Divine Mother or Supernal

FIGURE 4. *The tips of the Hebrew letter* shin *represent the first three* sefirot—Keter, Hokhmah *and* Binah.

Mother. *Hokhmah* and *Binah* are the original parents. Together they created the seven lower *sefirot* and then all creation, animate and inanimate. Kabbalists teach that just as *Binah* is the womb of the Great Mother from which all creation came forth, she is also the loving one to whom all will return at the end of time.

The first triad of *Keter, Hokhmah* and *Binah* represents the head in the human body and it also corresponds to the Hebrew letter *shin.* (fig. 4) *Shin* looks like a crown, the meaning of the word *Keter.* Kabbalists used the tips of the letter *shin* to represent *Keter, Hokhmah* and *Binah.* They also associated *shin* with the element of fire. The *Sefer Yetzirah* says that the heavens were created from fire.[16] The first triad of *Keter, Hokhmah* and *Binah* gives birth to the second triad.

The Second Triad: Hesed, Gevurah and Tiferet

The second triad is made up of *Hesed, Gevurah* and *Tiferet* and represents God's ethical perfection and moral power. (fig. 5) As the first triad represents the realm of the intellect, the second represents the realm of the soul.

Hesed is the fourth *sefirah.* The meaning of *Hesed,* like *Binah,* does not easily translate into English. It is usually translated as "Love" or "Mercy," but it can also be translated as "Grace" or "Loving-kindness." Kabbalists put the fourth *sefirah* in the center of the pillar that bears its name, the Pillar of Mercy. (fig. 2) They sometimes called the fourth *sefirah Gedullah* (Greatness) instead of *Hesed.*

The fifth *sefirah* is *Gevurah,* meaning "Power," "Strength" or "Severity." It is frequently called *Din,* meaning "Judgment" or "Justice." *Gevurah* is located in the center of the pillar that bears its name, the Pillar of Judgment or Severity. (fig. 2) Halevi teaches that together *Hesed* and *Gevurah* govern the level of emotion.[17]

Hesed and *Gevurah* act as a complementary pair. They represent the extremes of Love/Mercy *(Hesed)* on the one hand and Justice/Judgment *(Gevurah)* on the other. We can look at this pair as Kabbalah's system of checks and balances for the universe. *Hesed* and *Gevurah/Din,* says Matt, are "two sides of [the] divine personality: free-flowing love and strict judgment, grace and limitation. . . . Ideally a balance is achieved, symbolized by the central *sefirah, Tiferet.* . . . However, if Judgment is not softened by Love, *Din* lashes out and threatens to destroy life."[18]

Hesed tends to emanate and expand *Ein Sof's* essence without limit. *Gevurah* tends to do the opposite, to limit God's goodness by limiting *Hesed's* expansion. Poncé summarizes the Kabbalists' system of checks and balances:

> *Gevurah,* the Power of God, is the *sefirah* of Justice and Control, capable of also meting out punishment. Its nature is feminine, and it limits the abundance of Mercy. By the same token, the severities of Power are tempered by Mercy, so the two exist in a state of harmony.

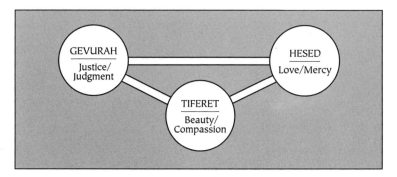

FIGURE 5. *The Second Triad*

[*Gevurah*] is representative of the contraction of the divine will. Because Mercy is a life-giving power, ever-productive in its activity, it would have been unwise to have let it express itself without setting some limit. It was for the reason that *Gevurah,* Judgment and Power, or Justice, holds things in check that it had to be created. Yet without the compassion and creativity of Mercy, Justice in its role of stern judge would cause things to contract to the point of nonexistence. [Judgment tempers mercy, and mercy tempers judgment.]

The fourth *sefirah's [Hesed's]* danger is to be found in its tendency to overexpand; the fifth *[Gevurah],* in contraction. The two together create a middle point. The marriage of these powers gives birth to Beauty *[Tiferet],* which is expressive of all that is harmoniously balanced.[19]

Kabbalists consider *Hesed* (Love/Mercy) to be masculine and *Gevurah* (Justice/Judgment) to be feminine. We can apply these archetypes of male and female to the roles of father and mother. I would say to mothers and fathers, accept your role as *Gevurah* when justice is appropriate and as *Hesed* when mercy is called for. Do not be too restrictive with your children lest you destroy them by your harsh judgments. On the other hand, do not be too giving lest you spoil them with too much mercy that becomes an indulgence.

Tiferet: The Son and Harmonizer

The sixth *sefirah* is *Tiferet,* which means "Beauty" or "Adornment." As the middle *sefirah* in the central Pillar of Compassion, *Tiferet* sits in the center of the Tree of Life. (fig. 2) The middle pillar takes its name from *Rahamim* (Compassion), another title for *Tiferet.*

Tiferet is the mediator who brings into harmony the extremes of Mercy and Judgment. This *sefirah* represents wholeness and balance.

Halevi describes *Tiferet* as "the point of equipoise, the perfect symmetrical center of the Tree of Life."[20] He says,

"Whenever the Tree diagram is applied—as it can be—to the dynamics of any organism or system, *Tiferet* is where the essence of the thing can be found. On the Divine Tree, *Tiferet* is the Heart of Hearts. . . . In the human psyche *Tiferet* is the Self, the core of the individual."[21]

In Kabbalah, *Tiferet* is referred to as "Heaven," "Sun," "King" and "the Blessed Holy One," which is the standard rabbinic name for God.[22] Kabbalists also see *Tiferet* as the son of *Hokhmah* and *Binah,* and the Zohar refers to *Tiferet* as the Son. One passage reads, "The Blessed Holy One has one Son who shines from one end of the world to the other. He is a great and mighty tree, whose head reaches toward heaven and whose roots are rooted in the holy ground."[23] The words *mighty tree* are a reference to *Tiferet,* which is considered to be the trunk of the body of the *sefirot.*

Another passage in the Zohar that describes *Tiferet* as the Son reads:

> The name of His son? Israel is his name, as it is written: "My firstborn son, Israel." All the keys of faith hang from Israel. . . . Father and Mother have crowned him and blessed him with countless crowns. . . . He has been crowned with judgment and compassion. Judgment for one who deserves judgment; compassion for one who deserves compassion. All the blessings of above and below belong to this son.[24]

"The son is not earthly Israel," explains Matt, "but its divine archetype, the central *sefirah* called Beauty of Israel *[Tiferet]*."[25]

The Zohar speaks of certain individuals who have become one with *Tiferet*. It says of Moses, "The Blessed Holy One *[Tiferet]* never departed from him. *Shekhinah* [another name for the last *sefirah, Malkhut*] joined with him constantly."[26] Matt says this is interpreted to mean that "Moses rose to the *sefirah* of *Tiferet* while still in his body" and thus "Moses and *Shekhinah* [the divine mate of *Tiferet*] were actually united in marriage."[27]

The Zohar says that Jacob too manifested *Tiferet:* "[Jacob] was saved and perfected, raised to a perfect sphere and called Israel. He attained a high rung, total perfection! He became the central pillar of whom it is written: 'The center bar in the middle of the planks shall run from end to end' (Exod. 26:28)."[28] The center bar, writes Matt, is *Tiferet,* "balancing right and left, joining the higher and lower *sefirot.* Jacob, now centered and whole, manifests *Tiferet Yisrael,* the Beauty of Israel."[29]

The Kabbalistic descriptions of *Tiferet*—Son, King, Compassion, Mediator—sound like the New Testament descriptions of Christ. But the Zohar endorses neither Christianity nor Jesus. Matt points out that the Zohar never mentions Jesus by name but rather makes it quite clear that the Jews do not need him. For the Zohar takes the position that *all* Jews are sons of God. It says, "Out of His love for [the children of

The Zohar, the major text of the Kabbalah, says that Moses and Jacob became one with Tiferet, *the sixth* sefirah. Tiferet *represents the force of Compassion that brings into harmony the extremes of Mercy and Judgment. (Left:* Moses Coming Down from Mount Sinai *by Gustave Doré. Right:* Jacob Hears the Voice of the Lord and Receives the Divine Sanction for His Journey into Egypt *by Frederick Sandys.)*

Israel], He called them 'My firstborn son, Israel.'"[30] Yet it is precisely Kabbalah that can help us understand Jesus' role and the real meaning of "the Son of God."

When the apostle John wrote of the "true Light, which lighteth every man that cometh into the world"[31] he was describing *Tiferet,* the Son, whom he believed dwelt bodily in Jesus Christ. The Light, the Son, *Tiferet,* is also known as the Word and the Universal Christ. The Universal Christ is individualized for each one of us as our Higher Self. You can think of your Higher Self as your Inner Christ or Inner Messiah. Your Higher Self represents your potential to realize God and to become one with him. (I will expand on the role of your Higher Self in chapter 4.)

In the opening chapter of his gospel, John wrote that "the Word was made flesh and dwelt among us."[32] Again he bore witness that the Son of God, *Tiferet,* the Universal Christ, dwelt bodily in Jesus' human frame—just as it will dwell bodily in your human frame when you have mastered the ten powers of the ten *sefirot.* Throughout his soul's incarnations and spiritual initiations, Jesus fully realized in the flesh the state of being that is *Tiferet.* Furthermore, he fully embodied the principles of the surrounding nine *sefirot.* As the apostle Paul wrote of Jesus, "in him dwelleth all the fullness of the Godhead bodily."[33]

He who fully internalizes *Tiferet* and the other nine *sefirot* is called the Son of God, with an uppercase *S.* He is also called Messiah (from the Hebrew *Mashiah,* meaning "anointed one") or Christ (from the Greek *Christos,* meaning "anointed"). A Messiah, or Christ, is one who is anointed with the ten lights of the ten *sefirot.* He *is* then the Tree of Life.

There is not one incarnation of Christ *(Tiferet)* or one incarnation of Messiah *(Tiferet).* Incarnating *Tiferet* is in reality the goal of the mystics of every religion, whether or not they express it in these terms; for all mystics seek the direct experience of and union with their Higher Self.

While Jesus and other Sons of God have realized the fullness of the *sefirot,* most of us are still working toward that goal. Most of us cannot yet say that we are "the Son of God," with an uppercase S. But we can say we are sons and daughters of God, with a lowercase *s* and *d,* who are in the process of fully developing our divine potential.

The term *Son of God* is therefore a title that all can earn by merit, by climbing the ladder of the Tree of Life. None can lay claim to this title on the grounds that he is a born Jew or a reborn Christian. Sonship is not automatic, for it is written: "God is no respecter of persons: but in every nation he that feareth him and worketh righteousness is accepted with him."[34]

Job, who maintained his sense of self-worth as a son of God throughout the testings of the Tempter, affirmed his goal of realizing the attributes of the ten *sefirot* in the flesh. With absolute conviction in the promises of God, he declared, "Though after my skin worms destroy this body, *yet in my flesh shall I see God.*"[35] Job looked to the day when he would be perfected in *Tiferet* in the flesh.[36]

What Job aspired to do, all can aspire to do. We who are sons and daughters of God by our spiritual birthright, whether our souls inhabit bodies black or white or red or yellow, are destined to mirror the Tree of Life not only in our spiritual body but also in our physical body.

The one who achieves this is blessed, as the Psalmist said, because he "walketh not in the counsel of the ungodly, nor standeth in the way of sinners, nor sitteth in the seat of the scornful. But his delight is in the law of the LORD; and in his law doth he meditate day and night. And he shall be like a tree planted by the rivers of water that bringeth forth his fruit in his season. His leaf also shall not wither; and whatsoever he doeth shall prosper."[37]

As the Psalmist suggests, we are made after the pattern of

the Tree of Life, which is nourished by the rivers of water of *Ein Sof.* It is when we assimilate the ten virtues represented in the *sefirot* and when we are bonded to *Tiferet* that we bring forth the ten fruits of the Tree of Life. The leaves of our Tree of Life will not wither and all that we do will prosper because we are rooted in the Heart of Hearts, *Tiferet,* the Son.

In his teachings on the mysteries of the kingdom, Jesus alludes to the Tree of Life and the seed of Christ that is in all. "The kingdom of heaven is like unto a grain of mustard seed, which a man took and sowed in his field, which indeed is the least of all seeds. But when it is grown, it is the greatest among herbs and becometh a tree, so that the birds of the air come and lodge in the branches thereof."[38]

Jesus gave this parable as an example of the growth of the spiritual kingdom within, as each of us self-realizes the seed of *Tiferet* and fully matures in the mantle of our divine Sonship. The birds that lodge in the branches of the tree are the souls that soar to the heart of *Tiferet* and find refuge among the Sons of God.

While there are other Sons of God in heaven, we can all claim a special relationship to Jesus Christ because he was and is the archetypal Christ, or avatar, for the 2,150-year period known as the age of Pisces. Approximately every 2,150 years the earth passes through an age, corresponding to one of the twelve signs of the zodiac. The length of an age is determined by a phenomenon called the precession of the equinoxes, which is the result of the slow backward rotation of earth around its polar axis. This backward rotation moves the point of the spring equinox backwards through the twelve signs of the zodiac. A new age begins when the point of the spring equinox moves from one sign of the zodiac to another.

During each age, a civilization or a continent or the entire planet is destined to assimilate a certain attribute of God. In about 2000 B.C., or 4,000 years ago, we entered the age of Aries.

This was the age of the patriarchs and the prophets. The age of Aries brought the awareness of God as Father, as Lawgiver. About 2,150 years ago we entered the age of Pisces. The Piscean age brought the awareness of God as the Son and was marked by the coming of Jesus Christ as the representative of the Son, *Tiferet.*

Today we are entering a new age. It is the age of Aquarius. This age will be marked by a universal awareness of the Holy Spirit and the Divine Mother. As we assimilate the initiations of the Holy Spirit and the teachings of the Divine Mother, we are preparing our mind, our soul and our heart to be the abode of both the Holy Spirit and the Divine Mother, just as we had the opportunity to embody the law of the Father and the Son in the preceding two ages.

Out of all the Sons of heaven, God chose Jesus to incarnate on earth to be the avatar of the Piscean age. In this role, Jesus has borne the weight of the sins, or negative karma,[39] of the world for the past 2,150 years, both prior to and after his birth. He has shielded us from the full consequences of our

misdeeds. Nevertheless, we are still responsible to atone for that sin, that karma.

By taking upon himself the burden of our sin, Jesus bore the sins of the world so that we could come of age spiritually and bear our own burdens. In effect, he pardoned our sin for the duration of the Piscean age. But his pardon did not cancel the debt: it only postponed our payment of it. We have had 2,150 years to pay it off. Now it has fallen due.

Today the people of planet earth are making the transition from the Piscean to the Aquarian age, and Jesus is turning over to us, one by one, the responsibility of bearing our own burden in dignity and in honor. Thus Paul taught that ultimately "every man shall bear his own burden." He warned, "Be not deceived; God is not mocked: for whatsoever a man soweth, that shall he also reap."[40] Paul also taught that each of us must work out our *own* salvation in fear of the LORD and with humility.[41]

Likewise, in Lurianic Kabbalah the Messiah is not cast in the role of a saviour who will save us and the world from the consequences of our actions. Kabbalists understand that personal and world salvation is not fundamentally the role of the Messiah. They know that each of us is responsible for redemption and that our every act and prayer can hasten or hamper this process. Scholem writes:

> The Messiah becomes a mere symbol, a pledge of the Messianic redemption of all things from their exile. For it is not the act of the Messiah..., as a person entrusted with the specific function of redemption, that brings Redemption, but

Kabbalists describe the sefirah Tiferet *as the Son, King, Compassion and Mediator, terms that sound like the New Testament's descriptions of Jesus (left). Jesus was the representative of and embodiment of* Tiferet *for the age of Pisces. He demonstrated the path of union with* Tiferet *so that we too could learn how to become one with* Tiferet. *(Jesus Healing the Sick by Gustave Doré.)*

your action and mine. . . . Redemption is no longer looked upon as a catastrophe, in which history itself comes to an end, but as the logical consequence of a process in which we are all participants. To Luria the coming of the Messiah means no more than a signature under a document that we ourselves write.[42]

As the representative of *Tiferet* for the Piscean age, Jesus is the Exemplar, the Wayshower of the path of Christhood, or *"Tiferethood,"* if you will. He came to demonstrate how to achieve union with the Higher Self and *Tiferet* so that we too would know how to become one with *Tiferet* and realize our own Christhood after his example. Jesus taught Paul that every son and daughter of God could "press toward the mark for the prize of the high calling of God."[43]

Since the Creation, we the sons and daughters of God have had the option of bonding to *Tiferet,* internalizing the ten *sefirot* and becoming one with the Tree of Life. While many sons have been called to this level of initiation, few have chosen to answer that call and merge with *Tiferet.* Yet our God has said that he will bring not one but many sons into the captivity of the law of the Tree of Life. At the conclusion of the Piscean age and in the new age of Aquarius, many are scheduled to realize the fullness of *Tiferet* dwelling in them bodily.

Kabbalah Illumines the New Testament

Now that we know that Jesus Christ incarnated *Tiferet,* the Son of God, and that we are also destined to incarnate *Tiferet,* we can appreciate many of the biblical statements concerning Jesus' role as "the Son of God" that have been misinterpreted by Christians and Jews—to the detriment of both. Based on passages such as those I will be citing and the truth that the Holy Spirit has unfolded in my heart, I do not believe that Jesus proclaimed he was the exclusive Son of God, as orthodox Christian tradition would have us believe.

When Jesus said, "I am the way, the truth, and the life: no man cometh unto the Father but by me,"[44] the "me" of whom he spoke was the universal Son of God, not his human self. The inner meaning of this statement is: No man comes unto the Father but by the way of the Universal Christ, *Tiferet*, the Mediator. The Universal Christ, personified in not one but many Sons of God, is the initiator of our souls whereby we also may attain union with God.

Another of Jesus' statements that takes on new meaning in light of Kabbalah is "Abide in me *[Tiferet]*, and I in you. As the branch cannot bear fruit of itself except it abide in the vine, no more can ye except ye abide in me. I am the vine, ye are the branches: He that abideth in me and I in him, the same bringeth forth much fruit: for without me ye can do nothing."[45]

The Universal Christ, embodied in Jesus and all Sons of God, is the vine, the Tree of Life. The disciples of the Christ are the branches. Just as the branches depend on the vine to nourish and sustain them, so we depend on the *sefirot,* which make up the Tree of Life, to conduct to us the life-giving essence of *Ein Sof.* The disciple who lives and moves and has his being in the Universal Christ, *Tiferet,* will have a rich spiritual life as he brings forth the many fruits of the *sefirot.* But without *Tiferet* and the other *sefirot,* he can do nothing.

Another way of interpreting the phrase "without me *[Tiferet]* ye can do nothing" is that unless we harmonize the qualities of mercy *(Hesed)* and justice *(Gevurah)* by embracing the compassion of the Son of God *(Tiferet),* we can do nothing. We need the wholeness and balance that comes through *Tiferet* to be effective in everything we do.

In the Book of John, Jesus promises at the Last Supper: "Verily, verily, I say unto you, he that believeth on me *[Tiferet],* the works that I do shall he do also; *and greater works than these shall he do,* because I go unto my Father."[46] Here it is apparent that Jesus intends each of us to do the same works he did and to walk our own path of personal Christhood.

Although this is not the portrait of Jesus that orthodox Christians have chosen to paint, there is plenty of evidence to support it. The Book of Matthew records that Jesus urged us to strive for perfection. "Be ye therefore perfect," Jesus said, "even as your Father which is in heaven is perfect."[47] Paul taught the Galatians, "I travail in birth again until Christ *[Tiferet]* be formed in you. . . . I live, yet not I, but Christ *[Tiferet]* liveth in me."[48]

Likewise Paul wrote to the Corinthians, "We have the mind of Christ,"[49] and to the Philippians, "Let this mind be in you which was also in Christ Jesus."[50] The mind of Christ is the trinity of *Keter/Hokhmah/Binah,* and because Jesus is one with *Tiferet* he is a vessel by which we can receive that mind.

Further evidence that Jesus taught that you, like him, are meant to realize your own Christhood is found in the Gnostic gospels and Christian texts unearthed in 1945 near Nag Hammadi, Egypt. *Gnosticism* is a term used to describe a diverse group of sects within Christianity that flourished in the second century, before the canon, doctrine and creeds of the Church were solidified.

The Gnostics claimed to possess an advanced teaching that had been secretly handed down to them from Jesus and his close circle of disciples. Some Gnostics offered a radically different view of Jesus' role and mission than did the churchmen of their day. Because the teachings of the Gnostics threatened the unity of the growing orthodox Church, Church leaders banned, suppressed and almost totally destroyed Gnostic scriptures.

The few Gnostic texts that have survived teach that a true disciple imitates his teacher in order to become equal to him or even surpass him. An early collection of wisdom sayings found at Nag Hammadi, called the Sentences of Sextus, instructs: "A good man is the good work of God. . . . A man who is worthy of God, he is God among men, and he is the son of God."[51]

In the Apocryphon (Secret Book) of James, Jesus says, "Verily I say unto you, no one will ever enter the kingdom of heaven at my bidding, but only because you yourselves are full. . . . Become better than I; make yourselves like the son of the Holy Spirit!"[52] The Gnostic Gospel of Philip describes the follower of Jesus who becomes "no longer a Christian but a Christ." It says: "You saw the spirit, you became spirit. You saw Christ, you became Christ. You saw the Father, you shall become Father."[53]

In the Gospel of Thomas, which claims to record the secret sayings of Jesus, the Master tells his disciples, "Because you have drunk, you have become intoxicated from the bubbling spring which I have measured out. . . . Whoever drinks from my mouth will become like me. I myself shall become he, and the things that are hidden will be revealed to him."[54]

The bubbling spring that Jesus speaks of is the fount of *Ein Sof* and the Universal Christ, *Tiferet*. Remember, Kabbalists describe the *sefirot* as vessels that channel *Ein Sof's* essence. You can picture that essence, as the Gospel of Thomas does, as a bubbling spring of light, energy and consciousness. *Tiferet* receives the essence of *Ein Sof* as it flows down through the upper *sefirot* and measures it out to those who are worthy. Jesus promises that when with love and gratitude you have drunk and assimilated those waters of everlasting life, "You will become like me, like *Tiferet*. I myself, the incarnation of *Tiferet,* shall become you."

The mystical paths of the world's religions bear witness to the universal truth that whoever drinks from the fount of the One Source will become one with that Source, whether we hear "You can become one with Brahman," "You can become one with the Tao," "You can become a Buddha," "You can cleave to *Ein Sof* and the *sefirot*" or "You can become the Son of God."

In the ancient Hindu epic the Mahabharata, the sage Sanat Kumara teaches that Brahman, the Absolute, "is awake in every creature. They that know Him know that Universal Father [who] dwelleth in the heart of every created thing!...The Brahman-knowing person... is equal unto Brahman."[55] The Chinese philosopher-sage Chu-hsi says, "If we would know the reality of Tao, we must seek it within our own nature. Each has within him the principle of right; this we call the Tao, the Way."[56]

One Buddhist text instructs, "The Germ of Buddhahood exists in every living being. Therefore, forever and anon, all that lives is endowed with the Essence of the Buddha."[57] The Buddhist teacher Saicho says, "When I worship thee, O Buddha, this is a Buddha worshiping another Buddha. And it is thou who makest this fact known to me, O Buddha."[58]

I believe that the New Testament and Christian Gnostic texts portray Jesus as an elder brother who teaches what all the great teachers of the mystical paths of the world's religions teach: that you can attain your own intimate and transforming relationship with God and that you can realize your potential to become a Son of God, one with *Tiferet*.

The Third Triad: Netzah, Hod and Yesod

The third triad consists of *Netzah, Hod* and *Yesod*. (fig. 6) As the first triad represents the realm of the intellect and the second triad the realm of the soul, the third triad signifies the realm of nature. *Netzah, Hod* and *Yesod* represent the governing and guidance of the world.

While Kabbalists write a great deal about *Ein Sof*, the unknowable God, and about the first six *sefirot*, they write very little about *Netzah* and *Hod*. *Netzah*, the seventh *sefirah*, is the lowest *sefirah* on the Pillar of Mercy. (fig. 2) *Netzah* means "Victory" or "Triumph" and is sometimes translated as "Endurance."

Hod, the eighth *sefirah*, is the lowest *sefirah* on the Pillar of Judgment. *Hod* means "Splendor" or "Majesty." Kabbalists consider *Netzah* to be a lower manifestation of *Hesed* (Love/ Mercy) and *Hod* to be a lower manifestation of *Gevurah* (Justice/Judgment). They describe *Netzah* and *Hod* not only as the instruments through which God governs the world but also as the source of prophecy. Halevi interprets *Netzah* and *Hod* as representing the operative, instrumental level of action. He says that in the human body *Netzah* governs the involuntary processes, including the autonomic system, and that *Hod* governs the voluntary processes.[59]

Yesod, the ninth *sefirah,* means "Foundation." Located on the middle pillar, the Pillar of Compassion, *Yesod* lies between *Tiferet* and *Malkhut,* between the Son and the Mother. (fig. 2) Some Kabbalists call it *Yesod Olam,* the "Foundation of the World." "*Yesod* represents. . . the procreative life force of the universe," writes Matt. "He is also called *Zaddiq* (Righteous One), and Proverbs 10:25 is applied to Him: 'The righteous one is the foundation of the world.'"[60] Those who wrote the scriptures were inserting verbal puzzles that could be solved only by those who had all the pieces, and some of those pieces can be found only in Kabbalah.

"*Yesod* is the *axis mundi,* the cosmic pillar," writes Matt. "The light and power of the preceding *sefirot* are channeled through Him to the last *sefirah, Malkhut.*"[61]

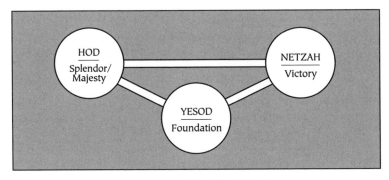

FIGURE 6. *The Third Triad*

Malkhut/Shekhinah
The Feminine Aspect of God

The tenth *sefirah* is *Malkhut* (Kingdom). It represents the physical universe and is the point where spiritual and physical forces meet. Scholem says the term *kingdom* in connection with *Malkhut* refers to "God's dominion or power in the world."[62] In relation to man, *Malkhut* corresponds to the physical body. *Malkhut* is at the base of the Pillar of Compassion and the base of the Tree of Life. (fig. 2)

"God reaches His complete individuation through His manifestation in *Malkhut,* where He is called 'I,'" writes Scholem. "This conception is summed up in the common statement that through the process of emanation 'Nothingness *[Ein Sof/Keter]* changes into I [personhood].'"[63]

Kabbalists used a play on words to show the transformation from "Nothingness" to "I." They recognized that the three Hebrew letters that make up *Ayin,* the Hebrew word for "Nothingness," also form *Ani,* the Hebrew word for "I." They saw the *Ayin* unfold step by step through the *sefirot* until it became *Ani,* the Divine Ego, or "I," in *Malkhut.*

Malkhut is at the nexus of two worlds. In the upper world, *Malkhut* is the lowest *sefirah* on the Tree of Life. In the lower world, our world, she is the uppermost point. Thus *Malkhut* serves as both the channel through which the divine forces of the *sefirot* flow downward to this world as well as the gate through which we on earth reach upward to God. *Malkhut,* says the Zohar, "is the agent for all, from the upper world to the lower world and from the lower world to the upper world."[64] She is also considered to be the most accessible aspect of God's being.

Malkhut is frequently referred to as *Shekhinah* (Divine Presence). In traditional Judaism, *Shekhinah* is the presence and activity of God in the world. Kabbalah adds an important new dimension: *Shekhinah* becomes the feminine aspect of God, a separate, divine entity, a feminine power. Scholem writes:

This discovery of a feminine element in God... is... one of the most significant steps [Kabbalists] took. Often regarded with the utmost misgiving by strictly Rabbinical, non-Kabbalistic Jews,... this mythical conception of the feminine principle of the *Shekhinah* as a providential guide of Creation achieved enormous popularity among the masses of the Jewish people, so showing that here the Kabbalists had uncovered one of the primordial religious impulses still latent in Judaism.[65]

As the uppermost point, the starting point, of the lower world, *Shekhinah* figures as the mother of the world and its ruler. In particular, she is the merciful mother of the nation Israel. She gives birth to our world and sustains it; she metes out rewards as well as punishments. One text says, "The creation is the work of the *Shekhinah,* who takes care of it as a mother cares for her children."[66] Both *Binah* and *Malkhut* are cast in the role of divine mothers, but *Binah* is known as the "upper mother" and the "upper *Shekhinah,*" and *Malkhut* is known as the "lower mother" and the "lower *Shekhinah.*"

In Kabbalah, *Shekhinah* also symbolizes the soul and the Community of Israel, which I interpret to be the mystical body of all sons and daughters of God. Kabbalistic texts refer to *Malkhut/Shekhinah* as the daughter of *Hokhmah* and *Binah. Malkhut/Shekhinah* is also the bride and consort of *Tiferet,* the King.

Just as the masculine and feminine *sefirot Hokhmah* and *Binah* are paired together, so are *Tiferet* and *Shekhinah.* But there is a distinct difference between the two couples. While *Hokhmah* and *Binah* are in a state of uninterrupted union, *Tiferet* and *Shekhinah* are not. They are torn from their loving embrace by the sins of Israel, which cause *Shekhinah* to go into exile along with her children.

Traditional Judaism also speaks of this exile, but Kabbalah's interpretation of *Shekhinah* as the feminine aspect of God gives this concept a unique twist. The Talmud, for instance, teaches that *Shekhinah* accompanies the children of Israel wherever they are in exile. "In the Talmud this means only that God's presence was always with Israel in its exiles," writes Scholem. "In the Kabbalah, however, it is taken to mean that *a part of God Himself is exiled from God.*"[67]

The Zohar pictures it in these terms: "It is like the king who was angry with his son, and for a punishment decreed that he should go far away from him to a distant land. The consort heard of this and said, 'Since my son has gone to a distant land and the king has expelled him from his palace, I shall not forsake him. Either we both return to the royal palace, or we both live together in another land.'"[68]

Elsewhere in the Zohar we are told that God sent *Shekhinah* to be with his exiled people as a guarantee that he would never forsake them, for God could not bear to leave his Beloved.[69] The Zohar compares God's devotion to *Shekhinah* to "a man who was in love with a woman who lived in the street of the tanners. If she had not been there, he would never have set foot in the place." But because the beloved of his soul lived there, that street was like "the street of the spice merchants, where all the finest perfumes in the world could be found."[70]

Kabbalistic texts depict the disruption of the union of *Tiferet* and *Shekhinah* as nothing short of a cosmic catastrophe, for their separation has stopped the flow of divine forces into this world. As I noted earlier, these forces flow from *Ein Sof* through the *sefirot* down into this world. The *sefirot* are the "bearers of *[Ein Sof's]* active and creative force," writes Scholem. *Malkhut/Shekhinah* is the last *sefirah* to conduct that force to our world. But ever since her exile, she has been cut off from her "constant union with the upper forces that she was supposed to carry and transmit to Creation."[71]

The Zohar describes the results of this cosmic imbalance. When *Shekhinah* went into exile, "all wept . . . and composed dirges and lamentations. . . . And just as she suffered a change from her earlier state, so too her husband *[Tiferet]:* his light no longer shone. . . . For from the day that the Temple was destroyed the heavens did not shine with their customary light. The secret of the matter is that blessings reside only in the place where male and female are together."[72]

With the exile of the feminine aspect of God, the floodgates of heaven have literally been stopped up. Only a tiny remnant of the flow of divine forces from the *sefirot* is able to seep through in order to sustain the world. *Shekhinah* begs to be reunited with her Beloved, for when she is, says the Zohar, "large numbers of the righteous come into their sacred inheritance, and a multitude of blessings are bestowed on the world."[73]

Thirteenth-century Kabbalist Rabbi Joseph Gikatilla portrays the catastrophe that resulted from the separation of *Shekhinah* from *Tiferet:*

> At the beginning of Creation, the essence of *Shekhinah* was in the lower worlds. . . . Since She was below, heaven and earth were united. . . perfecting one another, filling one another. The channels and wellsprings were working perfectly, conducting the flow from above to below. Thus *YHVH* [the LORD], may He be blessed, filled everything from above to below. . . . He was present equally in the upper and lower worlds. Then Adam came and sinned. The lines were ruined, the channels broken, the pools cut off; *Shekhinah* withdrew and the bond was severed.[74]

The all-important question posed by the Kabbalist is: Who or what can reunite *Shekhinah* with *Tiferet* and with the other *sefirot* in order to stimulate the flow of the divine into this world?

The answer: each one of us. For the permanent union of *Shekhinah* and *Tiferet* depends on the balance of virtue or sin in the world. The Zohar explains:

> When the righteous increase in the world, then the land *[Shekhinah]* produces fruit and is filled with everything. But when

the wicked increase in the world, then it is written "The waters disappear from the sea."[75]. . .

. . .*[Shekhinah]*. . . is she that gathers in from all the camps above, and holds in all that she gathers, letting it escape only by drops like dew, because there is not sufficient faith below. For if She were to find faith as it is found in her, She would pour the light on every side without restraint, and they would give to her also gifts and presents without stint. But it is those of the lower world who restrain them and restrain her, and then she is "closed up."[76]

So central to Kabbalists was their goal of reuniting *Shekhinah* with her Beloved, and thereby restoring the flow of the divine, that before performing a commandment they would say they were doing it "for the sake of the unification of the Holy One, blessed be He, and His *Shekhinah*."[77] "Under Kabbalistic influence," writes Scholem, "this formula was employed in all subsequent liturgical texts and books of later Judaism, down to the nineteenth century, when rationalistic Jews, horrified at a conception they no longer understood, deleted it from the prayer books destined for the use of Westernized minds."[78]

Another factor that can help repair the breach between *Shekhinah* and *Tiferet* is the holy marriage of man and woman. Kabbalists believe that human marriage not only symbolizes the divine marriage of *Shekhinah* and *Tiferet*, but it can also help bring it about.

The married mystics consider their sexual union to be a celebration of the divine union of *Tiferet* and *Shekhinah*. For instance, the Zohar says the desire of the parents of Moses "focused on joining *Shekhinah*."[79] According to Moses Cordovero, the meaning of that passage is: "Their desire, both his and hers, was to unite *Shekhinah*. He focused on *Tiferet*, and his wife on *Malkhut [Shekhinah]*. His union was to join *Shekhinah*; she focused correspondingly on being *Shekhinah* and uniting with Her Husband, *Tiferet*."[80]

Thus, unlike the Roman Catholic tendency to elevate the celibate lifestyle above the married, Kabbalism was "tempted to discover the mystery of sex within God himself," says Scholem. "It rejected asceticism and [like Judaism] continued to regard marriage not as a concession to the frailty of the flesh but as one of the most sacred mysteries. Every true marriage is a symbolical realization of the union of God and *Shekhinah*."[81]

Each one of us individually can have a special relationship with *Malkhut/Shekhinah*. Kabbalah teaches that when we are righteous, *Shekhinah* will dwell with us. One text says that righteous mystics are like "the limbs of the *Shekhinah*." The sinner, on the other hand, disfigures his body "so that the consort *[Shekhinah]* can find no dwelling-place there."[82]

I mentioned earlier that the Zohar describes Moses and *Shekhinah* as partners. It says that *Shekhinah* never left Moses; she "joined with him constantly." Moses was a prototype for us all. Matt writes:

> Can a human being experience *Shekhinah* directly? The Talmud had posed this question rhetorically: "Is it possible for a human being to walk behind *Shekhinah*?" "Is it possible to cleave to *Shekhinah*?" No. Rather, one should engage in good deeds and thus imitate God.
>
> Kabbalah is more daring. In the words of Joseph Gikatilla..., "As to what the Rabbis have said: 'Is it possible for a human being to cleave to *Shekhinah*?' it certainly is possible!"[83]

Cleaving to *Malkhut/Shekhinah* is the key to accessing the power of the *sefirot*. As the Zohar says, *Shekhinah* is the gate to *Tiferet* and all the *sefirot:*

> Who is "the way to the Tree of Life *[Tiferet]*"? It is the great consort; she is the way to that great and powerful tree. . . . If one does not enter through this gate *[Malkhut]*, one cannot gain entry to the worlds. It is like an exalted king *[Hokhmah]*, who is high, hidden and concealed, and who has made gates *[sefirot]* for himself, one upon the other, and at the end of all the gates

The holy marriage of man and woman not only symbolizes the divine union of Shekhinah *and* Tiferet, *but it can help bring it about.* Shekhinah *(another name for the tenth* sefirah, Malkhut*) is separated from her Beloved because of the sins of Adam and the Israelites. Whether or not they will be reunited depends on the balance of virtue or sin in the world.* (The Betrothal of the Virgin, *woodcut by Albrecht Dürer.*)

he has made one particular gate. . . . He says: Whoever desires to enter into my presence, this gate shall be the first [that leads] to me; and whoever enters by this gate shall enter. . . . Whoever takes one takes the other, and it is all one, for He is one.[84]

Isaiah Tishby says this last sentence means, "When one reaches *Malkhut*, it is as if one had already reached supernal *Hokhmah* as well, because the *sefirotic* system is the world of unification."[85]

How do we open the gate of *Malkhut?* According to Kabbalists, the keys that open the gate are prayer and performing good deeds, topics I will take up in later chapters. In addition, we need to understand our relationship to the feminine aspect of the Father-Mother God, the Divine Mother.

The Mother is your first Teacher. She, the Eternal Womb, has borne you since you came forth from the Great Central Sun, clothed in garments of light. When it became necessary for your soul to descend to the lower worlds, she fashioned other bodies for your journey through the dimensions of the spiritual and material universes. When you breathed your first breath of life from the Holy Spirit, it was her eyes that captured your gaze and her smile of radiant love that flooded your being. She was the Word "in the Beginning" who pronounced the first welcome to you as you entered your new body.

Your Mother-God fashioned your form and gave you the equipment to maneuver among the grids of mortality. She sealed within you the seed of everlasting life. It remains dormant until you choose to bathe it in the sunlight of your heart.

Just as she sent you out, the Divine Mother has set the cosmic stage for your ascent back to God through the four worlds by the doorway of *Malkhut/Shekhinah*. She is the wellspring of life. There is nothing in the matter universe that is not the province of the Divine Mother. She sustains the civilizations of the world and all the details of life that pertain to it. She is everywhere—in science, technology, government, the economy, health, education, the arts, the environment. She is fire, air, water and earth. She is nature.

We are living at a time when our need for the Divine Mother could not be greater—a time when women are having abortions at an unprecedented rate; when women are being raped and sexually harassed; when our children are not receiving a proper education; when they are surrounded by violence, not only in the streets but in school and at home; when governments and economies are falling apart because our leaders are spineless.

We can heal these afflictions by cleaving to the Divine Mother through prayer and service. We can increase the effectiveness of our prayers by establishing a strong tie of devotion to those who have personified the Divine Mother through the centuries—great lights such as Mary, the mother of Jesus; the Hindu goddesses Parvati and Lakshmi; Kuan Yin, the Bodhisattva of Compassion; and Saint Thérèse of Lisieux.

Understanding our relationship to the Divine Mother and her many incarnations also means coming to grips with our relationship to the feminine principle wherever it is found in life. Both men and women have a feminine side. It is the sensitive, intuitive side. It is the inner child, the soul. If we are to cleave to the Divine Mother, we must examine how we treat the feminine—how we care for our own soul and the souls of others.

Ask yourself: What is my relationship to *Binah* and to *Malkhut/Shekhinah,* to womankind and to the Woman clothed with the Sun, the moon under her feet?[86]

What is my relationship to the Mother's son, the Divine Manchild, whose Christ essence is aborning in my heart and the hearts of all her children?

What is my relationship to her seed, those throughout the earth who bear the light of the Manchild but are persecuted?

What am I doing, right where I am, to nurture the children

of the Divine Mother and all of her creation?

I urge you to read between the lines of your own psyche and wherever there is nonresolution make your peace with the Divine Mother. If necessary, work with a qualified professional to examine your relationship to the Mother, which may be reflected in your relationship to your human mother in this life.

Yes, "acquaint now thyself"[87] with the Divine Mother and let her peace quell the warring in your members. Enter the cosmic womb and know your rebirth through the Tree of Life that she zealously guards, letting only those who are ready pass through the gate. By and by, as you pursue a path of devotion

Cleaving to Malkhut/Shekhinah *is one of the keys to accessing the hidden power of the* sefirot. *Mystics of the world's religions know that by establishing a strong tie of devotion to those who have embodied the light of* Malkhut/Shekhinah—*such as Kuan Yin, the Chinese Bodhisattva of Compassion, and Mary, the mother of Jesus—we can heal the afflictions in the earth and increase the effectiveness of our prayers. (Left: Chinese sculpture, the Water and Moon Kuan-yin Bodhisattva. Right:* The Madonna of the Meadow *by Raphael.)*

to the Divine Mother and work with her to heal your psyche
and to heal the earth through service and good works, the Divine Mother will open the door to you—the door of *Malkhut/*
Shekhinah.

If you are ready, the Mother welcomes you to the disci-
plines of the tenth *sefirah.* But the Mother will not send for
you until you are ready to accept her invitation to walk
through the door. As the adage goes, when the pupil is ready,
the teacher appears.

The Mother opens the door to her heart when we open
the door to our own heart by extending mercy, justice and
compassion to ourselves and others. And once the door to
Malkhut has been opened to you, you will be able to enter the
gates of the *sefirot* as one by one you pass their initations.

Jesus spoke of the gate of *Malkhut/Shekhinah* when he
said, "Enter ye in at the strait gate: for wide is the gate and
broad is the way that leadeth to destruction, and many there
be which go in thereat: because strait is the gate and narrow
is the way which leadeth unto life, and few there be that
find it."[88]

When you are ready and the Divine Mother admits you in
full honor through the gate of *Malkhut/Shekhinah,* kiss her
blessed feet. Then stand on the first rung of the ladder of
eternal life. Fulfill there your reason for being until you hear
the call of *Yesod:* "Come up higher. Thou hast been faithful
over a few things in *Malkhut/Shekhinah.* Enter the gate of
Yesod and I will make you ready to rule over many things."[89]

The Quasi Sefirah, Da'at

Kabbalists tucked away a little surprise in the Tree of Life, a
secret attribute called *Da'at,* or "Knowledge." *Da'at* is located
on the central column of the tree. It is between *Keter* (Crown)
and *Tiferet* (Beauty/Compassion) and below *Hokhmah* (Wisdom) and *Binah* (Understanding). (fig. 7)

Scholem says *Da'at* appears between *Hokhmah* and *Binah* as "a kind of harmonizing of the two."[90] Kabbalists consider *Da'at* to be a non-*sefirah* or quasi *sefirah*. It is not a separate *sefirah* but "the external aspect of *Keter*."[91]

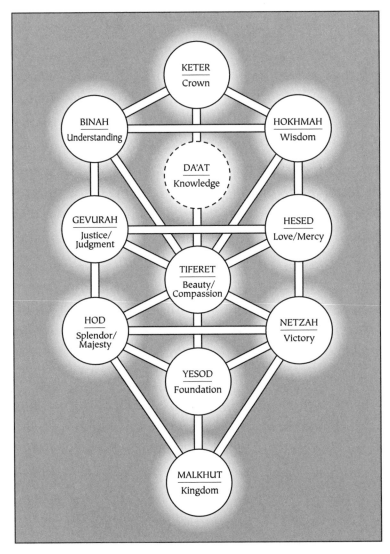

FIGURE 7. *Tree of Life with* Da'at

Halevi describes *Da'at* as divine inspiration. "In human terms *Da'at* is the Knowledge that emerges out of nowhere and comes direct from God," he writes. "It is quite different from the revelation of Wisdom *(Hokhmah)*; *Da'at* is not only seen but known. It is different, too, from what comes of Understanding *(Binah)* or deep pondering: *Da'at,* the child of the supernal *sefirot,* is not only observation but becoming."[92]

At least one tradition holds that *Da'at* is the source of miraculous powers. Perle Epstein says that some disciples of Isaac Luria "claimed to 'fly' through the air by drawing down the light of a secret attribute called *Da'at.*"[93]

The Lightning Flash

In addition to the Tree of Life, another diagram some later Kabbalists use to depict the emanation of the *sefirot* from *Keter* to *Malkhut* is the Lightning Flash. (fig. 8) As I quoted earlier, the *Sefer Yetzirah* says of the *sefirot,* "Their countenance is like the scintillating flame flashing in lightning, invisible and boundless." This has also been translated as: "The ten ineffable *sefirot* have the appearance of the Lightning Flash."[94]

Some take this description to mean the *sefirot* are luminescent or that they can only be seen for an instant, like a flash of lightning. Other Kabbalists believe the Lightning Flash describes the emanation of the *sefirot* as well as the continual descent of divine forces through the Tree of Life in a zigzag pattern like lightning.

The pattern of the Tree of Life, writes Halevi, "is the model on which everything that is to come into manifestation is based. . . . The relationships set forth in the Tree underlie the whole of existence; and so the properties of the *sefirot* may be seen in terms of any branch of knowledge.[95] The *sefirot* on the Tree might be regarded as a system of functions in a circuit through which flows a divine current."[96]

The divine flash continuously travels from a *sefirah* on the expansive Pillar of Mercy to a *sefirah* on the constrictive Pillar of Judgment then to a *sefirah* on the harmonizing Pillar of Compassion. The flash begins at *Keter,* flows to *Hokhmah* and *Binah* and then to *Da'at.* Next it travels to the expansive *sefirah Hesed,*

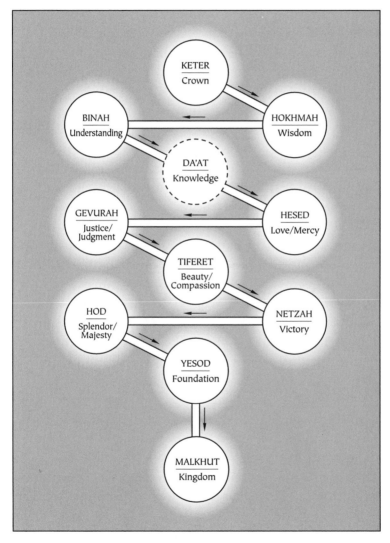

FIGURE 8. *The Lightning Flash*

then its constrictive opposite, *Gevurah,* then the balancing force of *Tiferet.* From there it moves to *Netzah, Hod, Yesod* and *Malkhut.*

To illustrate the creative process that occurs as the lightning flash travels through the *sefirot,* Halevi uses the example of writing a book. *Keter* (Crown), he says, is the creative principle. The idea is conceived in *Hokhmah* (Wisdom), but it is still formless. In *Binah* (Understanding) the idea takes shape. The author decides, for instance, to write a book (rather than a play or a short story) that will center on a certain theme.

This idea may be held in mind for years, but through *Da'at* (Knowledge) it becomes focused. At the point of *Hesed* (Love/Mercy), the writer begins an outline of the creative ideas that have been forming inside of him. Through *Gevurah* (Justice/Judgment) he continually judges and assesses what to include in the book. He shapes all the ideas of *Hesed* into a practical, finite concept.

As the book takes form, its distinctive essence or quality, *Tiferet* (Beauty/Compassion), starts to manifest. *Netzah* (Victory) is the point where the book is written down in its entirety. Through *Hod* (Splendor/Majesty) the vital forces of the body make the pen move over the paper. *Hod* also focuses knowledge or language into sentences. *Yesod* (Foundation) organizes the writing and polishes it with a personal style. *Malkhut* (Kingdom) is the physical manifestation of the book.

"In this illustration," says Halevi, "we have a brief outline of the Lightning Flash as described in the Human Tree of Life. All creative processes in the Universe follow the same pattern, though in the terms of their own level."[97]

Now that we have unveiled the character and function of each of the *sefirot,* let us look at how the Tree of Life relates to you.

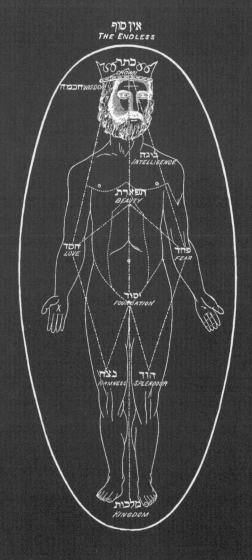

CHAPTER FOUR

A PORTRAIT OF
THE GOD WITHIN

He stretched forth His right hand and created the world above.
He stretched forth His left hand and created this world....
He made this world to match the world above, and whatever
exists above has its counterpart below.

THE ZOHAR

Kabbalists tell us that the *sefirot*
are the divine model for all of creation and that we ourselves
contain the ten *sefirot*. Everything in the universe, including
man, is created "according to the form that is above," says the
Zohar. "[God] made the lower world on the pattern of the
upper world, and they complement each other, forming one
whole, in a single unity."[1]

The *sefirot* relate to you personally on many different
levels. They are at once the archetypes of your inner, spiritual
being and of your physical body.

Adam Kadmon *from* Qabbalah *by Isaac Myer, 1888.*

Contemporary students of Kabbalah have described our relationship to the *sefirot* as follows:[2] *Keter* (Crown) is our divine essence. It also represents our free will and our awareness of God as the Divine Presence and First Cause. *Hokhmah* (Wisdom) in us is our knowledge of God. It is pure, undifferentiated thought. *Hokhmah* correlates with the right brain and is manifest as genius, inspiration, revelation and originality.

Binah (Understanding) represents the left brain, our ability to reason and discriminate. As a step-down from the internal thought processes of *Hokhmah* and *Binah, Da'at* (Knowledge) is our ability to express our thoughts. It is also spiritual knowledge and the omniscience and universal consciousness of God.

Hesed (Love/Mercy) manifests as love, tolerance, mercy and unconditional, unrestrained giving. *Hesed* is our "luminous nature which is always aspiring to the divine," says Schaya.[3] *Gevurah* (Justice/Judgment) is discipline, discrimination and true judgment. Aryeh Kaplan says *Gevurah* can manifest as the ability and the strength to overcome one's self, or it can be rigid, noncaring, withdrawn and totally self-contained.[4]

Tiferet (Beauty/Compassion) is the heart or core of each of us, our essential nature. It manifests as our inner and outer beauty and as harmony, balance and serenity. "*Tiferet* is a balanced giving," says Kaplan, "the ability to create a harmonious relationship."[5]

Netzah (Victory) governs our instinctual and involuntary processes and sustains our health. Some describe it as achievement or spiritual power. When out of balance, *Netzah* can manifest as dominance. *Hod* (Splendor/Majesty), on the other hand, applies to our voluntary processes. It is that part of our nature that learns, communicates and controls. When out of balance, *Hod* can manifest as passivity and submissiveness.

Yesod (Foundation) is the foundation of spiritual birth, physical procreation and the ego. It is the seat of physical and spiritual pleasure. By mastering the attribute of *Yesod,* says

Kaplan, the righteous are able to penetrate spiritual realms and attain an intimate union with God. *Malkhut/Shekhinah* (Kingdom/Divine Presence) represents our physical body and our receptivity, for as the last *sefirah* it receives the emanations of the preceding *sefirot*. It is the point where spiritual and physical forces meet.

Adam Kadmon: Our Divine Blueprint

In Kabbalah, the divine archetype of man and woman is known as *Adam Kadmon,* literally "Primordial Man." Some Kabbalists teach that when the *sefirot* emanated from *Ein Sof,* they first took the form of *Adam Kadmon.* Kabbalists describe him as "the concealed shape of the Godhead itself."[6] *Adam Kadmon* is androgynous; in him the male and female forces are in complete harmony and balance.

Kabbalists usually depict *Adam Kadmon* so that we are viewing his back. This is based on the passage from Exodus where Moses asks God to show him his glory but the LORD reveals only his back to Moses, saying: "Thou canst not see my face: for there shall no man see me and live. . . . And thou shalt see my back parts: but my face shall not be seen."[7]

Although Kabbalists do not always agree on how the *sefirot* correlate to *Adam Kadmon,* the most common scheme is shown in figure 9. *Keter, Hokhmah* and *Binah* (the three highest *sefirot*) represent *Adam Kadmon's* head. Some Kabbalists assign *Da'at,* the quasi *sefirah* of Knowledge, to *Adam Kadmon's* face and throat.[8] *Hesed* (the fourth *sefirah*) is his right arm and *Gevurah* (the fifth *sefirah*) is his left arm. *Tiferet* (the sixth *sefirah*) is associated with the trunk of *Adam Kadmon's* body. *Netzah* (the seventh *sefirah*) is his right leg, and *Hod* (the eighth *sefirah*) is his left leg. *Yesod* (the ninth *sefirah*) relates to the male sexual organ. *Malkhut* is at times depicted at the feet or mouth of *Adam Kadmon.* Sometimes *Malkhut* is not included in diagrams of *Adam Kadmon* at all.

Isaac Luria teaches that the body of *Adam Kadmon* was created when *Ein Sof* emitted a line or ray of light that became a series of concentric spheres that are the *sefirot*. (fig. 10) Rabbi Hayim Vital, Luria's closest disciple, describes the process:

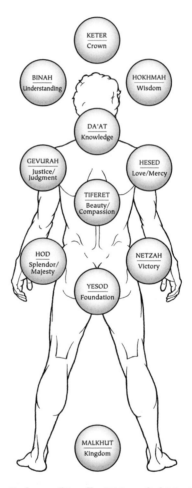

FIGURE 9. Adam Kadmon *(literally "Primordial Man") is the androgynous divine archetype of man, the primordial image and likeness of God in which we were made. Some Kabbalists teach that when the* sefirot *emanated from* Ein Sof, *they first took the form of* Adam Kadmon.

[The] first concentric sphere which adheres closely to *Ein Sof* is called *Keter* of primordial man. Then, the straight line continues briefly, then retreats and forms another concentric sphere within the other. This sphere is called the *Hokhmah* of primordial man.

This process is repeated as all the *sefirot* are unfolded. Vital says:

> That which joins all the spheres together is the subtle thin line which spreads out from *Ein Sof,* traversing, descending and joining each sphere to another until it reaches the very last.
>
> Next, the line spreads out in a straight way from the top to the bottom, from the highest point of the highest sphere to the very lowest and last of the spheres. It consists of ten *sefirot* arranged mysteriously in the image of an upright human figure.[9]

The Adam of the Garden of Eden was the anthropological counterpart of *Adam Kadmon.* Before he sinned, Adam's body was spiritual and ethereal. After he fell from his divine state in Eden, Adam took on a material body. But *Adam Kadmon* never descended below the realm of heavenly perfection.

I believe that *Adam Kadmon* was the primordial image and likeness of God in which we were made and that his body is the blueprint for the bodies of all sons and daughters of God. We have strayed from that blueprint, compromising our bodies by our negative thoughts, feelings, words and deeds. But the original matrix of perfection, the divine image and likeness, is there, sealed in our Higher Self.

Kabbalists say we can return to that divine image. "According to Genesis 1:27, the human being is created in the image of God," writes Daniel Matt. "The *sefirot* are the divine original of that image. As Primordial Adam, they are the mythical paragon of the human being, our archetypal nature. The human race has lost this nature, but if one were to purify himself, he would reconnect with the *sefirot* and become a vessel for them. This is what the Patriarchs attained and, to a greater degree, Moses."[10]

In later chapters I will be reviewing techniques you can use to purify yourself spiritually, reconnect with the *sefirot* and make yourself a vessel for the divine light.

FIGURE 10. *The process of creation, according to sixteenth-century Kabbalist Isaac Luria, started when* Ein Sof, *the Infinite, contracted itself to its centermost point and then withdrew to the sides surrounding that point in order to leave a vacuum in which its creation could exist. This process is called* tzimtzum. *Next, from the Infinite Light (Ein Sof Or) that enveloped the vacuum, Ein Sof emitted a ray of light (Kav) that formed a series of concentric spheres. These spheres are the ten* sefirot, *which compose the body of Primordial Man, Adam Kadmon.*

The I AM Presence: The Personal Presence of God

Like the Kabbalists of old, the ascended masters[11] have drawn a diagram that illustrates our divine nature and our relationship to God and the *sefirot.* This diagram is called the Chart of Your Divine Self. (p. 78) The ascended masters also refer to it as the Tree of Life.

The upper figure in the chart represents your I AM Presence. The I AM Presence corresponds to the Father-Mother God. The I AM Presence is the Presence of God individualized for each one of us. It is your personalized I AM THAT I AM. I AM THAT I AM is the name God revealed to Moses at Mount Sinai when he called to him out of the midst of the burning bush. In Kabbalah, I AM THAT I AM *(Ehyeh Asher Ehyeh)* is the name of God associated with *Keter.* So you can think of *Keter* (Crown) as corresponding to your I AM Presence.

What about *Ein Sof,* the "divine nothingness," the indescribable "Cause above all causes"? *Ein Sof* is hidden as the Sun behind the sun of the I AM Presence. That is why Kabbalists call *Ein Sof* the unmanifest and why the Zohar says "no trace may be found, nor can thought by any means or method reach it."[12]

Our I AM Presence is thus the closest and most personal Presence of God we can know while we are yet in our mortal body. Only when our soul has become one with *Keter* and I AM THAT I AM and has returned to the cosmos of pure Spirit will she be called to enter *Ein Sof,* the indescribable and unknowable God—the Supreme Source.

The light of I AM THAT I AM and *Keter* is a transforming light. Mark Prophet, my late husband and teacher, said that when the LORD told Moses, "Thou canst not see my face: for there shall no man see me and live," that meant: "No man can see God and still live *as man.*" If he survives the experience, he will be God in manifestation. Such is the power of the

The Chart of Your Divine Self

light of I AM THAT I AM and *Keter.* We may not yet be ready to stand in that Presence of God, but by reconnecting with the *sefirot,* by daily walking and talking with God, we are getting ready.

Before we can receive the light of *Keter* we must assimilate the essence of the nine lower *sefirot.* We can accomplish this under the tutelage of the ascended masters, who initiate us through the ten stages of the *sefirot* from the root of *Malkhut/ Shekhinah* to the crown of *Keter.* The soul's assimilation of the light of the *sefirot* may take numerous incarnations, perhaps with karmic digressions along the way. But, as Jesus said, "Blessed is the man that endureth temptation: for when he is tried, he shall receive the crown of life *[Keter],* which the Lord hath promised to them that love him."[13]

Your Unique Identity in God

If the Presence of God is individualized for each of us, then what makes one soul different from another? How you color, or qualify, the interpenetrating spheres of light surrounding your I AM Presence determines what's unique about you. Together, these spheres make up the Causal Body, also known as the Body of First Cause, which exists in higher levels of Spirit.

The spheres of your Causal Body are the storehouse of everything that is real and permanent about your unique identity. They contain the records of the virtuous acts you have performed to the glory of God and the blessing of man through your many incarnations on earth. These good works are your treasure stored in heaven.[14] Whenever you judiciously exercise your free will in love, harmony and creative endeavor, these energies, multiplied by your service to life, ascend to one of the seven spheres of your Causal Body.

Each sphere of the Causal Body is a different color, representing one of the seven spiritual "rays." Just as a ray of sunlight passing through a prism produces the seven colors of the rainbow, so spiritual light manifests as seven rays, or frequencies of light. Each ray has a specific color, quality and frequency that is associated with a different attribute or aspect of God's consciousness. In addition to the seven primary rays, there are five "secret" rays, which are "hidden" within the center sphere of the Causal Body.

The progression of the spheres of the Causal Body, from the center sphere to the outermost sphere, corresponds to the

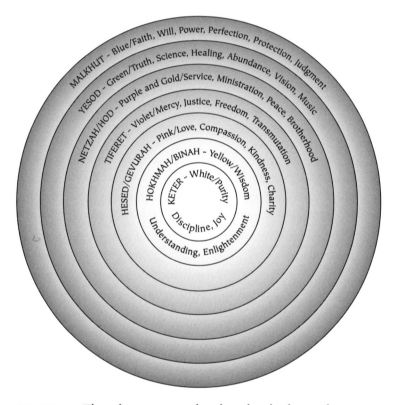

FIGURE 11. *The* sefirot *correspond to the colored spheres of your Causal Body that surround your I AM Presence (the Presence of God that is individualized for each one of us). As you imitate the divine attributes of the* sefirot, *you increase the power of the corresponding sphere of your Causal Body and you compel the corresponding frequency of God's light to descend into this world.*

progressive emanation of the *sefirot* that emanated from *Ein Sof* to form *Adam Kadmon*. (figs. 10, 11) The line, or ray of light, that connects the *sefirot* and runs right through the body of Primordial Man may be compared to the shaft of white light ("the crystal cord") that connects the three figures in the Chart of Your Divine Self. (p. 78)

When you embrace the attributes of each of the *sefirot*, you are creating a cosmic connection between your world and the heaven world. When you make the qualities of each of the *sefirot* your own, you increase the power and dominion of the corresponding sphere of your Causal Body as day by day the energy you have used for good ascends to the Causal Body. At the same time, your imitation of the divine attributes compels the corresponding frequency of God's light from the heaven world to descend through this world over the circuit of the *sefirot*.

For example, *Keter* (Crown) corresponds to the white sphere in the center of the Causal Body. The white sphere is the sphere of divine purity, discipline and joy. Whenever you act with a pure heart and an unblemished motive, desiring only to glorify God, you are multiplying the power of your white sphere and you are stimulating the flow of *Keter's* light into the world.

Hokhmah (Wisdom) and *Binah* (Understanding) correspond to the yellow sphere of divine wisdom, understanding and enlightenment. Whenever you bring spiritual understanding and illumination to anyone, you are multiplying the power of the yellow sphere of your Causal Body and increasing the flow of God's wisdom and understanding (the light of *Hokhmah* and *Binah*) into the world. The same pattern of interaction is true for each of the following spheres and attributes.

Hesed (Love/Mercy) and *Gevurah* (Justice/Judgment) correspond to the pink sphere of divine love, compassion, kindness and charity. *Tiferet* (Beauty/Compassion) corresponds to the violet sphere of divine mercy, justice, freedom and transmutation.

Netzah (Victory) and *Hod* (Splendor/Majesty) correspond to the purple-and-gold sphere of divine service, ministration, peace and brotherhood.

Yesod (Foundation) corresponds to the green sphere of divine truth, science, healing, abundance, vision and music. *Malkhut* (Kingdom) corresponds to the blue sphere of divine faith, will, power, perfection, protection and judgment. The quasi *sefirah, Da'at* (Knowledge), corresponds to the spheres of the five secret rays that are within the center sphere.

No two Causal Bodies are exactly alike because their shimmering spheres reflect the unique spiritual attainment of the soul. One person may have a greater momentum on expressing the love of *Hesed,* having perfected that quality over many lifetimes. Therefore the pink sphere of his Causal Body may be larger than the pink sphere of someone who has not developed that quality. One who embodies the attributes of *Hokhmah* and *Binah* may excel as a teacher of wisdom, and thus the yellow sphere of his Causal Body will shine as a star of great magnitude.

What relevance does our Causal Body have to our daily spiritual path? First, I said that as you perform good deeds, and thereby increase the spheres of your Causal Body, you are compelling divine light to descend to this world. In the famous words of the Zohar, "The impulse from below calls forth that from above."[15]

In addition, the particular attributes we have developed through hard work in our previous lives (reflected in the size of our Causal Body spheres) determine the gifts and talents we will be born with in our succeeding lives. These talents, sealed in our Causal Body, are made available to us today through our Higher Self (the middle figure in the Chart of Your Divine Self, p.78).

In my meditations, God has shown me that the progression of the Causal Body spheres is a logical unfoldment of the identity of our soul as God provides us with what we need to fulfill our assignment on earth. In the beginning (representing the white sphere), each of us is created out of a single white-fire ovoid with our twin flame, our "other half" with whom we share a unique blueprint. Together twin flames embody the masculine/feminine polarity of the Divine Whole.[16]

Next, we are clothed with the Mind of God (yellow sphere) and the love of God (pink sphere). Then God bestows upon us the gift of free will, which includes the freedom and ability to create (the violet sphere). Endowed with free will, we will be able to use our talents to serve others (purple-and-gold sphere).

The next step is setting the foundation of our physical form, the blueprint of *Adam Kadmon* (green sphere). And lastly, God gives us power, will and faith, qualities we need to evolve physically and spiritually in the physical dimension.

If we return to the vision of Ezekiel—the vision of the throne-chariot of God that the *Merkabah* mystics yearned to behold—what he saw sounds like nothing less than his own I AM Presence surrounded by the concentric spheres of his Causal Body. He saw the likeness of a man surrounded by "the appearance of fire" and a "brightness round about" the fire that resembled a rainbow.

Ezekiel describes his vision as "the appearance of the likeness of the glory of the LORD,"[17] and that is exactly what our Causal Body is. Each day, as we become closer and closer to God and reconnect with the ten *sefirot,* we are adding to that glory. And one day, when our soul has fully attained her goal of reunion with God, we will enter into the Causal Body and abide in the house of the LORD forever, nevermore to go out.

The Holy Christ Self: Your Inner Teacher

The middle figure in the Chart of Your Divine Self represents the Son of the Father-Mother God. That Son is the Universal Christ, corresponding to *Tiferet.* (fig. 12) There is only one Son

of God, one *Tiferet,* but God gave you and me and every son and daughter of God an exact replica of the original. The ascended masters call this likeness the "Holy Christ Self" or "Higher Self."

Your Holy Christ Self is your soul's advocate before the Father-Mother God. He is your inner teacher, guardian and dearest friend. He is also the voice of conscience that speaks within the precincts of your heart and soul.

Another name for the Holy Christ Self is the LORD Our Righteousness. Jeremiah prophesied that the LORD Our Righteousness would reign as king, executing judgment, justice and righteousness in the earth.[18] Thus the prophet depicted the LORD Our Righteousness as a Mediator. Your Holy Christ Self acts as the Mediator between you and I AM THAT I AM. He divides the way between good and evil within you, teaching you right from wrong.

Before sin/karma descended upon us, our souls were bonded to the Universal Christ, *Tiferet,* and we were clothed in the original, etheric pattern of *Adam Kadmon* in which we were made. But through succeeding incarnations in an imperfect world, we descended to the level of the lower figure in the chart and lost the enlightenment we had. Today our Holy Christ Self sustains for us the blueprint of *Adam Kadmon,* which Kabbalists say we are destined to manifest again.

FIGURE 12. *Kabbalah's diagram of the ten* sefirot *and the ascended masters' Chart of Your Divine Self are both referred to as the Tree of Life. Here the Kabbalists' Tree of Life is superimposed over the Chart of Your Divine Self. The uppermost* sefirah, Keter, *corresponds to the upper figure in the chart, the I AM Presence (the I AM THAT I AM individualized for each of us). The middle* sefirah, Tiferet, *corresponds to the Holy Christ Self (the Universal Christ individualized for each of us). The lower figure in the chart, representing your soul, corresponds to* Malkhut/Shekhinah—*the* sefirah *that represents the physical universe, the physical body, the soul, and the point where spiritual and physical forces meet.*

We can return to that archetypal pattern of perfection by bonding to our Holy Christ Self. This is the goal of every soul on the mystical path. What does it mean to be bonded to your Holy Christ Self? It means that through the steps and stages of the spiritualization of your consciousness, your soul has returned to the perfect pattern of your Holy Christ Self. This is "the alchemical marriage," whereby the soul attains union with her Bridegroom.

As you imitate the great spiritual teachers and rabbis of all time and as you develop the qualities of each of the *sefirot,* you can begin to know a greater fusion with your Holy Christ Self. Another way you can bond to your Holy Christ Self is to balance your karma. You do this by paying the debts you owe to those you have in some way wronged during this and past lifetimes. The most effective ways to balance karma are through (1) heartfelt prayer, including affirmations that invoke the violet flame of the Holy Spirit (see chapter 10), and (2) serving God, family and community.

The Flame of God in Your Heart

The Chart of Your Divine Self shows a shaft of white light descending from the I AM Presence through the Holy Christ Self to the lower figure in the chart. This is the "crystal cord." In Ecclesiastes 12:6 it is referred to as the silver cord. Through this umbilical cord flows a cascading stream of God's light, life and consciousness. It is called the "lifestream." The lifestream empowers you to think, feel, reason, experience life, work, play, grow and wax strong in spirit.[19]

As you exercise your freedom to be what you choose to be, you are making your mark on your lifestream. You are coloring that crystal-clear stream with your thoughts, feelings, words, works and desires. Either you color the stream with pure colors, representing talents and virtues from God that you are developing day by day, or you taint the stream with the putrid, muddied perversions of an off-color state of consciousness.

The energy of your crystal cord also nourishes and sustains the flame of God that is ensconced in the secret chamber of your heart. This flame is called the "threefold flame" or "divine spark." It is literally a spark of sacred fire from God's own heart. It is your soul's point of contact with the Supreme Source of all life, *Ein Sof.*

In a discourse on the threefold flame and the secret chamber of the heart, the Ascended Master Saint Germain says:

> Your heart is indeed one of the choicest gifts of God. Within it there is a central chamber surrounded by such light and protection that we call it a "cosmic interval." It is a chamber separated from matter, and no probing could ever discover it. It occupies simultaneously not only the third and fourth dimensions but also other dimensions unknown to man. It is thus the connecting point of the mighty silver cord of light that descends from your God Presence to sustain the beating of your physical heart, giving you life, purpose and cosmic integration.[20]

The threefold flame has three "plumes" that embody the three primary attributes of God and that correspond to the Trinity. The blue plume (on your left) embodies God's Power and corresponds to the Father. The yellow plume (in the center) embodies God's Wisdom and corresponds to the Son. The pink plume (on your right) embodies God's Love and corresponds to the Holy Spirit. By accessing the Power, Wisdom and Love of the Godhead anchored in your threefold flame, you can fulfill your reason for being.

Your Soul and Four Lower Bodies

The lower figure in the Chart of Your Divine Self represents your soul. Your soul is sheathed in four different "bodies," called the "four lower bodies": (1) the etheric body, (2) the mental body, (3) the desire, or emotional, body and (4) the physical body. These are the vehicles your soul uses in her journey on earth. (They are called "lower bodies" in contrast to the three "higher bodies," which are the I AM Presence, Causal Body and Holy Christ Self.) The lower figure in the chart corresponds to the Holy Spirit, for your soul and four lower bodies are intended to be the temple of the Holy Spirit.[21]

Your etheric body, also called the memory body, houses the blueprint of your identity. It also contains the memory of all that has ever transpired in your soul and all impulses you have ever sent out through your soul since you were created. Your mental body is the vessel of your cognitive faculties. When it is purified it can become the vessel of the Mind of God. The desire body houses your higher and lower desires and records your emotions. Your physical body is the miracle of flesh and blood that enables your soul to progress in the material universe.

The Chart of Your Divine Self shows the lower figure standing in the violet flame. (p. 78) The violet flame is the spiritual fire of the Holy Spirit that can help your soul find her way back to God. It has the purifying power to consume negative thoughts, negative feelings and negative karma. As you invoke it, the violet flame will penetrate your mind and heart, your unconscious and subconscious to transmute your past "sins" (or misuses of the light of the ten *sefirot*) and bring all things into harmony and balance.

When you use the violet flame to transmute the imperfections of your etheric, mental, emotional and physical bodies, you are clearing the way for the blueprint of *Adam Kadmon* to be manifest in those bodies. And you will find that you are able to anchor in your body greater and greater increments of light to offset the darkness in the earth. (See the last chapter for affirmations you can use to invoke the violet flame.)

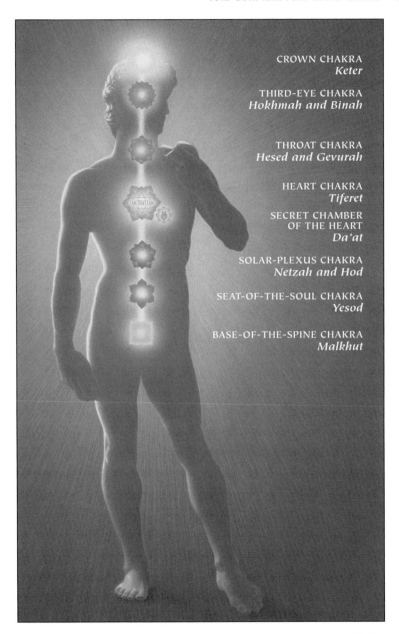

CROWN CHAKRA
Keter

THIRD-EYE CHAKRA
Hokhmah and Binah

THROAT CHAKRA
Hesed and Gevurah

HEART CHAKRA
Tiferet

SECRET CHAMBER
OF THE HEART
Da'at

SOLAR-PLEXUS CHAKRA
Netzah and Hod

SEAT-OF-THE-SOUL CHAKRA
Yesod

BASE-OF-THE-SPINE CHAKRA
Malkhut

FIGURE 13. *The* sefirot *correspond to the chakras (the centers of light in your etheric body). Both the* sefirot *and the chakras step down God's energy for our use.*

The Sefirot and the Chakras

We have seen how the *sefirot* correspond to the spheres of the Causal Body that surround the upper figure in the Chart of Your Divine Self. The *sefirot* also relate to the lower figure in the chart because they correspond to your *chakras,* a Sanskrit term for the centers of light in your etheric body.

Your chakras receive the energy that flows from *Ein Sof* through your I AM Presence and the *sefirot,* and then they distribute it to your four lower bodies. Each chakra regulates the energy flow to a different area of the body, and each chakra externalizes that energy flow through one of the endocrine glands.

Although Kabbalists did not use the term *chakra,* Perle Epstein notes that they meditated on the body's energy centers to enhance their meditation.[22]

The seven major chakras are positioned along the spinal column from the base of the spine to the crown (see fig. 13). Just as the *sefirot* are step-down transformers that transform God's energy for our use, so the chakras are internal step-down transformers that regulate God's energy according to the needs of our four lower bodies.

Chakra means "wheel" or "disc." The more energy that flows through a chakra, the faster it spins. Each chakra has a unique function and frequency and represents a different level of consciousness. These differences are denoted by the number of petals of each chakra. The more petals the chakra has, the higher its frequency.

Some modern Kabbalists have correlated the *sefirot* to specific chakras. (fig. 13) (Earlier I correlated the Causal Body spheres and their corresponding rays to the *sefirot.* What follows is a different way of correlating the rays to the *sefirot* but one that also has value for your meditation on the *sefirot.*)

Keter (Crown) corresponds to the crown chakra. The crown chakra has 972 petals and is located at the top of the head.

The yellow ray of illumination is focused in the crown chakra. *Hokhmah* (Wisdom) and *Binah* (Understanding) correspond to the ninety-six-petaled third-eye chakra, located at the center of the brow. The green ray of truth, science, healing, abundance, vision and music is focused in this chakra.

Hesed (Love/Mercy) and *Gevurah* (Justice/Judgment) correspond to the sixteen-petaled throat chakra, where the blue ray of God's will, faith, power, protection, perfection and judgment is focused. *Tiferet* (Beauty/Compassion) corresponds to the twelve-petaled heart chakra, where the roseate ray of divine love is focused.

Netzah (Victory) and *Hod* (Splendor/Majesty) correspond to the ten-petaled solar-plexus chakra at the navel. The purple-and-gold ray of ministration and service is focused there. *Yesod* (Foundation) corresponds to the six-petaled seat-of-the-soul chakra, located halfway between the navel and base of the spine. Here the violet ray of transmutation is focused.

Malkhut (Kingdom) corresponds to the four-petaled base-of-the-spine chakra, the lowest chakra on the spinal column. The white ray focused in this chakra is known as the sacred fire and the flame of the ascension. When a soul pays off her karma, fulfills her divine plan and bonds to her Holy Christ Self, she returns to God in the ritual of the ascension, as Jesus and the other ascended masters have done.

Rabbi Yonassan Gershom says that *Malkhut* can correspond to the base of the spine or the feet. "Through the *sefirah Malkhut* you touch the physical world," he says. "It is the connection to the earth. Yogis sit on the ground, but in Kabbalah *Malkhut* corresponds to the point of the feet because we stand when we pray."[23]

As for the quasi *sefirah, Da'at,* I associate it with the eight-petaled secret chamber of the heart, that special place where you commune with your Holy Christ Self and fan the fires of your threefold flame. Here you can also invoke the light of

SEFIRAH	ATTRIBUTE	ADAM KADMON'S BODY	CHAKRA	COLOR/ATTRIBUTE OF CHAKRA
KETER	Crown	Head	Crown	Yellow/Wisdom, Understanding, Enlightenment
HOKHMAH	Wisdom	Head	Third eye	Green/Truth, Science, Healing, Abundance, Vision, Music
BINAH	Understanding	Head	Third eye	Green/Truth, Science, Healing, Abundance, Vision, Music
DA'AT	Knowledge	Face and Throat	Secret Chamber of the Heart	Peach/ Self-Knowledge, Threefold Flame
HESED	Love, Mercy	Right Arm	Throat	Blue/Faith, Will, Power, Perfection, Protection, Judgment
GEVURAH	Justice, Judgment	Left Arm	Throat	Blue/Faith, Will, Power, Perfection, Protection, Judgment
TIFERET	Beauty, Compassion	Trunk	Heart	Pink/Love, Compassion, Kindness, Charity
NETZAH	Victory	Right Leg	Solar Plexus	Purple and Gold/ Service, Ministration, Peace, Brotherhood
HOD	Splendor, Majesty	Left Leg	Solar Plexus	Purple and Gold/ Service, Ministration, Peace, Brotherhood
YESOD	Foundation	Male Sexual Organ	Seat of the soul	Violet/Mercy, Justice, Freedom, Transmutation
MALKHUT/ SHEKHINAH	Kingdom/ Divine Presence	Feet or Mouth	Base of the spine	White/Purity, Discipline, Joy

FIGURE 14. *Attributes of and Correspondences to the* Sefirot

Da'at to gain self-knowledge, truly the knowledge of your inner child, your very soul.

You automatically intensify light in a chakra when you perform the good works that accrue to the corresponding sphere of your Causal Body. For example, when you perform good works that accrue to the white sphere of your Causal Body, you also intensify the light in your white (base-of-the-spine) chakra; when you perform good works that accrue to your yellow sphere, you also intensify the light in your yellow (crown) chakra.

If you misuse the energies of your chakras—through selfishness, hatred, criticism, anger or any perversion of the virtues of the *sefirot*—your chakras will become clogged. This blocks the currents of *Ein Sof's* energy that vitalize your four lower bodies and can cause sluggishness or illness in your mental, emotional and physical bodies.

Although diagrams of the chakras and the *sefirot* of necessity depict them as static forces, when you meditate on them remember to see them as vibrant and dynamic. God's energy is constantly pulsing through your body and the network of your chakras, just as it is pulsing through the network of the *sefirot*. The *sefirot*, says Isaiah Tishby, are not like

> fixed, solid rungs on the ladder of the progressive revelation of the divine attributes. They are, on the contrary, dynamic forces, ascending and descending, and extending themselves within the area of the Godhead. . . . They are in continuous motion, involved in innumerable processes of interweaving, interlinking, and union. . . . The lower *sefirot* elevate themselves in their yearning to return and cleave to their source, and the upper *sefirot* move downward in order to give sustenance to the lower, and to transmit divine influence to the worlds below.[24]

The more we attune to the activity of the *sefirot,* which undergirds the entire universe, the more the Tree of Life of the *sefirot* will become a part of our daily walk with God. "Gradually, as the aspirant comes to appreciate the interaction of Laws—the flows, circulations, interchanges, transformations and levels—the Tree becomes less and less like an external abstraction and more like a living organism," writes Halevi. "When it has begun to be part of the aspirant's own being, he can say that he knows something of Kabbalah."[25]

The Kabbalists, along with mystics of all the world's religions, never lose sight of the principle that the divine pattern of the world above is reflected in their own bodies and souls and in the world all around them. The mystic lives and breathes the truth of the ancient Hermetic axiom "As Above, so below." And as Ralph Waldo Emerson once said, "What lies behind us and what lies before us are tiny matters compared to what lies within us."

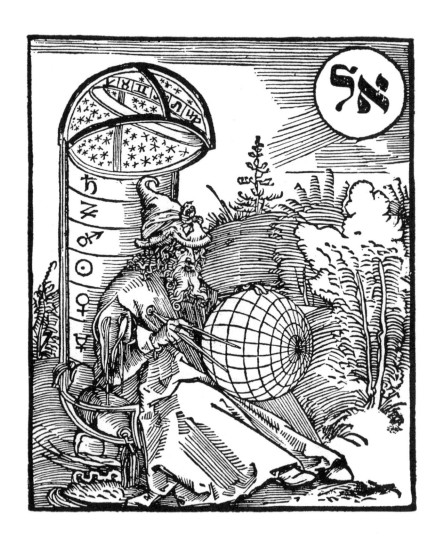

CHAPTER FIVE

MYSTERIES OF THE SOUL

*From the beginning of Time, through eternities, I was among
His hidden treasures. From Nothing He called me forth,
but at the End of Time I shall be recalled by the King.*

NAHMANIDES

Since we are patterned after
the *sefirot,* Kabbalists believe that the more we know about our
human form and our soul, the more we will know about the
divine world of the *sefirot.* "The man who intends to penetrate
the royal palace needs first to know his own soul. . . [which]
is modeled on its Creator who created it," writes Moses de León.
"Therefore, when man knows the eminence and nature of the
soul, his thoughts and understanding will spread from there to
the secrets of royal matters,"[1] that is, the secrets of the *sefirot.*

What is the soul? According to Kabbalists, the soul is a mirror
in which the *sefirot* are reflected, a spark of the divine essence.
De León writes, "The body is not an image of the Creator.

*Kabbalists teach that if we desire to penetrate the secret world of the
sefirot, we must first explore the mysteries of our own soul and spirit,
for we are patterned after the sefirot. (Astronomer, printed by Johann
Weissenburger, Nuremberg, 1504.)*

. . . What, then, is His image and His counterpart? The soul, without a doubt." The soul, he says, is God's "own essential being."[2]

The Zohar tells us that our body is nothing more than a garment for our soul: "How does Scripture describe the creation of man? 'You have clothed me with skin and flesh' (Job 10:11). What then is man? If you say that he is nothing but skin and flesh, and bones and sinews, you are wrong; for, in actual truth, the real part of man is his soul. Clothes belong to man, but they are not man, and when man departs he is stripped of the clothes that he has put on."[3]

The Three Parts of the Soul

The Zohar says the soul has three parts: *nefesh, ruah* and *neshamah*. Each part comes from a different *sefirah*. Nefesh is the part of the soul that gives life to and sustains the body. Its source is the *sefirah Malkhut*. The Zohar says the *nefesh* stimulates the body to observe the commandments.

The second part of the soul, *ruah,* is the spirit, the seat of intellect and reason that allows us to transcend mere human existence. The *ruah* originates in *Tiferet.* It is "the ethical power to distinguish between good and evil," writes Scholem.[4]

The third part of the soul, *neshamah,* is known as the spiritual soul, holy soul or divine spark. It is described in the Zohar as a spark of *Binah,* for it comes from that *sefirah.*[5] Author Sidney Spencer writes:

Neshamah is literally "breathing": it is the "breath of higher spirituality, the bridge which connects man with the heavenly world." It is an emanation of *Binah,* the divine Intelligence, and unites man with God.

. . . It is an individualized expression of the divine. As the Zohar says, it is in its essence "the Supernal Soul, the Soul of all souls, inscrutable and unknowable, veiled in a covering of exceeding brightness" (2:245a). In entering into the depths of his own being, man thus becomes aware of the presence of God.[6]

We all have the potential to realize the three grades of the soul, say Kabbalists, but these grades are not automatically active in all people. The *nefesh* is active in everyone, but the other two parts are activated only when merited. Scholem says that the *ruah* and *neshamah*

> are found only in the man who has awakened spiritually and made a special effort to develop his intellectual powers and religious sensibilities. The *ruah*. . . is aroused at an unspecified time when a man succeeds in rising above his purely vitalistic side. But it is the highest of the three parts of the soul, the *neshamah* or *spiritus,* which is the most important of all. It is aroused in a man when he occupies himself with the Torah and its commandments, and it opens his higher powers of apprehension, especially his ability to mystically apprehend the Godhead and the secrets of the universe.[7] By acquiring *[neshamah],* the Kabbalist thus realizes something of the divine in his own nature.[8]

The Zohar says that the *neshamah* is activated within us when we strive for righteousness and purity and that by observing the grades of the soul we can learn about the *sefirot:*

> The *nefesh* and the *ruah* are intertwined together, whereas the *neshamah* resides in a man's character—an abode which cannot be discovered or located. Should a man strive towards purity of life, he is aided thereto by a holy *neshamah,* whereby he is purified and sanctified and attains the title of "saint." But should he not strive for righteousness and purity of life, he is animated only by the two grades, *nefesh* and *ruah,* and is devoid of a holy *neshamah.* What is more, he who commences to defile himself is led further into defilement, and heavenly help is withdrawn from him. Thus each is led along the path which he chooses.[9]. . .
> Happy are the righteous in this world and in the next, because they are altogether holy. Their body is holy, their soul *(nefesh)* is holy, their spirit *(ruah)* is holy, their super-soul *(neshamah)* is holy of holies. These are three grades indissolubly united.

If a man does well with his soul *(nefesh)*, there descends upon him a certain crown called spirit *(ruah)*, which stirs him to a deeper contemplation of the laws of the Holy King. If he does well with this spirit, he is invested with a noble holy crown called super-soul *(neshamah)*, which can contemplate all.[10]. . .

From observing these grades of the soul, you will obtain an insight into the higher Wisdom, and everything is Wisdom, so that you might perceive in this way matters that are sealed[11] [i.e., perceive the *sefirot*[12]].

The Zohar goes on to say that Abraham attained the highest level of the soul. It interprets certain events in Abraham's life as symbolic of the soul testings he had to face as he sought to cleave to God. These teachings are profound and they are immediately relevant to your soul's ascent up the Tree of Life today. For every soul who seeks to cleave to God must pass through the same initiations that Abraham did.

At the time when Abram [Abraham] entered the land, God appeared to him and he received there a *nefesh,* and built an altar to the corresponding grade (of divinity) [to the corresponding *sefirah*]. Then "he journeyed to the South," receiving a *ruah*. Finally he rose to the height of cleaving to God through the medium of the *neshamah,* whereupon he "built an altar to the Lord," indicating the most recondite grade corresponding to the *neshamah*.

He then found that it was requisite for him to test himself and endow himself with grades, so he went down to Egypt [a country of magicians, symbolizing the domain of evil forces and magic; worldliness; the material world]. There he preserved himself from being seduced by those bright essences, and after testing himself he returned to his place: he "went up" from Egypt literally, strengthened and confirmed in faith, and reached the highest grade of faith. Thenceforth Abram was acquainted with the higher Wisdom and clung to God and became the right hand of the world.[13]

What happens to the parts of the soul after death? Since the *neshamah* is a spark of the divine, the Zohar says that it cannot sin and therefore cannot be punished after death. The *nefesh* and sometimes the *ruah* can be punished after death. Scholem says Kabbalists teach that after death "the *nefesh* remains for a while in the grave, brooding over the body; the *ruah* ascends to the terrestrial paradise in accordance with its merits; and the *neshamah* goes directly back to its native home."[14]

Kabbalists after the Zohar, including Isaac Luria, name two additional levels of the soul that are higher than the *nefesh, ruah* and *neshamah:* the *hayyah* and *yehidah.* These two tiers of the soul, writes Scholem, "were considered to represent the sublimest levels of intuitive cognition and to be within the grasp only of a few chosen individuals."[15]

The Difference between Your Soul and Your Divine Spark

Like the Kabbalists, mystics the world around believe that a part of God resides within each of us. The apostle Paul told the Corinthians, "Know ye not that ye are the temple of God, and that the Spirit of God dwelleth in you?"[16] Peter said that through the goodness and glory of Christ we could be "partakers of the divine nature."[17]

In a teaching that resembles that of Kabbalah, fourteenth-century Christian theologian and mystic Meister Eckhart taught: "There is something in the soul that is so akin to God that it is one with Him.[18] God's seed is within us.[19] There is a part of the soul that is untouched by time or mortality: it proceeds out of the Spirit and remains eternally in the Spirit and is divine. . . . Here God glows and flames without ceasing, in all His abundance and sweetness and rapture."[20]

Similarly, Buddhists teach that all men have within them the potential for Buddhahood, which they call the Buddha-nature or the "Germ of Buddhahood." One Buddhist text says, "The road to Buddhahood is open to all. At all times have all living beings the Germ of Buddhahood in them."[21]

Hinduism calls the indwelling God "the Atman." The Atman is the imperishable, undecaying core of man. It is identical with Brahman, the Absolute, hence the famous Hindu affirmation: *Tat Tvam Asi,* "That thou art," meaning: Thou art the Absolute. Thou art Brahman. Thou art God. *That* is what thou art.

Although mystics like Meister Eckhart sometimes refer to the soul and the divine spark as identical, there is a difference between them. The Jewish mystics approach this understanding when they make a distinction between the holy spark, *neshamah,* and the other two grades of the soul, *nefesh* and *ruah.*

You can think of the divine spark as pure Spirit. It can never die. But the soul can be lost; she can self-destruct by her own actions. If the soul does not exercise her free will to realize her potential, she may ultimately lose that potential and cease to exist.

The Book of Ezekiel and the Book of Revelation explain what happens to the soul in this case: "The soul that sinneth, it shall die."[22] "He that overcometh shall inherit all things; and I will be his God and he shall be my son. But the fearful and unbelieving and the abominable and murderers and whoremongers and sorcerers and idolaters and all liars shall have their part in the lake which burneth with fire and brimstone: which is the second death."[23]

Mark Prophet and I explain the difference between the soul and the Spirit in *Climb the Highest Mountain:*

> God is a Spirit and the soul is the living potential of God. The soul's demand for free will and her separation from God resulted in the descent of this potential into the lowly estate of the flesh. Sown in dishonor, the soul is destined to be raised in honor to the fullness of that God-estate which is the one Spirit of all Life. The soul can be lost; Spirit can never die. . . .
>
> The soul, then, remains a fallen potential that must be imbued with the Reality of Spirit, purified through prayer and

supplication, and returned to the glory from which it descended and to the unity of the Whole. This rejoining of soul to Spirit is the alchemical marriage which determines the destiny of the self and makes it one with immortal Truth. When this ritual is fulfilled, the highest Self is enthroned as the Lord of Life; and the potential of God, realized in man, is found to be the All-in-all.[24]

Mark liked to talk about a drop of water taken from the ocean to describe the relationship of the soul to God. In a lecture he once gave he said:

I like to think that God is a Spirit—like a great big ocean. And I like to think of all of us as being like drops of water in a vast sea of light.

Reciting the great mysteries of the universe, the Hindu sage used to say, "God is the ocean. . ."—it was his favorite similitude, and he would hold up his finger with one little drop of water glistening on the end of it as he continued—"and this drop is the soul. This is a part of the ocean of God. It lacks only the quantity of God but none of the quality."

. . . Do you know that all of the elements of the whole ocean are to be found in that drop of water?

So you see, you have all of the shining qualities of God, of the Creator of a living soul which has the real potential—the *real*izable potential—of the Spirit. . . .

That means that you have within yourself a glisteringly beautiful spark of the Son of God, of the Christ consciousness —of Reality. It's right there in front of you. That's you! You're a drop in an infinite ocean of God. Isn't that something to think about![25]

The concept in Kabbalah that we have within us a part of God and that we are composed of the ten *sefirot* has far-reaching implications. Our divine nature confers upon us unparalleled opportunities: we not only have tremendous power to change our own lives and the world around us, but, astonishingly, we have the power to change the world of the Godhead as well. Scholem writes:

> Man is the perfecting agent in the structure of the cosmos; like all the other created beings, only even more so, he is composed of all ten *sefirot* and "of all spiritual things," that is, of the supernal principles that constitute the attributes of the Godhead. If the forces of the *sefirot* are reflected in him, he is also the "transformer" who through his own life and deeds amplifies these forces to their highest level of manifestation and redirects them to their original source. To use the neoplatonic formula, the process of creation involves the departure of [the] all from the One and its return to the One.[26]

In short, Kabbalists have come up with the very unique idea that we can use our spiritual power to strengthen or to weaken, to unite or to disrupt the divine world. This is a subject I will discuss further in later chapters.

Soul Travel to Celestial Academies
"With My Soul Have I Desired Thee in the Night"

The Zohar and other Kabbalistic writings describe the mystic ascent of the soul to heavenly realms. They say that while the body is asleep the soul can take flight to "celestial academies," where she is tutored in the sublime mysteries of God. Hayim Vital says that Luria was one whose soul was worthy to ascend to the celestial academies nightly. Vital writes:

> Troops of angels would greet him to safeguard his way, bringing him to the celestial academies. These angels would ask him which academy he chose to visit. Sometimes he said that he wished to visit the academy of Rabbi Simeon bar Yohai, or the academy of Rabbi Akiva or that of Rabbi Eliezer the Great or those of other *tannaim* and *amoraim*,[27] or of the prophets. And to whichever of those academies he wished to go, the angels would take him. The next day he would disclose to the sages what he received in that academy.[28]

Moshe Idel, a contemporary expert on Kabbalah, says, "This perception of Luria is no doubt closely connected to the huge amount of Kabbalistic material he communicated that produced the extensive Lurianic literature."[29]

Idel says that the Kabbalist Rabbi Shem Tov ibn Gaon also speaks of sharing knowledge gained during mystic ascents. "Rabbi Shem Tov mentions the need to fathom intellectually the secrets of the *Merkabah* [the throne-chariot of God] and the structures of the Creation," writes Idel. "The result is not only beatific or divine visions but also an impressive explosion of literary creativity, consisting in 'copying' the contents revealed in his mind as if from a book. The affinity of this description to Luria's own creativity is startling."[30] The ideal for the mystic, according to Rabbi Shem Tov, is "to ascend from the lower academy to the supernal academy and to subsist from the splendor of the *Shekhinah*."[31]

Idel also cites an entry made by Vital in his diary that alludes to the soul's ascent to spiritual realms to commune with heavenly beings. Here Vital is recording the dream of Rabbi Isaac Alatif.

> Once I fainted deeply for an hour, and a huge number of old men and many women came to watch me, and the house was completely full of them, and they all were worried for me. Afterwards the swoon passed and I opened my eyes and said, "Know that just now my soul ascended to the seat of glory, and they sent my soul back to this world in order to preach before you and lead you in the way of repentance and in matters of charity."[32]

The celestial academies that the Jewish mystics write about are what the ascended masters call "retreats" or "universities of the Spirit." They are located in the heaven world, known as the etheric plane. As your soul takes leave of your body while you sleep at night, you can travel to these academies to study with angels and masters of wisdom who have gained mastery in their fields of specialization.

If you keep your mind and heart attuned to the sendings of your soul, you may recall the lessons you have learned at night in the etheric retreats or you may awaken in the morning with a clear direction to do this or that. You may even feel that the burdens you have prayed to God about the night before are resolved, or you will arise knowing precisely what steps to take to resolve them.

Keep a journal with pen or pencil handy on your nightstand. Record instructions and revelations you receive right

Kabbalists say that while the body is asleep, the soul can take flight, escorted by angels, to "celestial academies." At these academies the soul is tutored in the sublime mysteries of God. (The New Jerusalem by Gustave Doré.)

away, either when you are awakened in the night or when you arise in the morning. Some dreams are encoded material presented symbolically by your Holy Christ Self. You can ask your Holy Christ Self to decode your dreams and to show you how to apply their lessons to your daily life. Sift through the material and act on what feels right to you and is consistent with ethical standards. Then discard what is neither plausible nor rational.

The Zohar wisely warns that the ascent of the soul during sleep is not without its dangers. In one passage it describes how "certain bright but unclean essences" attempt to prevent the soul from soaring to the heights:

> Rabbi Simeon was on a journey with Rabbi Eleazar, his son, Rabbi Abba, and Rabbi Judah. As they went along Rabbi Simeon said: It surprises me how people fail to pay attention to the study of the words of Torah, and of the very foundation of their lives.
>
> He proceeded to discourse on the text: "With my soul have I desired thee in the night, yea, with my spirit within me will I seek thee early" (Isa. 26:9). He said: The inner meaning of this verse is as follows.
>
> When a man lies down in bed, his vital spirit *(nefesh)* leaves him and begins to mount on high. But do all [souls] really ascend [that is, reach the highest levels[33]]? No. Not every one sees the countenance of the king [that is, contemplates the divine *sefirot*[34]]. But the soul does ascend, leaving with the body only the impression of a receptacle which contains the heartbeat. The rest of it tries to soar from grade to grade, and in doing so it encounters certain bright but unclean essences.
>
> If [the *nefesh*] is pure and has not defiled itself by day, it rises above [the unclean essences] to the higher realms, but if not, it becomes defiled among them and cleaves to them and does not rise any further. There they show her certain things which are going to happen in the near future: and sometimes they delude her and show her false things. Thus she goes

about the whole night until the man wakes up, when she returns to her place. Happy are the righteous to whom God reveals His secrets in dreams, so that they may be on their guard against sin! Woe to the sinners who defile their bodies and their souls![35]

When we travel out of our body at night on our way to the etheric realm, we must beware of getting caught in what is known as "the astral plane." Here bright essences of disembodied spirits will try to lure us to their level with baubles and trinkets. These spirits are also called "discarnate entities." Some have lost their souls and would draw us to themselves to steal our light. Do not allow them to pull on you. Resist their animal magnetism.

The above passage from the Zohar tells us that whatever we bring back from the astral plane and from the "bright but unclean essences" is not reliable and is not a revelation from God. Rather than seeking communications from disembodied spirits on the astral plane, seek the direct communication of your God Presence through your Holy Christ Self. Pray to the Holy Spirit for the gift of discernment of spirits and heed the warnings of your Holy Christ Self. Accept his guidance to stay away from the negative influences of the astral plane.

Aware of the wiles of discarnate entities and malevolent spirits, Paul said:

> Be strong in the Lord, and in the power of his might. Put on the whole armour of God, that ye may be able to stand against the wiles of the devil. . . .
>
> Stand therefore, having your loins girt about with truth, and having on the breastplate of righteousness; and your feet shod with the preparation of the gospel of peace; above all, taking the shield of faith, wherewith ye shall be able to quench all the fiery darts of the wicked.
>
> And take the helmet of salvation, and the sword of the Spirit, which is the word of God: praying always with all prayer and supplication in the Spirit.[36]

The Royal Teton Retreat, a university of the Spirit in the heaven world, is congruent with the Grand Teton in the Teton Range near Jackson Hole, Wyoming. Souls travel to this retreat during sleep or between incarnations to be tutored by masters of wisdom.

To help you reach the heaven world safely as you journey out of your body at night, you can pray to Archangel Michael to protect your soul from getting entangled with the bright essences of disembodied spirits.* In addition, as you go to sleep, fix your mind straight as an arrow and let it fly unerringly to its mark. Focus your inner sight on your destination, preferably an etheric retreat of the Great White Brotherhood, such as the Royal Teton Retreat.

The Royal Teton Retreat, congruent with the Grand Teton near Jackson Hole, Wyoming, is the retreat the ascended masters recommend spiritual seekers aim for. Put up a poster, painting or photo of the Grand Teton opposite your bed so it is the last thing you see just before you turn out your light.

---

*See chapter 10 for prayers you can give to invoke the intercession of Archangel Michael.

Then visualize your soul clothed in your etheric body of light being escorted to the Royal Teton Retreat by a cordon of angels assigned to you by Archangel Michael.

After warning of the bright but unclean essences that ensnare and delude souls who have defiled themselves during the day, the Zohar goes on to describe the ascent of pure souls.

> As for those who have not defiled themselves during the day, when they fall asleep at night their soul begins to ascend, and first enters those grades which we have mentioned, but it does not cleave to them and continues to mount further. And it moves on subsequently, rising in its own way [depending on the virtues that it has[37]]. The soul which is privileged thus to rise finally appears before the gate of the celestial palace and yearns with all its might to behold the beauty of the King and to visit His sanctuary.
>
> This is the man who ever hath a portion in the world to come, and this is the soul whose yearning when she ascends is for the Holy One, blessed be He, and who does not cleave to those other bright essences but seeks out the holy essence in the place from which she (originally) issued. Therefore it is written, "With my soul have I desired thee in the night," to pursue after thee and not to be enticed away after false powers.[38]

Twin Flames and Soul Mates

Another mystery of the soul unveiled in Kabbalah is the mystery of you and your soul partner. The Zohar teaches that your soul has a twin who was created with you in the beginning. God will bring the two of you together, it says, if you live a life of purity and good works.

> All the souls in the world, which are the fruit of the handiwork of the Almighty, are mystically one, but when they descend to this world they are separated into male and female, though these are still conjoined.
>
> When they first issue forth, they issue as male and female together. Subsequently, when they descend [to this world] they

separate, one to one side and the other to the other, and God afterwards unites them—God and no other, He alone knowing the mate proper to each. Happy the man who is upright in his works [or pure] and walks in the way of truth, so that his soul may find its original mate, for then he becomes indeed perfect,* and through his perfection the whole world is blessed.[39]

Centuries before the Zohar was written, Plato taught that each of us is half of a divine whole and that is why we are always searching for our original partner. In his *Symposium* he writes:

Ancient is the desire of one another which is implanted in us, reuniting our original nature, making one of two, and healing the state of man.

Each of us when separated, having one side only, like a flat fish, is but the indenture [indentation] of a man, and he is always looking for his other half. . . .

When one of them meets with his other half, the actual half of himself, . . . the pair are lost in an amazement of love and friendship and intimacy. . . .These are the people who pass their whole lives together; yet they could not explain what they desire of one another. For the intense yearning which each of them has towards the other does not appear to be the desire of lover's intercourse, but of something else which the soul of either evidently desires and cannot tell.[40]

Plato's image of the lone soul as a flat fish, having only one side, reminds me of statues of the Hindu god Shiva that depict him as half man and half woman. According to legend, Shiva was determined that there be no separation between himself and his consort Parvati. He therefore decreed that his right side represent Shiva and that his left side represent Parvati in an eternal union. That eternal union with one's divine counterpart and with God is what every soul, consciously or unconsciously, yearns for.

---

*also translated "for if he performs good deeds, he is the proper, whole man" (Tishby, *Wisdom of the Zohar* 3:1382)

Like the Zohar, Plato says our search for our divine partner will end only if we are pious and avoid evil:

> Human nature was originally one and we were a whole, and the desire and pursuit of the whole is called love. There was a time, I say, when we were one, but now because of the wickedness of mankind God has dispersed us. . . .
>
> Wherefore let us exhort all men to piety, that we may avoid evil, and obtain the good, of which Love is to us the lord and minister. . . .If we are friends of the god [Love] and at peace with him, we shall find our own true loves, which rarely happens in this world at present. . . .
>
> I believe that if our loves were perfectly accomplished, and each one returning to his primeval nature had his original true love, then our race would be happy. . . .[The god Love] promises that if we are pious, he will restore us to our original state, and heal us and make us happy and blessed.[41]

The term the ascended masters use to describe you and your "other half" is "twin flames." God created your twin flames out of a single "white fire body." He separated this ovoid into two spheres of being—one with a masculine polarity and the other with a feminine polarity. For the purpose of the soul's evolution, each half of the divine whole has its own Causal Body, I AM Presence, Holy Christ Self and soul. Twin flames are twin flames because they have the same spiritual origin and unique pattern of identity.

We would have continued to share the beauty of the relationship of cosmic lovers with our twin flame throughout our many incarnations on earth if we had remained in harmony with each other and with God. But we fell from the state of perfection by misusing God's light. In the process, we created negative karma—coils of energy and layers of density in our aura that have separated us from our twin flame. We found ourselves farther and farther apart until we passed as ships in the night, not knowing how near and yet how far we were from one another.

Thus before God can bring you and your twin flame together, you may have karmic obligations to others that you must fulfill. The sooner you balance your karma through service to life, the sooner you and your twin flame will be liberated for the next step in the saga of your destiny. This is one of the reasons why we find ourselves inexplicably drawn into certain circumstances, relationships or marriages. We may have something very important to give to another or to receive from another before we can move on with the divine plan of our twin flames.

In chapter 4, I said that the most effective way to fulfill karmic obligations is through prayer, especially by invoking

God originally created each soul with a mate, says the Zohar, but they became separated when they descended into this world. God will bring soul partners together again if they live a life of purity and good works.

the violet flame, and through service to God, family and community. This is what Plato and the Zohar mean when they say we must be pious and upright in our works in order to be reunited with our other half.

The first step toward your soul's union with her twin flame is to seek union with your Holy Christ Self and I AM Presence—to cleave to God, as the Jewish mystics would say. For you want to be able to bring to your twin flame the highest gift of your love, your true self and your spiritual attainment. And it is the light of God you garner as you ascend the ladder of the *sefirot* that will magnetize your twin flame to you or liberate you both to move closer to that goal.

Not all beautiful and soul-fulfilling loves are those of twin flames. There is also the love of kindred souls, who are called "soul mates." Whereas twin flames share a common spiritual origin, soul mates share a complementary calling in life. They are mates in the sense of being partners for the journey, co-workers. Soul mates are very compatible and very much alike. They are, in a sense, playmates in the schoolroom of life. You may have a number of such associations in the history of your soul's incarnations. But you only have one twin flame, and your twin flame is your greatest love.

Although you may be separated from your twin flame on earth, you are always one in Spirit. If karma must keep you apart for a season, at spiritual levels you may still work with your twin flame, amplifying the combined momentum of your love to minister to life.[42]

The Baal Shem Tov, founder of Hasidism, a Jewish religious movement that began in Poland in the eighteenth century, expressed the beauty and power of the relationship of twin flames when he wrote: "From every human being there rises a light that reaches straight to heaven. And when two souls that are destined to be together find each other, their streams of light flow together and a single brighter light goes forth from their united being."

Devekut, Mystical Cleaving to God

Kabbalists believe that because the soul has her origin in the divine realm, she naturally desires to return to her source. Kabbalists seek this return through *devekut,* mystical cleaving to God. *Devekut* is the ultimate goal of the Jewish mystic. Scholem says *devekut* is "continuous attachment or adhesion to God," "a perpetual being-with-God, an intimate union and conformity of the human and the divine will."[43]

Isaac of Acco delineates degrees of *devekut,* including equanimity (the indifference of the soul to praise or blame), concentration or solitude (being alone with God), the Holy Spirit (a general term for enlightenment and inspiration), and prophecy.[44]

The thirteenth-century mystic philosopher Rabbi Nahmanides says that *devekut* means that

> you should remember God and the love of Him always, that you should not cease thinking of Him, when you are on a journey, when you lie down or when you arise; so that when you converse with people you should do so with your mouth and your tongue, but your heart should be with God. And it is possible that the souls of men who achieve this state are bound up in the bond of eternal life even during their lifetime, for they are in themselves the abode of the *Shekhinah.*[45]

Nahmanides says that if you cleave to your Creator in this way, you are eligible to receive the Holy Spirit.[46] The twelfth-century Jewish philosopher and scholar Maimonides says that the person who has merited receiving the Holy Spirit is transformed and can perceive things that are not normally accessible:

> His soul becomes bound up on the level of the angels. . . and he becomes a completely different person. He can now understand things with a knowledge completely different than anything that he ever experienced previously. The level that he has attained is far above that of other men, who can merely use their intellect. This is the meaning of what [the prophet Samuel told] King Saul, "[The spirit of God shall descend

upon you,] you shall prophesy with them, and you shall be transformed into a different man" (I Sam. 10:6).[47]

Moses Luzzatto also describes the Holy Spirit as a form of enlightenment that is above human reason and intellect. He calls it "bestowed enlightenment." "Bestowed enlightenment consists of an influence granted by God through various means," says Luzzatto. "When such influence enters a person's mind, certain information becomes fixed in his intellect. He perceives this information clearly, without any doubt or error, understanding it completely, with all its causes and effects, as well as its place in the general scheme."[48]

Like Isaac of Acco, Luzzatto describes an even higher form of *devekut* than enlightenment—"the level of true prophecy." He says:

> This is a degree of inspiration in which the individual reaches a level where he literally binds himself to God in such a way that he actually feels this attachment. He then clearly realizes that the One to whom he is bound is God. This is sensed with complete clarity, with an awareness that leaves no room for any doubt whatsoever. The individual is as certain of it as he would be if it were a physical object observed with his physical senses.
>
> The main concept of true prophecy, then, is that a living human being achieves such an attachment and bond with God. This in itself is an extremely high state of perfection. Besides this, however, it is also often accompanied by certain information and enlightenment. Through prophecy, one can gain knowledge of many lofty truths among God's hidden mysteries. These things are perceived very clearly, just as all knowledge gained through bestowed enlightenment. Prophecy, however, comes with much greater intensity than *Ruah HaKodesh* [Holy Spirit].[49]

Kabbalists say that the opportunity to receive the Holy Spirit is not limited to Kabbalists or Jews. Elijah is said to have taught his disciples, "I call heaven and earth to bear witness

The ultimate goal of the Jewish mystic is an intimate oneness with God, known as devekut, *or mystical cleaving to God. Some Kabbalists describe prophecy as the highest level of* devekut. *The prophetess Deborah (above) was one of the greatest judges of Israel. The judges were charismatic leaders and military heroes, deliverers endowed with the Spirit of God. Deborah with Barak led the Israelites into battle and foretold their victory.* (The Prophetess Deborah *by Edwin Austin Abbey.*)

that any person, Jew or Gentile, man or woman, freeman or slave, if his deeds are worthy, then *Ruah HaKodesh* will descend upon him."[50]

Aryeh Kaplan points to the promise in the Book of Joel as evidence that God intends all humanity to receive his Holy Spirit: "I will pour out my spirit upon all flesh; and your sons and your daughters shall prophesy, your old men shall dream dreams, your young men shall see visions. And also upon the servants and upon the handmaids in those days will I pour out my spirit."[51]

According to Scholem, Kabbalists unanimously agree that *devekut,* mystical cleaving to God, is the ultimate goal of the spiritual path. However, there is disagreement among scholars as to whether Kabbalists taught that *devekut* leads to total union with God.

Moshe Idel notes, "Gershom Scholem stressed, time and again, that a total union with the Divine is absent in Jewish texts."[52] Scholem wrote in his book *Major Trends in Jewish Mysticism:* "It is only in extremely rare cases that ecstasy signifies actual union with God, in which the human individuality abandons itself to the rapture of complete submersion in the divine stream. Even in this ecstatic frame of mind, the Jewish mystic almost invariably retains a sense of the distance between the Creator and His creature."[53]

However, as Idel points out, Scholem was such a fine scholar of Jewish mysticism that many other scholars have accepted his views uncritically.[54] Using Kabbalistic texts for evidence, Idel shows that some Kabbalists did in fact pursue complete union with God.

For instance, Isaac of Acco uses a variation of the drop-in-the-ocean metaphor to describe the soul's union with God: "[The soul] will cleave to the divine intellect, and it will cleave to her. . . and she and the intellect become one entity, as if somebody pours out a jug of water into a flowing spring, so that all becomes one. . . . And this is the secret meaning of [the phrase] 'a fire devouring fire.'"[55]

In the same text Isaac of Acco writes: "This [rational] soul will cleave to the *Ein Sof* and will become total and universal, after she had been individual, due to her [experience in the] palace, while she was yet imprisoned in it, and she will become universal because of the nature of her real source."[56]

The Hasidic master Rabbi Menahem Nahum of Chernobyl also speaks of the union of the soul with its source: "He becomes attached to the divine unity by means of the union of the part to the all, which is *Ein Sof.* Consequently, the light of the holiness of *Ein Sof* shines in him, as the part cleaves to its root."[57]

The Soul's Journey after Life

The Zohar says the soul's journey beyond her earthly life is determined by the type of *devekut* she pursues in her life on earth. The soul chooses her own fate by cleaving to holy forces or to unholy forces.

> Blessed are the righteous, whose desire is perpetual *devekut* to the Holy One, blessed be He, and as they cleave to Him continually, so He cleaves to them and never leaves them. Alas for the wicked, whose desire and *devekut* separate them from Him. And it is not enough that they separate themselves from Him, but they cleave to "the other side" [the domain of demonic powers]. . . .
>
> When the righteous depart from the world, their souls all ascend, and the Holy One, blessed be He, prepares for them another form that they can put on, and that reflects their existence in this world.[58]

Tishby interprets this to mean that "the garment that the souls don after death in the Garden of Eden is woven from the commandments that were fulfilled and the good deeds that were done in the physical world."[59] The Zohar continues:

> It is the path taken by man in this world that determines the path of the soul on her departure. Thus, if a man is drawn towards the Holy One, and is filled with longing towards Him in this world, the soul in departing from him is carried upward towards the higher realms by the impetus given her each day in this world.[60]

Elaborating on the same theme, Rabbi Abba says in the Zohar that when he was in a town inhabited by descendants of the "children of the East," they imparted to him "some of the Wisdom of antiquity with which they were acquainted." One of the things they told him was that after the death of the body the soul who has cleaved to holiness while on earth will stand among "holy beings," but the soul who has cleaved to uncleanness while on earth will be attached to "unclean company." Rabbi Abba says:

> They showed me one [of their books of wisdom] in which it was written that, according to the goal which a man sets himself in this world, so does he draw to himself a spirit from on high. If he strives to attain some holy and lofty object, he draws that object from on high to himself below. But if his desire is to cleave to the other side, and he makes this his whole intent, then he draws to himself from above the other influence. They said, further, that all depends on the kind of speech, action, and intention to which a man habituates himself, for he draws to himself here below from on high that side to which he habitually cleaves.

> I found also in the same book the rites and ceremonies pertaining to the worship of the stars, with the requisite formulas and the directions for concentrating the thought upon them so as to draw them near the worshipper. The same principle applies to him who seeks to be attached to the sacred spirit on high. For it is by his acts, by his words, and by his fervency and devotion that he can draw to himself that spirit from on high.

> They further said that if a man follows a certain direction in this world, he will be led further in the same direction when he departs this world; as that to which he attaches himself in this world, so is that to which he will find himself attached in the other world: if holy, holy, and if defiled, defiled.

> If he cleaves to holiness he will on high be drawn to that side and be made a servant to minister before the Holy One among the angels, and will stand among those holy beings. . . . Similarly if he clings here to uncleanness, he will be drawn there towards that side and be made one of the unclean company and be attached to them. These are called "pests of mankind."[61]

The ascended masters, like the Jewish mystics, teach that the goal of the soul is to reunite with God. When the soul passes on through the change called death but is not ready for this ultimate reunion, she will spend time on interim planes before her next incarnation. Advanced souls who have led a life dedicated to God are taken by angels to retreats in the heaven world. Here they progress spiritually and prepare to meet the challenges of their next life.

Not everyone, however, reaches these schoolrooms between their incarnations. Some souls get stuck in the astral plane, which the Zohar describes as the side of uncleanness. In the astral plane they become entangled with disembodied spirits (what the Zohar calls the "pests of mankind"), whose energies vibrate at the lowest common denominator of humanity.

The formula that the Zohar spells out is simple: if you cleave to earthly things while you are on earth—material goods, power, position, ambition, base desire—when you die your soul will not be free to rise to the realms of light. If you get into the habit of cleaving to heavenly things—meditating on the *sefirot,* communing with ascended masters, befriending the angels—then when your soul departs this world you will be magnetized to the light and, as the Zohar says, you will stand among holy beings.

The Soul's Final Ascent

Mystical cleaving to God is a day-by-day process of attaching oneself to God through prayer, devotion, meditation and good works. But, as I said, Kabbalists also speak of the soul's ultimate cleaving to God when she ascends back to her source at the end of her tenure on earth. Like Plato, de León describes the soul as a prisoner in the body.[62] The Zohar frequently depicts the soul as a fugitive or exile who has only one longing: "for the place from which it was taken."[63] Spencer writes:

> As an emanation from the *sefirot,* the soul pre-exists in the heavenly world, "hidden in the divine Idea." Before its descent to earth, it vows to fulfill its task—to re-unite itself with God. During its earthly life, it weaves the garment of light, which it is to wear after death in the "realm of radiance," from its righteous acts. In its final blessedness, when it has completed its growth,

the soul ascends to its source, and is re-united with God.

This union is described in terms of love. The soul is united with "the Queen," the *Shekhinah,* or with the "heavenly King, the Holy One," in "the Palace of Love." But it is only "if a man is drawn towards the Holy One, and is filled with longing for Him in this world" that the soul is "carried upwards towards the higher realms" (Zohar 1:99). Otherwise men have to undergo reincarnation on earth, or to be purified in "the fiery stream of Gehenna," or even destroyed. Reincarnation, first taught in the Bahir, is apparently an exceptional destiny in the Zohar, though regarded by later Kabbalists as universal.[64]

Scholem says that as Kabbalah developed, "transmigration [reincarnation] ceased to be considered merely a punishment and came also to be viewed as an opportunity for the soul to fulfill its mission and make up for its failures in previous transmigrations."[65] The soul may go through numerous incarnations before she is perfected and is thereby worthy to reunite with God. If she does not willingly undergo the tests of the Holy Spirit lifetime after lifetime, her opportunity to do so will come to an end and she may ultimately cease to retain any identification with God. This is what is meant by the second death.[66]

The ascended masters teach that the soul is made permanent when after lifetimes of service to life she ascends back to God and reunites with her I AM Presence. This Jesus and other ascended masters have done. The prerequisites for this graduation from earth's schoolroom are (1) the soul must be bonded to her Holy Christ Self, (2) she must have balanced at least 51 percent of her karma, and (3) she must have fulfilled her mission on earth according to her divine plan. The reunion with the I AM Presence through the ascension is the ultimate goal of life for every living soul.

Kabbalists interpret certain Bible passages as referring to the union of the soul and God. Idel cites a passage from a work by one Jewish mystic: "He told me: 'Thou art my son, this day I have begotten thee' [Ps. 2:7], and also: 'See now that I, even I, am He' [Deut. 32:39]. And the secret [of these verses] is the cleaving of the power—that is, the supernal divine power called the circle of prophecy—with the human power." Idel says that "I, even I, am He" stands for "the union of the Divine with the human."[67]

Idel also cites the work of one of the disciples of the Spanish Kabbalist Abraham Abulafia, which gives an interesting image for the soul's ascent and ultimate union with God. Abulafia's disciple says that the Hebrew letter *yod* stands for a person seeking union with God: "He is the *yod* in this world who has received the power from the all, and he comprises the all, like the *yod* in [the realm of] the *sefirot*. Understand, therefore, that there is no discernible difference between this *yod* and that *yod* but a very fine one, from the aspect of spirituality. . . . And this is the secret [of] 'and cleave unto Him' [Deut. 13:4]—the cleaving of *yod* to *yod* in order to complete the circle."[68] (fig. 15)

The metaphor of the circle, explains Idel, is a symbol of the union of the human and the divine. He writes: "Each of the two *yods* are explicitly defined as halves of the circle, which is completed by the ascension of the lower man and his turning into 'the higher man, the man who [sits] on the throne and shall be called: "The LORD our righteousness.'" Man, then,

FIGURE 15. *A disciple of the thirteenth-century Kabbalist Abraham Abulafia said that a* yod *cleaving to a* yod *symbolized union with God. The* yod *(above left) is the tenth letter of the Hebrew alphabet. The union of the two* yods *forms a circle (middle), resembling the ancient Chinese* yin-yang, *or T'ai Chi, symbol (right). The* yin-yang *symbol represents the harmonious interaction and integration of the* yin *(female) and* yang *(male) forces in the universe.*

is but half of a greater unit, the circle, and by his ascent he can reconstruct it."[69]

The "cleaving of *yod* to *yod*" is the God in you below cleaving to the God in you above. In other words, by accessing the power of God that is within you, you can transform your lower self into your Higher Self. You can become one with the LORD Our Righteousness, your Holy Christ Self, and ultimately one with your I AM Presence.

When you look at the Chart of Your Divine Self, in your mind's eye draw an ellipse around it and see inside the ellipse a figure eight. (fig. 16) The I AM Presence represents the upper half of the figure eight and the soul represents the lower half. At the nexus of the figure eight is the Son of God, *Tiferet,* the LORD Our Righteousness. Through *Tiferet,* your soul (the *yod* below) is magnetized to your I AM Presence (the *yod* above), until you are no longer two but one.

Cleave to your I AM Presence. Cleave to the rock of your Divine Reality. For that which you cleave to, you shall become.

FIGURE 16. *The Fiery Ovoid Uniting God and the Soul. Mystical cleaving to God is portrayed here by the flow of light over the figure eight between the I AM Presence and the soul through the nexus of the Holy Christ Self. As your soul (the lower figure) bonds to your Holy Christ Self (the middle figure, corresponding to* Tiferet*), you are becoming one with God.*

CHAPTER SIX

THE ORIGIN OF EVIL

*Know that when all of God's works are each in its place, they
are good in this place of their creation, as assigned to them and
predetermined for them; but when they rebel and leave their
legitimate places, then they are evil.*

JOSEPH GIKATILLA

Where does evil come from?
And why does God allow it to exist? For these age-old conun-
drums Kabbalists have offered innovative answers—extraordinary in their implications.

Kabbalists speak about the "evil urge," the dark side of
human nature that entices man to sin, and about demonic
powers, whose domain they call the "Other Side." But if a
cardinal principle of Kabbalah is that everything ultimately
has its roots in the Infinite God, *Ein Sof,* how do Kabbalists
account for evil in the universe?

*The Zohar uses the image of the snake to symbolize the power of evil
that ambushes human beings, entices them to sin and persecutes*
Shekhinah. (The Serpent *by Gustave Doré.*)

They give several different explanations. One of the most prevalent is that evil is rooted in judgment untempered by love and mercy. This view is presented in the Zohar and then reappears, with a new twist, in the influential doctrines of Isaac Luria.

Evil Emerged from Gevurah/Din

The Zohar says that evil emerged out of the fifth *sefirah*, *Gevurah* (also called *Din*), the *sefirah* of Power, Judgment and Justice. Specifically, the Zohar portrays evil as a by-product of the emanation of the *sefirot*. As I outlined in chapter 2, *Ein Sof* emanated *Keter*, *Keter* emanated *Hokhmah*, and *Hokhmah* emanated *Binah*. The remaining *sefirot* emanated from *Binah*, starting with *Hesed* (Love/Mercy) and *Gevurah* (Justice/Judgment). Arthur Green explains the Zohar's conception of how evil was born as the by-product of the creative tension between *Hesed* and *Gevurah/Din:*

> [There is a] necessary tension that exists as the fourth and fifth *sefirot*, *Hesed* and *Din*, emerge from *Binah*. *Din*, the force of divine rigor or judgment, resents being tied to *Hesed*, the unmitigated flow of love. In the very moment of its emanation it broke forth from the *sefirotic* system, saying, in the words of the Zohar, "I shall rule!" The measuring rod of the *sefirot*. . . used the power of *Ein Sof* to quickly force *Din* back into line, but in that moment of escape some portion of its power was released that could not be retrieved. That portion of *Din*, now turned against God, began its own *sefirotic* emanation in mocking imitation of the divine world. It too has ten emanated rungs. . . .
>
> . . . The Zohar sees evil as originating in justice itself, when that justice is not tempered with compassionate loving-kindness. The force of *Din* within God has a legitimate role, punishing the wicked and setting out to limit the indiscriminate love-flow of *Hesed*, which itself can be destructive if not held in proper balance. But once *Din* has escaped the demands of

love, it is no longer to be trusted. It then becomes a perversion of God's justice, one that would use his punishing powers to wreak destruction without cause.[1]

The counterfeit emanation that resulted from the rebellion of *Din* is what Kabbalists refer to as *Sitra Ahra,* the Other Side. It is also called the Emanation of the Left Hand or the Emanation of the Left because it emanated from *Din,* which is on the left side of the Tree of Life. The Zohar teaches that everything in the divine world, including the *sefirot,* has its counterpart on the Other Side: "Just as there are ten crowns of faith above, so there are ten crowns of sorcery of uncleanness below."[2]

The Zohar portrays the creation of the Other Side from *Gevurah/Din* as a single point that rises from the smoke of anger:

> When the smoke started to come out of the furious anger, the smoke spread farther and farther, anger after anger, one upon another, and one rode upon and dominated the other, like the appearance of male and female, so that all was a furious anger. And when the smoke began to spread it emitted from the anger the emission of a single point, that it might spread. Subsequently, the smoke of the anger spread out in a curling fashion, like the cunning snake, in order to do evil.[3]

Just as Genesis depicts the snake as the seducer of Eve and Jewish legend portrays Satan as a primordial snake, the Zohar uses the image of the snake to symbolize the Other Side. The snake, sometimes male and sometimes female, lures human beings into licentiousness, persecutes *Shekhinah* (the feminine aspect of God), and is the source of witchcraft. In one passage, the primordial snake is surrounded by his emissaries—a troop of snakes, including "the small snake that brings up the rear." These snakes "go out to ambush mankind with sins that repel them backward."[4]

The Counterfeit Din

The original act of rebellion took place when *Din* said, "I want to be the supreme judge without being forced to qualify my judgment with mercy." Fallen angels who personify stern judgment have attempted to usurp the authority of the true *Gevurah/Din*.[5] By refusing to qualify judgment with mercy, they have stripped *Gevurah* of its garments of Divine Justice, deposed it from its throne and blackened the name *Hesed*. Their battle cry is that of the rebellious *Din*, "I shall rule!"

Those who are aligned with the counterfeit *Din* perpetrate wrongful judgment in all areas of life—judgment that rears its ugly head as racism, bigotry and prejudice. Judgment that ends in bloodbaths between Jews and Arabs, Catholics and Protestants, Hindus and Muslims, Serbs and Croats, Hutus and Tutsis. Judgment that maligns the innocent and glorifies the guilty through the misuse of the power of the bench and the press. Judgment that tears down the soul's self-esteem, destroys lives, and defies hope and faith and charity.

Think about stern judgment in your own life: If you judge another but your judgment is not just, you are sowing seeds of evil between you and your brother. You have arrived at the gate of bitterness and some part of you has become the slave of the unjust *Din*.

The Ascended Master El Morya has warned us again and again that we must not criticize, condemn or judge others. Jesus said, "Judge not, that ye be not judged."[6] Because we are not yet fully bonded to *Tiferet*, we do not always have the wisdom or the discernment to rightly judge another. But the portion of *Din* that turned against God is more than willing to enter into collusion with us to unjustly judge our neighbor. And once we enmesh ourselves in the roots of the counterfeit *Din*, we will have to wage war against it to extricate ourselves from its tangles.

If we become enslaved by *Din*, or if we have become the

victims of those who are enslaved by it, we must turn to *Tiferet*. For it is only through the compassionate heart of *Tiferet* (Beauty/ Compassion) that we can balance and harmonize the contending forces of *Hesed* (Love/Mercy) and *Gevurah* (Justice/Judgment). Jesus Christ and all Sons of God who have embodied the compassion of *Tiferet* were sent by God to counteract the forces of harsh judgment. As John said, "God sent not his Son *[Tiferet]* into the world to condemn the world, but that the world through him *[Tiferet]* might be saved."[7]

As we imitate the path of the rabbis and saints who have become one with *Tiferet,* we are increasing the light of *Tiferet* within us. It is this light that will turn back the force of wrongful judgment. And as we develop the inner beauty and compassion of *Tiferet,* we will be able to judge true and righteous judgments, because our Holy Christ Self will counsel us as we separate out the Light from the Darkness, the Good from the Evil.

Balancing the Masculine and Feminine Qualities of Hesed and Gevurah

Some Kabbalists refer to *Gevurah/Din* as a feminine *sefirah*. It is on the left, or feminine, pillar of the Tree of Life. This connotes that the true and exalted nature of Justice as well as the perversion of Justice is feminine. Interestingly, Justice is traditionally symbolized by the female figure who holds a sword in one hand and scales in the other. To ensure impartiality, she is blindfolded.

Shakespeare gave Justice a body and breathed life into her when he created the character Portia in *The Merchant of Venice*. Portia disguises herself as a young lawyer and argues a case for her husband's friend Antonio, who after forfeiting a bond payment to Shylock is legally bound to give him a pound of flesh. In her plea for Antonio's life, Portia extols mercy when it seasons justice:

The quality of mercy is not strained;
It droppeth as the gentle rain from heaven
Upon the place beneath. It is twice blest;
It blesseth him that gives and him that takes.
'Tis mightiest in the mightiest; it becomes
The thronèd monarch better than his crown.
His scepter shows the force of temporal power,
The attribute to awe and majesty,
Wherein doth sit the dread and fear of kings;
But mercy is above this scept'red sway;
It is enthronèd in the hearts of kings,
It is an attribute to God Himself,
And earthly power doth then show likest God's
When mercy seasons justice.[8]

As Portia says, earthly power is most like God's when, like *Tiferet,* it balances the opposing qualities of the masculine *Hesed* (Love/Mercy) and the feminine *Gevurah* (Justice/Judgment).

Like the Kabbalists, mystics of many of the world's religions recognize that everything in the spiritual and material worlds moves to the rhythmic dance of male and female forces. Chinese philosophy also speaks of two opposite but complementary energies—*yin* and *yang*—whose interaction produces all phenomena in the universe. In their ideal state, *yin* (feminine) and *yang* (masculine) are in balance. These same forces are at work within our own body and soul and the components of our identity.

All of us, both men and women, have a part of our nature that is masculine and a part of our nature that is feminine. Carl Jung called the feminine side of a man his anima and the masculine side of a woman her animus. The masculine side of our nature, corresponding to the left brain, is mental, reasoning and analytical. The feminine side of our nature, corresponding to the right brain, is caring, nurturing, sensitive and intuitive, and therein lies its strength. Yet this intuitive

Shakespeare's Portia champions the balance of the masculine and feminine virtues of Justice (Gevurah) *and Mercy* (Hesed) *when she eloquently pleads for Antonio's life, saying, "Mercy. . . is an attribute to God Himself, and earthly power doth then show likest God's when mercy seasons justice"* (The Merchant of Venice, *act 4, sc. 1*).

(yin) quality is what also leaves the feminine part of us vulnerable, because she must remain open.

In the account of Adam and Eve in Genesis, Eve represents our feminine, intuitive side. In her openness, Eve was receptive to the serpent. But she lost her objectivity and got sucked in to the perversion of the left-brain, male logic of that cunning agent of the Other Side.

Whether we are male or female, our goal is to balance the masculine and feminine parts of ourselves and bond to the great harmonizer, *Tiferet.* Only then will we be whole. When we have bonded to *Tiferet,* we will be open to others, yet we will have the discrimination to reject false logic with the authority of a son or daughter of God.

Shakespeare's Portia balanced the feminine and masculine sides of her nature. She showed an impeccable knowledge of the law and a commitment to justice, yet pleaded for mercy, saying to Shylock, "Though justice be thy plea, consider this: that, in the course of justice, none of us should see salvation."[9]

The battle between stern judgment and mercy that the Zohar pictures in mythical terms is not just a symbolic one. The battle goes on within and without. It takes place in ourselves as we struggle to balance our masculine and feminine sides to become spiritually and psychologically whole. It takes place in the streets and in the courts of law and in the schools every day as sons and daughters of God champion the meek of the earth. Everyone who takes a stand for truth, wherever it is found, is reinforcing the divine power of *Gevurah/Din.*

The equation is simple: Whenever someone champions justice, the power of the divine *Gevurah/Din* is amplified and the power of the Other Side is diminished. And whenever someone aligns with the unjust judges of the fallen *Din,* the power of the Other Side intensifies and the power of Divine Justice declines. As the Zohar puts it, our sins restore legs to the serpent, who was punished for seducing Adam and Eve by having his legs cut off. The serpent, representing the Other Side, literally had "no leg to stand on" after the episode in the Garden of Eden. But when we sin, says the Zohar, we "give him supports and legs to stand upon, and he derives strength from them."[10]

Defeating the forces of the counterfeit *Din* is the work God has set before us. When we have accomplished it, the Other Side will be rolled up as a scroll and put to the torch of Divine Justice. May she reign supreme and may we, her children, know the glory of vindicating her cause.

Escaping the Clutches of the Other Side and the Evil Urge

In the Zohar, the evil urge, or "evil inclination," is the agent of the Other Side. At times the Zohar depicts the evil urge as an internal power that perpetually wars against our "good inclination." (The good inclination springs from the *neshamah,* the spark of the divine that resides within us.) But the Zohar also depicts the evil urge as an external power—a demonic person, a snake or a harlot who lies in wait to ensnare and annihilate the soul.

The war between good and evil has been symbolized in the literature of the world since ancient times. In a popular, contemporary setting, we can see the powers of the Other Side symbolized in Walt Disney's *Snow White and the Seven Dwarfs.* The beautiful princess Snow White escapes from her stepmother, the wicked queen, because the kindhearted huntsman warns her that the queen is jealous of her and has ordered him to kill her. Snow White flees, running through the forest. The tree trunks sprout evil faces, their branches grow fingers and they try to grab her. Snow White keeps running but finally falls to the ground weeping.

Fortunately Snow White has friends in the forest—the gentle animals who escort her to the cottage of the seven dwarfs. The dwarfs invite Snow White to stay in their cottage, where she will be safe. When they leave for work the next morning, they warn her to be careful not to let anyone inside. But the queen transforms herself into an old peddler woman and tricks the naive princess into eating a poisoned apple. Snow White falls into a deep sleep, and the dwarfs think she has died. Only when the handsome prince finds Snow White and gives her "love's first kiss" is the spell broken.

The wicked queen represents the fallen *Din* and the evil urge, the evil spirits of the forest represent the deputies of *Din,* and Snow White represents the soul. Like the queen and the evil spirits, *Din* and its agents are jealous of the light of God within us. They try to snag our soul and steal our light. The kind animals, the dwarfs and the prince are like the Kabbalists, the ascended masters and the angels. They awaken us to the dangers and the illusions of the Other Side. They give us the knowledge, the guidance and the love we need to survive the wiles of the Tempter and the circumstances of our karma.

The first line of defense against the evil urge is to be aware that it exists. Like Snow White, the soul has to be warned that someone is after her. The Baal Shem Tov teaches that the wise are always alert to the trickery of the evil urge:

> The righteous man who serves God. . . is fully aware of the battle waged by the evil urge. [The evil urge is like] the robber lying on the path [that leads] to the worship of God. [The righteous man] is aware of the danger, and is constantly alert to avoid a trap. He also knows how to warn others of the danger of these robbers. . . .The wicked man, however, . . . constantly enjoys the snares of the evil urge, and says, "I am at peace—there is no danger in this world."[11]

Those who are blind to the snares of the evil urge are like the unwary people of Judah, who were lulled to sleep by the false prophets who proclaimed, "Peace, peace," when there was no peace.[12] That is what the evil urge whispers in our ear as it tempts us to stray from the path of oneness with our Higher Self.

According to the Kabbalists, we can escape the clutches of the evil urge and attract angels of light to protect us by observing the commandments *(mitzvot)* outlined in the Torah. The Zohar says:

> When a person sees that evil imaginings are assailing him, he should occupy himself with Torah and they will pass away.[13]. . .
>
> Whenever man goes toward the right, the protection of the Holy One, blessed be He, is always with him, and the Other Side can have no power over him. This evil is humiliated before him and cannot dominate him. But when the protection of the Holy One, blessed be He, passes from him, because of his attachment

to evil, then this evil, seeing that he is without protection, immediately takes control of him, and comes to destroy him. Then authority is given to [evil], and he takes away his soul.[14]

When we keep the commandments of God and have compassion toward our brother, we are one with *Tiferet*. Our oneness with *Tiferet* brings us to the feet of I AM THAT I AM and connects us to *Keter*. And when we are one with *Tiferet* and *Keter*, we are empowered to defeat the fallen *Din*.

The Zohar warns that we must be careful not to give any part of ourselves to the Other Side:

> It is forbidden to a man to abandon any vessel of his house into the possession of the Other Side, for many emissaries [of the Other Side] are ready to receive it, and from that time blessings do not rest upon him—all the more if he assigns to the Other Side the most precious part of himself. For from that time he belongs to [the Other Side], and when the time comes for the celestial form which has been given to him to depart from this world, the evil spirit to which he had become daily devoted comes and takes it, and it is never again restored to him.[15]

This sounds very much like the proverbial "selling your soul to the devil." In light of Kabbalah and the Teachings of the Ascended Masters, the "vessels" of our house that we should not abandon to the Other Side can be interpreted in several ways. We can think of our vessels as our four lower bodies, mentioned in chapter 4 (the etheric, mental, desire and physical bodies). These are the vehicles our soul uses to increase in the strength of the Lord and to fulfill her reason for being.

We can think of our vessels as our chakras because they receive and distribute the light of God to our four lower bodies. When we misuse the light of our chakras, we stop up the flow of God's light and increase the power of the Other Side.

We can also think of our vessels as our organs. When they are working properly, our organs are instruments for the dynamic interchange of *yin/yang* energy in our body. When we abuse our organs by eating unhealthy foods, we reduce the quotient of God's light our body can carry. The Zohar goes so far as to say that "man's soul can be known only through the organs of the body," for the organs "are the levels that perform the work of the soul."[16]

Remember, you—body, mind and soul—were created by *Elohim* to be a vessel for the sacred energies of *Ein Sof.* You have a divine spark. The seed of Abraham is alive within your very breast. You are nobly endowed, and you must not surrender any part of yourself to the evil urge or to the Other Side.

Why Does God Allow Evil to Exist?

We have seen how the Zohar answers the question: Where does evil come from? But once evil emerges, why does God allow it to exist?

Some Kabbalists believe that rather than destroy evil out-right, God assigns the righteous to destroy evil in his name. As I understand it, we are in the lower world because some-time, somewhere we gave a part of ourselves to the Other Side. God sends us back to the lower world so that we might balance the karma we made when we allowed the light of the *sefirot* to be stolen by the forces of the fallen *Din*. The process of bal-ancing our karma must include championing justice and challenging stern, unmerciful judgment.

The Zohar also teaches that God uses evil to punish the wicked and to test the mettle of our determination to return to the Tree of Everlasting Life. In order to illustrate how God uses the evil inclination to initiate us, the Zohar uses an alle-gory of a prince who is tested by his father. The king com-mands his only son not to consort with an evil woman. Out of his love for his father, the son agrees to obey his father's will. One day the king decides to test his son. He orders a beautiful seductress to entice the prince.

If the son is worthy and attentive to his father's commands, says the Zohar, he will rebuke her and send her away. Then the king will rejoice, invite his son into the innermost room of the palace and give him gifts and great honor. "Who will have brought all this glory upon the son?" asks the Zohar. "The whore, without a doubt!... She should be praised on every side... because she enabled the son to earn all this goodness and the deep love of the king."[17]

When you are tempted to stray from the paths of right-eousness and violate God's laws in small ways or great, think of the king, the prince and the whore. And remember that

Evil literally has no leg to stand on, says the Zohar, because the serpent's legs were cut off as punishment for seducing Adam and Eve. Our negative thoughts, feelings, words and deeds are what restore legs to the serpent and empower the Other Side. (Eve Tempted by Lucien Lévy-Dhurmer.)

God has a right to test us, we have a right to be tested, and we have a right to pass—or fail—our tests.

The Zohar also cites the trials of Abraham and the Israelites in Egypt to show that God uses evil to test and purify his children.

> Abraham went down to the "lower degrees" in Egypt, and probed them to the bottom, but clave not to them and returned unto his Master. He was not seduced by them, as was Adam, who reached that level and was then seduced by the serpent, and brought death into the world. Nor was he seduced like Noah, who became intoxicated. . . . But of Abraham it is written, "And Abram went up out of Egypt" (Gen. 13:1). He went up and not down, and returned to his place, to the upper level to which he had attached himself at the beginning [that is, the *sefirah Hesed* (Love), the first of the seven lower *sefirot*[18]]. . . .
>
> The mystery of the matter is: If Abram had not gone down into Egypt and had not been purified there first, he would not have had a portion in the Holy One, blessed be He. Similarly with his descendants: the Holy One, blessed be He, wished to make

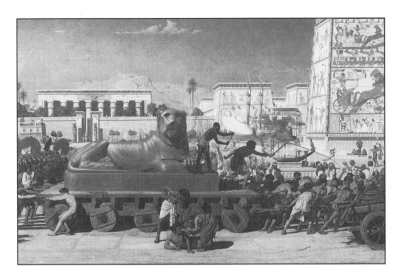

of them a single people, a perfect people, and to draw them near to Him. But if they had not gone down into Egypt first and been tested there, they would not have been God's chosen people.[19]

"Abraham's descent into Egypt and safe return is a rite of passage," writes Daniel Matt. "Having confronted and experienced the Abyss, he is transmuted into a divine hero, apotheosized as *Hesed,* the Love of God."[20] Kabbalah teaches that Abraham embodied the *sefirah Hesed* and that he represents the attribute of Love, just as Isaac represents *Gevurah/Din* and Jacob represents *Tiferet.* This means that Abraham, by his spiritual attainment, was the vehicle through which the light and energy of *Hesed* was able to come to earth.

Isaiah Tishby says the Zohar's teaching on Abraham's and

In Kabbalah, Abraham's and the Israelites' journeys to Egypt are symbolic of the tests and trials we, too, must face in our encounters with evil. Abraham successfully passed his tests and so emulated the divine attribute of Love that Kabbalists say he actually embodied and represented the sefirah Hesed. *(Left: Abram Draws Near to Shechem in the Promised Land by Julius Schnorr. Above: from Israel in Egypt by Sir Edward J. Poynter.)*

the Israelites' descent into Egypt means that we are all tested and purified through our contact with the power of evil. "In order to achieve perfection in his desire to serve God, man must first enter the domain of evil and purify himself there as in a refiner's crucible," he writes. "Only after this can he ascend to the level of perfect goodness. . . . Man has to prove his devotion to God by going out to fight God's adversary, and by returning victorious from the fray."[21]

Aiding and Abetting the Other Side

Although the Zohar says that God allows evil to exist in order to punish the wicked and to test us, it reminds us that it is not God that empowers evil but man. The Other Side was cut off from *Ein Sof's* life-giving energies, says the Zohar, and therefore evil has no power of its own. It literally lives off of the energies we feed it.

We energize the Other Side when we channel the precious energy God gives us daily into negative thoughts, feelings, words and deeds. And it is not just the "big" sins, like stealing or murder, that energize the Other Side. When we mentally put people down or make fun of them, when we curse them or are jealous of their accomplishments, we knowingly aid and abet the forces of the counterfeit *Din.* Conversely, when we generate good works, kind thoughts and daring deeds in defense of Truth and Justice, we vitalize the world of the *sefirot* and fasten our soul to the Tree of Life.

A powerful mantra that I often recommend (to be given in multiples of nine) to challenge the appearance of evil and its claim to power is "In the name of God, *Elohim:* Evil is not real and its appearance has no power!" Evil cannot exist unless we feed it the divine energies that come to us from *Ein Sof* through our I AM Presence and the ten *sefirot.* The fallen angels who align with the fallen *Din* are also cut off from the Tree of Life; we must not turn around and give them our precious lifeblood by perverting the light of any one of the ten *sefirot.*

Now we can see that the real reason we should avoid "sinning" is not for fear of roasting in "hell" for eternity. It is because the energy that we misuse empowers the forces of wrongful judgment in the earth—the same evil forces that kill and maim children, that rape and harass women, that cause brother to kill brother. Yes, the same forces that engineered the Holocaust.

So before we attempt to climb the Tree of Life, we must make sure that we are not a sieve, that we are not allowing the emissaries of the Other Side to receive the windfall of *Ein Sof's* light that comes to us through the *sefirot.* We must protect the light we have garnered in our chakras by disciplining our mind and heart so that only God lives within us.

The Hasidic leader Menahem Mendel of Kotsk once asked some visitors, "Where is the dwelling place of God?" They laughed and replied, "What a thing to ask! Is not the whole world full of God's glory?" But he replied that this was not true, because God only dwells where people let God in. When we think the thoughts of God and do his deeds on earth, God dwells within us. When we think negative thoughts and do negative deeds, the forces of the Other Side control our soul.

The Zohar says that because evil requires a steady flow of God's energy to exist, it tempts us to keep sinning. Once evil convinces us to commit a sin of injustice, it tries to make us reinforce that injustice by doing it again and again. Its hold on us becomes stronger and stronger. Finally we are its prisoner and it is able to siphon off our life-essence as easily as sipping cider through a straw.

The Zohar compares the evil inclination to a man who breaks into a house and takes control of it when no one challenges him.

When the evil inclination starts to attach itself to a man it is like someone coming to the door [of a house]. When he sees that no one tries to stop him, he enters the house and becomes a guest. He notices that no one tries to stop him or send him on his way. Once he has entered the house, and still no one tries to stop him, he gains the upper hand and becomes the master of the house, so that in time he exercises control over the whole household. . . .

So it is with the evil inclination. He approaches a man like someone coming to the door. He interests him in a minor sin, and is then like a mere passer-by. . . . He then interests him in graver sins for a day or two, like a guest who is invited to stay in the house just for a day or two. [When he sees that no one tries to stop him] he becomes. . . the master of the house. The man has enslaved himself to him.[22]

If we do not challenge the evil inclination when it first knocks at our door, it will step by step gain the upper hand and eventually become the master of our soul.

In other passages, the Zohar depicts how the Other Side continually tries to subjugate *Shekhinah,* the divine mother who sustains our world, and how our actions on earth can spell defeat or victory for the Other Side. Tishby writes:

The large amount of sin in the world helps [the Other Side] to reach its goal, while the power of the commandments and good deeds protects the *Shekhinah,* and helps to defeat the Other Side. In other words, human conduct holds the balance in this conflict between good and evil. When the power of the Other Side is at its greatest, it subdues the *Shekhinah.* This means that the light of the upper *sefirot* is removed from the *Shekhinah,* the channels that transmit the flow of influence to the lower worlds are stopped up, and the powers of the *Shekhinah* are transferred to the Other Side and give it additional strength.[23]

As Tishby puts it, our world is a kind of "battle zone in the war between the two contestants"—the side of holiness and the Other Side.[24] The Zohar says, "When this side, the holy side, begins to prevail, *Sitra Ahra* [the Other Side], the unclean side, grows weak. One prevails; the other grows weak. . . .When one is full, the other is ruined."[25] In short, Kabbalah teaches that *we* determine how much power evil exercises over the world. Since the advent of evil, we have been faced with two choices: we can submit to the evil urge and fortify the power of evil or we can obey the precepts of the Torah and strengthen the power of good.

Adam's Sin

As we have seen, the Zohar's first theory of the origin of evil is that evil was a by-product of the emanation of the *sefirot*. A second view of the origin of evil stated in the Zohar and by the Gerona Kabbalists is that evil can be traced back to Adam's sin in the Garden of Eden. But they describe Adam's sin very differently than do most interpreters of the Genesis story, for to Kabbalists the words of scripture are symbolic of much deeper mysteries.

According to this theory, Adam sinned by worshiping *Malkhut/Shekhinah* apart from the other *sefirot*. "Instead of penetrating the vast unity and totality of the *sefirot* in his contemplation," writes Gershom Scholem, "Adam, when faced with the choice, took the easier course of contemplating only the last *sefirah* (since it seemed to represent everything else) separately from the other *sefirot*, and of mistaking it for the whole of the Godhead."[26] As a result *Shekhinah*, the feminine aspect of God, was cut off from the upper *sefirot*, divorced from her husband, *Tiferet*, and forced to go with Adam into exile.

How did Adam's sin affect mankind? Before Adam sinned, he had enjoyed a steady, direct contact with God. But his sin severed that tie. "Had it not been for Adam's sin," writes Scholem, "the supreme divine will would have continued to work unbroken in Adam and Eve and all their descendants, and all of creation would have functioned in. . .harmony, transmitting the divine influx downward from above and upward from below, so that there would have been no separation between the Creator and His creation."[27]

The exile of *Shekhinah* symbolizes the separation of the masculine and feminine principles of God. The reunion of God and his *Shekhinah* will reunite the masculine and the feminine principles and restore harmony and the unimpeded flow of God's energy between the divine and human realms.

The reunion of God and his *Shekhinah,* and God and man, is the goal of the Kabbalist. Scholem writes:

> It is the function of good in the world, whose tools are the Torah and its commandments, to bridge the abyss of separation that was formed by man's sin and to restore all existence to its original harmony and unity. The final goal, in other words, is the reunification of the divine and the human wills. . . .Unlike [the] Christian dogma of original sin, the Kabbalah does not reject the idea that every man has the power to overcome this state of corruption, to the extent that he too is affected by it, by means of his own innate powers and with . . .divine aid.[28]

It is up to us to reestablish the tie between God and man. By accessing the power of the *sefirot* and our own inner power, we can bring harmony and wholeness to both the divine and human worlds.

The Kings That Died

A third theory of the origin of evil found in the Zohar is that the Other Side originated from the leftovers of previous worlds that had been destroyed because they contained the forces of stern judgment untempered by mercy. These imperfect worlds emanated from *Keter* before the other *sefirot* were emanated. The Zohar says: "Before *[Keter]* prepared his attributes, he constructed kings, inscribed kings, and conjectured kings [that is, *Keter* attempted to set up the structure of emanation], but they could not survive, so that after a time he concealed them."[29]

The Zohar goes on to say that our world was not able to survive until the emanation of the *sefirot* had been completed in the form of Primordial Man, *Adam Kadmon*. Why? Because in Primordial Man there was a harmonious balance of male and female forces, and only through a balanced partnership of male and female, mercy and judgment, could the world sustain itself.

Tishby explains the Zohar's theory of how the Other Side sprang from the leftovers of defective worlds:

> These early judgments [that existed in the imperfect worlds] . . . contained the root of evil in the form, as it were, of refuse. And the properly ordered system of emanation could not be established until the refuse had been removed from the divine realm. This removal was effected when the worlds were destroyed. The holy lights that were extinguished during this destruction were then rekindled and included among the *sefirot,* while the fragments of the destroyed worlds that were beyond repair were left mutilated and covered in darkness outside the divine system. It is from these fragments that the system of *Sitra Ahra* [the Other Side] was constructed.[30]

The Zohar refers to the previous worlds that had to be destroyed as "the kings that died."[31] It says these imperfect worlds are symbolized in Genesis 36 as the kings who were descendants of Esau and who reigned in Edom before there were kings in Israel. As Tishby notes, "one of the root meanings of *Edom* is 'red,' which is the color of strict judgment."[32]

The Breaking of the Vessels

In the sixteenth century, Luria proposed yet another theory of the origin of evil, one of the most radical ever conceived. Evil, he said, emerged from *Ein Sof* itself. Furthermore, he claimed that both the domain of evil and our world were born as a result of a cosmic catastrophe that accompanied the Creation. Luria wrote down little of his own teachings, and the writings of his disciples give differing and even conflicting versions of his profound doctrines. Some of Luria's students view the disaster that spawned evil as an unplanned mishap. Others believe that God planned this catastrophe as a way to cleanse himself of the harsh elements of judgment *(Din)*. Here is what happened according to this theory.

The Creation was a two-step process of contraction and emanation. Luria starts with the premise that *Ein Sof,* who is infinite, could not create a finite world without first creating a space apart from its infinity where its creation could exist. In order to do that, *Ein Sof* first contracted itself to its centermost point and then withdrew to the sides surrounding that point, leaving an empty sphere. This process is called *tzimtzum.* Although *tzimtzum* is commonly referred to as "contraction," for Luria it does not mean that God is contracting, or concentrating, himself *in* a place, but that he is withdrawing *from* a place.

The space that was left behind after *Ein Sof's* withdrawal contained a residue of the divine light *(reshimu)*. Luria says this is like the residue of oil or wine left in a bottle after it is emptied of its contents. In the process of *tzimtzum, Ein Sof* separated out from itself "roots of judgment," or roots of *Din,* and left them behind in the empty space as well. Some Lurianic Kabbalists say that *Ein Sof* discharged the roots of judgment to purge itself of these elements of inharmony, elements of potential evil.

But the question still remains: How could *Ein Sof*—the infinite, perfect God—have had within itself any elements of inharmony in the first place? Some Kabbalists claim that the act of *tzimtzum* created the inharmony. Before *Ein Sof* contracted itself, all the forces within it were in perfect balance, including the opposing forces of *Din* (Judgment) and *Hesed*

(Love/Mercy). These elements were in such harmony that they were not distinguishable from each other. However, when *Ein Sof* contracted, *Din* became concentrated and crystallized. The reason for this is that the very act of *tzimtzum,* whereby *Ein Sof* was limiting and restricting its infinity, was an act of *Din,* the force of limitation and restriction. Thus as *Ein Sof* contracted itself, *Din* automatically became more powerful.

The activation of *Din* upset the delicate equilibrium of forces within *Ein Sof.* The only way to restore harmony to the Godhead was to separate out and expel the "roots of *Din.*" These roots of *Din,* or judgment, which were left in the empty space after *Ein Sof's* contraction, were what eventually took shape as the forces of evil.

Ein Sof's contraction and withdrawal was step one in the process of the Creation. Next *Ein Sof* began to emanate within the empty space that contained the mixture of light and the roots of judgment. When the divine light of *Ein Sof* first flowed forth, the *sefirot* took the form of *Adam Kadmon,* Primordial Man. Luria says that lights burst from the ears, nose and mouth of *Adam Kadmon* in an undifferentiated form. But the light that issued from his eyes was different. It separated into distinct *sefirot,* each requiring its own vessel to hold its light.

The light flowed into the vessels of the first three *sefirot—Keter, Hokhmah* and *Binah*—without any problem. But the vessels that were supposed to contain the light of the lower *sefirot,* from *Hesed* through *Yesod,* were not strong enough to hold the light and they shattered. The vessel containing *Malkhut* cracked but did not shatter. In this disaster, shards of the broken vessels scattered and fell. Some Kabbalists believe that the vessels were weak and broke because they were made up of the roots of judgment.

What happened to the light that was in the vessels? Some of it found its way back to its source. Some of the light, however, fell along with the shards of the broken vessels and became attached to them. From these shards, the dark forces of the Other Side were formed. These dark forces are called *kelippot,* "shells" or "husks" of evil.

The husks of evil have no power of their own, says Luria. It is the sparks of light that are trapped among the husks that give life and power to the Other Side. Luria teaches that the breaking of the vessels not only animated evil but also inaugurated the creation of the material world, for the broken shards are the basis of all matter.

Luria associates the breaking of the vessels with the death of the primordial kings—the name the Zohar gives to the early, imperfect worlds that were destroyed because they contained an excess of stern judgment and lacked a harmonious balance of male and female forces. The same can be said of Luria's breaking of the vessels, where the out-of-balance force of judgment, activated through *Ein Sof's* contraction, had to be expelled from God.

Parallels with Hindu Cosmology

Luria's theory that the Creation was a two-step process of contraction and expansion resembles the theory in Hindu cosmology that the universe is continually evolving through alternating cycles of creation and dissolution.

According to Hindu cosmology, the universe evolves during the day of Brahma, who is the God of Creation. This is followed by the night of Brahma, during which all matter in the universe is absorbed into the Universal Spirit. The day of Brahma is thus a period of expansion, and the night of Brahma is a period of involution, or contraction. This rhythm of expansion and contraction is repeated as the universe continues to evolve during each day of Brahma and to dissolve during each night of Brahma.

Kabbalists, too, say that the two steps of contraction and

expansion are cyclically repeated. Scholem says that in Lurianic Kabbalah, "just as the first movement in creation was in
reality composed of two movements—the ascent of *Ein Sof*
into the depths of itself [contraction, *tzimtzum*] and its partial
descent [that is, expansion] into the space [left behind after]
tzimtzum—so this double rhythm is a necessarily recurring
feature of every stage in the universal process."[33] Kabbalists
term this ebb and flow "regression" and "egression." Regression is *Ein Sof's* desire to return to itself (its contraction), and
egression is the expanding movement of *Ein Sof.*

Another way Hindus describe creation and dissolution is
to portray it as the outbreath and inbreath of Brahma. Creation
occurs during the outbreath, or exhalation, of Brahma and dissolution occurs during his inbreath, or inhalation. Scholem uses
the same terminology to describe Kabbalah's drama of creation:
"Just as the human organism exists through the double process
of inhaling and exhaling and the one cannot be conceived
without the other, so also the whole of Creation constitutes a
gigantic process of divine inhalation and exhalation."[34] I see
this cosmic process as the eternal movement of the Great Tao
as all of creation dances to the rhythm of *yang* and *yin*—
contraction and expansion, dissolution and creation.

Liberating the Sparks

Luria teaches that with the catastrophe of the breaking of the
vessels, nothing has remained in its proper place. "Everything
is somewhere else," says Scholem. "Since that primordial act,
all being has been . . . in exile, in need of being led back and
redeemed."[35] As David Biale writes, *tzimtzum* and the breaking
of the vessels can be seen as "two stages in the same process where
God is shattered and parts of him are exiled from the rest."[36]

Following the breaking of the vessels, the *sefirot* reorga-
nized themselves in an attempt to restore their original harmony. But, Biale writes, "in place of the *Adam Kadmon*

(primordial man) out of which emanated the original *sefirot,* a series of 'faces' *(partzufim)* constitute the divine realm. Luria suggests that the *sefirot* system described in the earlier Kabbalah does not exist in its ideal form after the [breaking of the vessels]. In general, the whole order of creation is demoted to a lower level as a result of the breaking of the vessels."[37]

Luria says the first man, Adam, had the opportunity to completely separate the sparks from their shells and set the world back in order because his body was a microcosm of *Adam Kadmon.* But he failed. In Luria's scheme, Adam's sin was not the origin of evil; his sin was a second fall that repeated and reinforced the original catastrophe (the breaking of the vessels) that had given birth to evil. Scholem writes:

> Adam was by nature a purely spiritual figure, a 'great soul,' whose very body was a spiritual substance, an ethereal body, or body of light.[38] The soul of Adam was composed of all the worlds and was destined to uplift and reintegrate all the sparks of holiness that were left in the *kelippot* [shells or husks]. [His soul's] garment was of spiritual ether and it contained within it all of the souls of the human race in perfect condition. . . . Had Adam fulfilled his mission through the spiritual works of which he was capable, which called for contemplative action and deep meditation, . . . the power of evil, the *kelippah,* would have undergone. . . complete separation from holiness. . . .
>
> Instead of uplifting everything, however, he caused it to fall even further. . . . As a result. . . Adam assumed a material body. . . . His soul shattered and its unity was smashed to pieces. . . . The bulk of the souls that were in Adam. . . fell from him and were subjugated by the *kelippot.* . . . In a manner of speaking, Adam's fall when he sinned was a repetition of the catastrophe of the breaking of the vessels.[39] Each sin [of man] repeats the primordial event in part, just as each good deed contributes to the homecoming of the banished souls.[40]

According to Luria's theory, Adam's soul contained all the souls that were ever to be a part of humanity. Each of these souls, including our own souls, is a spark of Adam's great soul. Luria also taught that the souls within Adam are divided into a number of groups, or "soul families," and that each family shares a common "root." "Only sparks from the same root... are able to assist and strengthen one another," writes Scholem. "They suffer with one another, and anything done by one of them, good or bad, affects all the others. Their destiny is determined by a deep, invisible connection of 'soul affinity.'[41] It is the task of man to seek out...the sparks of his root."[42]

The goal of the Kabbalist is to repair the cleavage that took place in the Godhead as a result of the breaking of the vessels and Adam's fall. The process of restoring the universe to its original design is called *tikkun,* which means literally "fixing," "repair" or "restoration."

Tikkun is essentially the work of man not God. To perform *tikkun,* we must find the sparks embedded here, there and everywhere and liberate them to return to their divine source. *Tikkun* will not only "repair" the Godhead, but it will spell defeat for the Other Side. For the sparks of light that are attached to the shells of evil are what give power to the Other Side. Once the sparks are liberated, the Other Side cannot continue to exist.

Luria teaches, then, that there are two kinds of sparks to rescue: the sparks that fell when the vessels broke and the sparks that were once a part of Adam's soul. Luria says that anyone can strive to raise up the sparks of light that fell when the vessels broke. As for the sparks of Adam's soul, we can raise up only those sparks that belong to our own soul family, or soul root.

Therefore, in Luria's scheme our task is to raise up the sparks of the *sefirot* that are scattered throughout the creation, to raise up the sparks that belong to our soul family, and to perfect and thereby liberate our own soul. All who are part of the mystical body of God have a collective mission to rescue the sparks, but each son and daughter of God has a unique role to play in that great drama.

How do we perform *tikkun?* Through prayer and obedience to the commandments of God—by living spiritually. This brings us full circle to the Zohar's equation: When we do good, we energize the divine world and diminish the power of the Other Side; when we do evil, we energize the Other Side and weaken the harmony of the divine world.

"Every evil deed not only keeps the holy sparks imprisoned among the *kelippot* but also sends baneful impulses on high to disturb further the harmony among the *sefirot*," writes Rabbi Louis Jacobs. "Conversely, every good deed sends beneficent impulses on high to promote harmony among the *sefirot* and to reclaim the holy sparks."[43]

The Hasidic View:
Your Unique Role in Rescuing the Sparks

The Hasidic movement that blossomed in the eighteenth century transformed Luria's teaching on uplifting the sparks of light. According to Hasidism, the sparks that you and you alone can liberate are to be found in your environment—in food, drink and other material objects as well as in the people you come in contact with. As twentieth-century Kabbalist Hillel Zeitlin puts it, "Every man is the Redeemer of a world that is all his own."[44]

The idea that each person is responsible to redeem the sparks within his own personal sphere is well-developed in the teachings of the Baal Shem Tov. He says that God makes certain that we will meet the sparks that belong to the root of our soul. The grandson of the Baal Shem Tov writes:

> I have heard from my grandfather that all that belongs to a man, be it his servants and animals, be it even his household effects—they are all of his sparks which belong to the root of his soul and he has to lift them up to their upper root. For the

beginnings of a thing are tied to its ultimate end, and even the lowest sparks still have some communion with their beginning within the infinite being. If, then, the man to whose root they belong experiences spiritual uplift, they all rise with him, and this is brought about through *devekut* [mystical cleaving to God], for it is *devekut* that enables him to lift them up.[45]

For the Baal Shem Tov, cleaving to God, *devekut,* is the key to our fulfilling our mission of redeeming the sparks. The Baal Shem says of the man who is not in a state of *devekut,* "If a man walks irregularly with God, . . . then [God] walks irregularly with him and does not prepare for him clothing and food that contain sparks of his own soul root so that he may perform their *tikkun* [restoration]."[46]

Rabbi Jacob Joseph of Polonnoye, a disciple of the Baal Shem, writes: "As is well known from the writings, all that a person eats and his house and his business and his contemporaries and his wife—all these come to the person according to his nature, that is, from his sparks. If a person deserves it by his good deeds, then he meets the sparks which by his very nature belong to him in order that he may restore them to their rightful place."[47]

Hasidism's personal approach to rescuing the sparks led to a unique understanding of how to pursue the spiritual quest midst the challenges of living in the world. The Hasidic devotee believes that the rescue operation does not take place exclusively while we pray, study, and observe the commandments; it also takes place while we engage in necessary worldly pursuits, as long as our mind is stayed on God. "When attending to his material needs for the sake of God, the Hasid is carrying out acts of divine worship," writes Jacobs. "The Hasidic ideal, to which all else is subordinated, is that of *devekut,* wherein the total concentration of the mind is on God."[48]

As eighteenth-century Hasidic rabbi Levi Isaac of Berdichev says, "When you desire to eat or drink, or to fulfill other

worldly desires, and you focus your awareness on the love of God, then you elevate that physical desire to spiritual desire. Thereby you draw out the holy spark that dwells within. You bring forth holy sparks from the material world. There is no path greater than this. For wherever you go and whatever you do—even mundane activities—you serve God."[49]

The exile and dispersion of the Jews took on new meaning with Isaac Luria's theory that sparks of God had scattered with the breaking of the vessels of the sefirot. Kabbalists no longer saw the exile of the Jews as a punishment or a test. Instead, they saw it as a way to fulfill their mission of rescuing the sparks that had been scattered throughout the creation. (Above: Jeremiah at the Fall of Jerusalem *by Eduard Bendemann. Right:* The Sorrowing Jews in Exile *by Eduard Bendemann.)*

The Exile Takes On New Meaning

Luria's theory of the exile of the divine sparks from the rest of God struck a responsive chord among the Jews of his age. Ever since the Assyrians had deported the Israelites in 734 B.C. and 722 B.C. and the Babylonians had burned the Temple in Jerusalem and deported the people of Judah in 586 B.C., the Jews had been exiled from their homeland and scattered among the nations. But with Luria's theory of the shattering of the vessels, the exile of the Jews became a symbol for something larger. It signified the crisis of cosmic proportions that God himself was still experiencing—the exile of his sparks of light.

Furthermore, for Luria the Jewish exile is no longer a punishment or a test. It is a mission. In fact, the exile and dispersion are crucial to the redemption of souls. "One needed the exile of Israel among all the seventy nations, where the sparks fell," says Jacob Joseph of Polonnoye. "Each individual in Israel must be exiled. . . in that place which contains sparks from the root of his soul, [in order] to separate and uplift them."[50]

"In the course of its exile Israel must go everywhere, to every corner of the world, for everywhere a spark... is waiting to be found, gathered, and restored by a religious act," says Scholem. "Fundamentally every man and especially every Jew participates in the process of the *tikkun.*"[51]

Scholem also notes that the exile of the Jews "has its parallel in the exile of the soul in its migrations from embodiment to embodiment, from one form of being to another. The doctrine of metempsychosis [reincarnation], as the exile of the soul, acquired unprecedented popularity among the Jewish masses of the generations following the Lurianic period."[52]

From this perspective, in each of our incarnations we must play the role of the shepherd who goes after the lost sheep, those souls for whom we are responsible and to whom we are tied, by good karma or bad or because they belong to our soul family. Thus, the circumstances into which we are born—including those who are destined to be our parents or children, our work mates, playmates or soul mates—are no accident.

I think of the process of *tikkun* as taking a cosmic tweezer and pulling out little specks of gold embedded in dense matter. Kabbalists regard *tikkun* primarily as the work of the Jews, but I believe that *tikkun* is the mighty work of the mystics of all ages and all religions.

Thus, our daily striving to cleave to God is not merely to exalt our soul or even to escape from the concerns of this world. It has a far greater purpose. Our mystical cleaving to God will confer upon us the spiritual empowerment we must have to rescue the souls, as well as the sparks, who cry out to us for help.

CHAPTER SEVEN

THE PRACTICAL PATH OF THE MYSTIC

Be persistent in learning how to sanctify what you do.
In the end, the Blessed Holy One will ... impart holiness to you,
so that you become holy. Then you will succeed, attaining union
continuously. Even your bodily actions are transformed into holy
deeds. You are walking in the presence of God while being right
here in this world. You become a dwelling place of the divine.

MOSES LUZZATTO

To the Kabbalist, the concept that we are patterned after the *sefirot* is not an abstract idea. It is the starting point of a way of life. For, above all, the mystic is practical. His soul may soar to the heights to commune with God, but his feet remain firmly planted in the earth so that he can translate something of the sacred to others.

Moses Cordovero was one of the greatest exponents of the

Kabbalists were practical mystics who infused their daily life with spiritual meaning. They believed that by embodying the virtues of the sefirot, *we stimulate the flow of God's blessings to this world. (The Blessing over the Candles by Isidor Kaufmann.)*

practical path of Kabbalah. He taught that the mystic can bring heaven to earth by imitating the virtues of the *sefirot*. To set the stage for Cordovero's teachings, we must travel back in time to sixteenth-century Palestine—to a thriving community called Safed in the mountains of Upper Galilee, about twenty-five miles from Nazareth.

A Golden Age of Kabbalah

There had been a Jewish community at Safed since ancient times, but when the Jews were expelled from Spain in 1492 during the Spanish Inquisition, Safed became a haven for Jewish exiles. The town grew into a flourishing economic and spiritual hub.

Great rabbinical and Talmudic scholars as well as the leaders of Spain's Kabbalistic movement settled in Safed. This rare mixture of scholars and mystics, of old traditions and new aspirations gave birth to a religious awakening. The teachings of the sages of Safed spread throughout the Jewish world, and for two generations the city was the spiritual center of the scattered Jewish nation. It became known as one of the four holy cities of Judaism.

In its heyday, Safed produced nothing less than a golden age of Kabbalah. Among the luminaries of Kabbalah who walked its streets were Isaac Luria, Joseph Caro, Solomon Alkabetz, Hayim Vital and Moses Cordovero. The Kabbalists of Safed were not merely scholars and theorists engaged in speculative thinking; they were practical mystics, determined to live their religion.

In 1607 a biographer of Luria wrote of Safed: "Here live great scholars, saints and men of action. . . .None among them is ashamed to go to the well and draw water and carry the pitcher on his shoulders, or go to the market to buy bread, oil and vegetables. All the work in the house is done by themselves."[1]

Just as the scholars fused their spirituality to the work of their hands, so the people of Safed infused their daily lives with the work of the spirit. Perle Epstein describes the utterly spiritual complexion of the town:

In the sixteenth century the Palestinian community of Safed, in the mountains of upper Galilee, gave birth to a golden age of Kabbalah. Here mystics, scholars and families lived and worked together, dedicating themselves first and foremost to the spiritual life.

When Joseph Caro arrived in 1536, he found an entire town devoted primarily to spiritual life and only incidentally to earning a living. Some citizens fasted, others prayed all night, still others practiced strict vegetarianism. Yet the asceticism prevailing in Safed never emphasized mortification for its own sake; putting the Torah into practice was its primary aim. Thus, citizens distributed charity daily; orphans were immediately adopted and raised by more fortunate families; holidays were entirely communal, entirely mystical occasions for rejoicing....

...It was a place where Isaac Luria, the greatest of the town's masters, contributed huge sums to its treasury from his family's trade in textiles, and where Spanish-born Joseph Caro ...could function as an inspired mystic by night and practical attorney by day.[2]

The Kabbalists of Safed showed us that we do not necessarily need to choose between a spiritual life and a secular life, for our soul needs both paths. On the one hand, our spiritual devotions intensify the light of God within us and draw us nearer to God. On the other hand, our labor in the streets of life enables us to contribute to the welfare of society and to balance the karma we have with others.

Mirroring the Sefirot in Our Virtues and Deeds

The man who was largely responsible for making Safed into a renowned center of Kabbalah was Moses Cordovero, Safed's chief systematic theologian of Kabbalah. Cordovero was either born in Safed or settled there after the Spanish Inquisition. He was known for his profound religious thinking as well as his ability to elucidate the teachings of Kabbalah. A prolific author, Cordovero wrote about thirty works in his short life. He died at the age of forty-eight in 1570, two years before the death of Isaac Luria.

One of Cordovero's popular works is *The Palm Tree of Deborah*. Found among Cordovero's manuscripts after his death, it was first published in 1588. This classic is a step-by-step guide to cultivating the attributes of the *sefirot* within ourselves, and its advice is as practical today as it was four hundred years ago.

Cordovero's premise is that since we were made in the image and likeness of God, we are supposed to imitate our Creator through our virtues and our deeds. Thus the goal of the mystic, says Cordovero, is not simply to contemplate the attributes of the ten *sefirot* but to actually embody those attributes—to become a chalice for God's (1) mercy and humility *(Keter)*, (2) wisdom *(Hokhmah)*, (3) understanding *(Binah)*, (4) love *(Hesed)*, (5) justice and judgment *(Gevurah)*, (6) beauty and compassion *(Tiferet)*, (7) victory and endurance *(Netzah)*, (8) majesty *(Hod)*, (9) foundation *(Yesod)*, and (10) sovereignty *(Malkhut)*.

Here we see at play the ancient Hermetic axiom "As Above, so below": as God exhibits divine attributes in dealing with us, so we must exhibit those same attributes in dealing with others. But *The Palm Tree of Deborah* also reflects the corollary axiom, "As below, so Above." For it is founded on the unique Kabbalistic principle that every action we take in this world produces a corresponding reaction in the divine world, whether for good or for ill.

In other words, we affect the activity of the *sefirot*. By embodying their attributes, we activate those attributes in the world above and thereby stimulate the flow of God's blessings into the world below. When we do not imitate the divine attributes, we disrupt the world of the *sefirot* above and thereby block the flow of God's blessings into the world below.

Thus the Kabbalist believes that the quotient of spiritual blessings that God bestows upon mankind depends entirely on how we live our lives. As Cordovero describes it, if we imitate the qualities of the *sefirot*, those qualities will "shine upon earth."[3] But if we don't imitate those qualities, they will disappear from this world.

Whenever you are kind to another, for example, you are keeping *Hesed's* quality of loving-kindness alive on earth because you are empowering *Hesed* to convey more love into the world. And every act of kindness, however big or small, creates a snowball effect.

Did you ever notice how, if you're not on guard, a cantankerous co-worker can infect you and everyone else in the vicinity with his irritability and his irascibility? Conversely, when you meet a happy face and feel the warmth of someone's heart touching your own, you're much more inclined to be loving toward others. Loving-kindness begets loving-kindness.

Cordovero teaches that we are not just interconnected with the divine world, but we are interconnected with each other. "In everyone there is something of his fellowman," he writes. "Therefore whoever sins injures not only himself but also that part of himself which belongs to another."[4] He says the real reason the Torah commands us to "love thy neighbor as thyself"[5] is because we and our neighbor are one. "All Israel [i.e., the children of God] are related one to the other," he writes, "for their souls are united, and in each soul there is a portion of all the others."[6]

This sentiment is echoed by John Donne. In 1623, the acclaimed Anglican preacher and poet expressed the very Kabbalistic precept of the oneness of humanity when he wrote:

> The church is catholic, universal, so are all her actions; all that she does belongs to all. When she baptizes a child, that action concerns me. . . . And when she buries a man, that action concerns me: all mankind is of one author and is one volume. . . . No man is an island, entire of itself; every man is a piece of the continent, a part of the main. . . . Any man's death diminishes me because I am involved in mankind, and therefore never send to know for whom the bell tolls; it tolls for thee.[7]

To Imitate Keter,
Develop the Thirteen Attributes of Mercy

Cordovero begins his spiritual guidebook by showing us that we can imitate *Keter* (Crown) by acquiring "the thirteen highest attributes of mercy."[8] Just as God exhibits these qualities in dealing with us, he says, so we must exhibit these qualities in dealing with our neighbors.

The thirteen attributes of mercy are:

1. Patiently bear insult and be good to those who insult you.

2. Patiently endure evils performed by your neighbor.

3. Pardon sin and wash its stain away.

4. Regard yourself and your neighbor as one. Always wish your neighbor well. Never say anything negative about him and never desire to see him suffer or be disgraced. Rejoice in your neighbor's good fortune and be grieved at his misfortunes as if they were your own.

5. Do not stay angry with others, even when they persist in sinning. "It is a religious duty," says Cordovero, "to encourage [your neighbor] lovingly, and perhaps this way of dealing with him will succeed." On a parallel track, the author of Proverbs said, "A soft answer turneth away wrath: but grievous words stir up anger."[9] And a Taoist sage advised, "If you do not contend with anyone, no one can contend with you."[10]

6. Show mercy to those who offend or provoke you by recalling their good qualities.

7. Do not harbor resentment against anyone who offends you. If your neighbor repents of a misdeed, "show him a greater degree of kindness and love than formerly."

8. Always remember the good your neighbor has done and forget the evil he has done.

9. Do not hate or judge those who suffer. Welcome those who suffer and are punished, and save them from their enemies. Do not say of one who is suffering, "His sufferings are the result of his sins," but have compassion upon him.

10. Be truthful and upright.

11. Go beyond the letter of the law when dealing with the good and saintly. We should choose as our friends those who are good, and we should be extremely compassionate and patient with them.

12. Do not behave cruelly towards the wicked or insult them, but have mercy upon them and try to help them improve.

13. Recall the good deeds others have done from the day of their birth. When someone is unworthy, remember that there was a time—even if it was in his infancy—when he did not sin. If we get into the habit of thinking like this, says Cordovero, everyone will be found worthy of our prayers and mercy.

The Folly of Taking Offense

When I studied Cordovero's guide on how to acquire the thirteen attributes of mercy, I was reminded of an essay by Mary Baker Eddy, the founder of Christian Science. It parallels Cordovero's advice not to harbor resentment or anger no matter how evil another's actions have been. Her essay, entitled "Taking Offense," had a profound impact on me when I read it as a college student. Mrs. Eddy writes:

> The mental arrow shot from another's bow is practically harmless, unless our own thought barbs it. It is our pride that makes another's criticism rankle, our self-will that makes another's deed offensive, our egotism that feels hurt by another's self-assertion. Well may we feel wounded by our own faults; but we can hardly afford to be miserable for the faults of others.
>
> A courtier told Constantine that a mob had broken the head of his statue with stones. The emperor lifted his hands to his head, saying: "It is very surprising, but I don't feel hurt in the least."
>
> We should remember that the world is wide; that there are a thousand million different human wills, opinions, ambitions, tastes, and loves; that each person has a different history,

constitution, culture, character, from all the rest; that human life is the work, the play, the ceaseless action and reaction upon each other of these different atoms. Then, we should go forth into life with the smallest expectations, but with the largest patience; with a keen relish for and appreciation of everything beautiful, great, and good, but with a temper so genial that the friction of the world shall not wear upon our sensibilities. . . .

Nothing short of our own errors should offend us. He who can willfully attempt to injure another, is an object of pity rather than of resentment.[11]

When I read this essay on a wintry day at Antioch College, a great burden was lifted from me. Then and there I adopted Jesus' admonishment to Peter. It was as though he were speaking directly to me: "What is that to thee? Follow thou me."[12]

I found that no matter what anyone said or did to me, I simply could not find it in my heart to take offense. Oh, what a joyous liberation that was!

I have learned that being angry or resentful is a vicious circle, because it ties us to the person or object of our dislike. And it drains our energy, because part of us is always focused on that unresolved situation. If you continually revolve the past, you just aren't free to move on. But when you forgive and forget, you free up 100 percent of your energy for constructive endeavor.

Sometimes when people wrong us it has everything to do with them and nothing to do with us. Perhaps someone's sharp words are a result of a deep inner pain that won't go away. Perhaps a frustrated friend is carrying a burden too hard to bear and his soul is crying out for help.

On the other hand, when someone criticizes me I take a lesson from it. Over the years I have learned much about myself from my enemies as well as from my friends. Every encounter, however unpleasant, offers us an opportunity to learn something new about ourselves—if we are open to it.

The Ascended Master El Morya puts it this way: "If the messenger be an ant, heed him!" Look beyond the messenger to the message itself.

The Karmic Factor

A second teaching that dovetails with Cordovero's attributes of mercy is Jesus' challenge to the popular view of his day that suffering was always a punishment for sin:

> There were present at that season some that told [Jesus] of the Galileans, whose blood Pilate had mingled with their sacrifices.*
>
> And Jesus answering said unto them, "Suppose ye that these Galileans were sinners above all the Galileans, because they suffered such things?
>
> "I tell you, Nay: but except ye repent, ye shall all likewise perish.
>
> "Or those eighteen, upon whom the tower in Siloam fell, and slew them, think ye that they were sinners above all men that dwelt in Jerusalem?
>
> "I tell you, Nay: but, except ye repent, ye shall all likewise perish."[13]

Just as Cordovero warns us never to say of one who suffers, "His sufferings are the result of his sins," so Jesus warns us not to point the accusing finger at those who suffer calamity and say, "Aha! They must have sinned greatly. It is because of their sins that this calamity has come upon them."

Our neighbor's afflictions may not be the result of his sin at all. In imitation of the mercy of *Keter,* those who suffer may, in fact, be angels of mercy, bearing a burden on behalf of others.

On the other hand, our neighbor's afflictions may be the result of an ancient karma come due from one or more past lives. When we see the misfortunes of another, we must remind

---

*These Galileans were murdered while offering their sacrifices, probably at the Temple in Jerusalem.

ourselves, "There but for the grace of God go I." For we never know the day or the hour when we, too, may be visited by some past karma that brings calamity or illness to our doorstep.

A Two-Step Process of Resolution: Mercy and Justice

If I were to encapsulate in one word the thread that runs through Cordovero's thirteen attributes of mercy, I would say it is forgiveness. Yet how hard it is for us to forgive those who have inflicted deep pain or committed ultimate crimes against the soul, the mind, the body.

This came home to me as never before when a devout woman once poured out her heart to me in a letter. "Try as hard as I can, I cannot forgive my former husband for molesting my daughters," she wrote. "They have suffered all their lives as a result of this. They have problems in their marriages. They have not been able to work through the trauma of it all and I cannot forgive him. What shall I do?"

Haven't we all faced the same question when a mother like Susan Smith drowns her two small sons or a serial killer like Jeffrey Dahmer brutally murders and dismembers seventeen young men?

After receiving this woman's letter, I asked El Morya what the appropriate response of the spiritual seeker should be to the evildoer. He explained that resolution is a two-step process. The first step is to invoke the law of divine mercy for the forgiveness of the soul of the evildoer. The second step is to invoke the law of divine justice for the judgment of the "not-self" of the evildoer.

Forgiveness is always the first step on the spiritual path. If we withhold our forgiveness from friend or foe, God will withhold his forgiveness from us. Jesus stated the law on this point: "If ye forgive men their trespasses, your heavenly Father will also forgive you: but if ye forgive not men their trespasses, neither will your Father forgive your trespasses."[14]

Some people think of forgiveness as an act of surrender to the enemy. But, in fact, not to forgive is the real act of surrender to the enemy. By refusing to forgive someone, we literally surrender a part of ourselves to him—we tie ourselves to that person until we ultimately do forgive him. That is one very important reason why when Peter asked Jesus, "How often shall my brother sin against me and I forgive him? As many as seven times?" Jesus replied, "I do not say to you seven times, but seventy times seven."[15]

Many people go to their graves refusing to make peace with their enemies. This is a tragic mistake, for they will carry their resentment into their next life—and their next and their next—until they finally decide to let go of it. Lifetime after lifetime, they can choose to perpetuate an ages-old feud or one day they can say, "Enough is enough. I will forgive and forget and I will rest my case in the LORD."

Paul taught a sure way to avoid karmic entanglements that tie us to others and thereby stunt our spiritual growth. He said: "Never avenge yourselves, but leave it to the wrath of God; for it is written [in the Old Testament], 'Vengeance is mine; I will repay saith the LORD.' Therefore if thine enemy hunger, feed him; if he thirst, give him drink. . . .Be not overcome of evil, but overcome evil with good."[16]

The soul of the one who has wronged you may be imperfect, but that soul still has the potential to one day return to a state of perfection. Therefore, no matter how bad a person's deeds are, you can always forgive the soul.

With this done, you can take step two: Ask the Lord to send his archangels to bind and judge the not-self of the evildoer. The not-self is akin to the evil urge (see chapter 6). It is the force of evil that impels the soul to disobey the commandments of God. It is the portion of a person's being that is not of God, that is evil, and therefore can be judged. Once the not-self is bound, the soul has a better chance of transforming herself.

You can ask God to give the soul of the evildoer the opportunity to repent of her evil deeds and strengthen herself under the shadow of the Almighty so she can resist the evil urge when it knocks again at her door. Ask the Lord to exorcise the discarnate entities and demons that have infested the soul and to free the evildoer from the negative patterns of his psychology that induce him to sin.

There is one thing, however, that we cannot do: we cannot interfere with anyone's free will. If the soul is still determined to commit crimes against herself and humanity, then the mercy she has withheld from others shall be withheld from her.

El Morya's two-step process of resolution is both liberating and empowering because it frees us to forgive the soul, even as it empowers us to wage war against the forces of evil that hold that soul in their grip. It activates the mercy of *Hesed* and the justice of *Gevurah* through the compassion of *Tiferet*. And when your spiritual work is done, you can be certain that, in God's own time and way, the soul will be assisted and given new opportunity, and justice will be meted out.

The Banner of Humility

In addition to the thirteen attributes of mercy, Cordovero lists eight more ways we can imitate *Keter*. They are all under the "banner of humility." He says humility is the chief quality we should aim for because it is the key to all other qualities. Each of his eight ways to develop humility corresponds to a different part of the head.

1. With your head, imitate God by being humble and good to all. "The proud man lifts his head upwards," but we should look upon and help anyone in need of our goodness, no matter what his past sins or misdeeds.

2. With your mind, think the thoughts of God. Contemplate God's majesty, the Torah and how to do good. Do not let negative thoughts enter your mind.

3. With your forehead, imitate the quality of God that accepts everyone and is pleasant to everyone. Your forehead should "have no hardness whatsoever." Even if others provoke you, "appease them and quiet them with good will." If you are harsh to others, you will not succeed in soothing them.

4. Let your ears be open to hear good and useful things but be shut to rumors, gossip, ugly reports or things that incite your anger.

5. With your eyes, be alert to the suffering of others and avoid gazing at evil. When you see the poor suffer, "give as much thought to their predicament as lies in [your] power, and awaken the pity of heaven and of humans upon them."

6. Your nose should never bespeak anger. (The word *anger* in Hebrew means literally "snorting with the nose.") Always be willing to forgive. Be patient with everyone, revive those who suffer, and desire to fulfill the requests of others (as long as they are in accordance with God's laws).

7. Let your face shine constantly. Welcome everyone with joy and a friendly countenance.

8. With your mouth, speak well of everyone. Your words should always engender goodness and blessing. Never allow an ugly comment, a curse, anger or frivolous talk to escape from your mouth.

To Acquire Wisdom, Be a Father to All

The next attribute the mystic must learn to make his own is wisdom, the attribute of *Hokhmah*. Cordovero says you can acquire wisdom by being "a father to all the creatures of the Holy One." Pray constantly to alleviate suffering as if those who suffer were your own children.

To add to your wisdom and perfect it, spend time in solitude with your Creator. Then share that wisdom with others by being an "effective teacher."

To Acquire Understanding, Root Yourself in Repentance

You can acquire understanding, the attribute of *Binah,* through "perfect repentance" and by rectifying every flaw. No matter how evil you have been, "do not think that there is no hope for you," says Cordovero. "If you do well, you can root yourself in the secret of repentance."

To Acquire Mercy and Love, Make Your First Priority to Serve God

To acquire mercy and love, the attributes of *Hesed,* make your first priority to serve God. The best way to "enter into the secret of Loving-kindness *[Hesed],*" says Cordovero, "is to love God with perfect love so as not to forsake his service for any reason whatsoever, for nothing has any value at all. . .compared with the Blessed One's love. Therefore, [we] should primarily attend to the requirements of God's service and the rest of [our] time may be for other needs."

Firmly fix in your heart love for God, he says, whether you experience good or whether you experience sufferings and rebukes, for both are tokens of God's love. As the Proverbs of Solomon tell us, "Despise not the chastening of the LORD; neither be weary of his correction: for whom the LORD loveth he correcteth, even as a father [correcteth] the son in whom he delighteth."[17]

To Acquire Power, Do Not Excite the Evil Urge

Cordovero says that in order to acquire power, which is the attribute of *Gevurah,* we must be careful not to excite the evil urge—the dark side of human nature that tempts us to sin. "The evil inclination [evil urge] should be bound and tied down," he says, so that we don't become angry or desire money or honor. Walking the spiritual path requires constant vigilance, for any one of us can be tempted by the evil urge until we are perfected in God.

Don't seek to derive pleasure from the evil urge, says Cordovero. "However, for his wife's sake [a man] should gently bestir his evil inclination in the direction of the sweet Powers, to provide her with clothes and with a house, for example." For by adorning his wife, a man is really adorning *Shekhinah,* the feminine aspect of God.

But if we seek power for our own sake, we awaken strong and destructive powers in the world of the *sefirot.* And power without the necessary balance of love can destroy the world. Therefore, says Cordovero, "one can observe how ugly is anger and suchlike, for it causes the strong Powers to prevail."

If we allow sudden anger to overtake us, our spiritual progress will be compromised. God wants to entrust us with his light, but he will withhold it from us as long as we allow anger to occupy our mind and spirit; for anger funnels God's light to the Other Side and ignites the forces of evil.

Our anger hurts not only our own souls but also the souls of others within the field of our aura. And that is only the beginning of our troubles. Anger is, in reality, a highly infectious disease.

Like a wild forest fire that begins with a single match and leaps from ridge to ridge, anger can leap from mind to mind, igniting a veritable conflagration within the collective unconscious. That is why the ascended masters teach that there will never be an end to war on earth until enough people who are spiritual put an end to the warring within and among themselves. As Gandhi once said, "*You* must be the change you wish to see in the world."

Sometimes anger can be caused by the psychological condition of the soul and records of past karma. These records may be sealed for lifetimes at subconscious or unconscious levels of our being. But one day we will be required to deal with them, and we can begin to prepare for this test today by building a strong foundation of inner peace.

Diet can also be a factor in dealing with anger. An off-balance diet can increase a person's tendency to be angry and irritated. According to macrobiotic theory, based on ancient Chinese medicine, a toxic liver tends to make people ill-tempered and aggressive. Conversely, a healthy liver tends to make people patient and thoughtful. We can harm our liver—and therefore make ourselves more susceptible to irritability and anger—when we overconsume drugs, alcohol, caffeine, soft drinks or fatty foods such as meat and dairy products.

I have seen the Eastern diet of macrobiotics help many people restore equilibrium in their emotions because this diet balances *yin* and *yang* in the body. *Yin* and *yang* are the opposing but complementary forces of the universe. *Yang* is a tight, constrictive, warming force. *Yin* is a relaxed, expansive, cooling force. Eating too many *yang* foods, such as red meat, may cause you to become hot, bothered and angry more easily.

If you moderate your intake of meat and eat more whole grains and vegetables (which are more *yin*), you may notice that you are slower to anger and more balanced. And the more balanced you are, the better equipped you will be to triumph in the face of your returning negative karma. As the author of Proverbs said, "He that is slow to anger is better than the mighty; and he that ruleth his spirit than he that taketh a city."

To help us control runaway emotions and "riptides" of negative energy that come up from time to time, the ascended masters have given a simple prayer called "Count to Nine." It invokes *Hesed* (Love) to balance the overbearing forces of *Gevurah* (Power/Judgment). No matter what your spiritual path, you can use this prayer as a safety valve when you feel yourself or others around you "heating up."

If you are attending a meeting, for instance, and find yourself or someone else getting hot under the collar, try suggesting a fifteen-minute break. Cool down with a glass of water, get outside for some fresh air, do some slow deep breathing and make contact with the earth if possible. Resolve that you will not be moved to inharmony by anyone or anything connected with your meeting. Affirm three times out loud with love and determination, "I shall not be moved!" Then affirm, "I shall not be moved from the harmony of the God who lives within me!"

Having so resolved, consciously turn over to God the matter at hand. Remind yourself of Cordovero's thirteen attributes of mercy, starting with patiently bearing insult and being good to those who insult you. And determine not to unleash the "strong Powers," as Cordovero calls them.

Then give the following prayer with fervor and know that your Higher Self is in total control of your energies, your meeting and your life. Once you have regained your equilibrium, return to your meeting and solve the problem, having centered yourself in the beauty and harmony of *Tiferet*.

Count to Nine

In the name I AM THAT I AM, I command my I AM Presence and Holy Christ Self and all hosts of heaven to reestablish peace and to halt all aggression, anger, arrogance, argumentation, accusation, agitation and aggravation here and now!

Come now by Love divine,   (Visualize the white
Guard thou this soul of mine,   light filling your
Make now my world all thine,   aura)
God's light around me shine.

I count one,   (Visualize a band of
It is done.   white fire around the
O feeling world, Be still!   solar plexus)
Two and three,
I AM free,
Peace, it is God's Will.

I count four,
I do adore
My Presence all divine.
Five and six,
O God, affix
My gaze on Thee sublime!

(Visualize a band of white fire around the neck and throat chakra)

I count seven,
Come, O Heaven,
My energies take hold!
Eight and nine,
Completely thine,
My mental world enfold!

(Visualize a band of white fire around the head and third eye)

The white-fire light now encircles me,
All riptides are rejected!
With God's own might around me bright
I AM by Love protected!   (give this prayer three times)

(Visualize the white light encircling all of the chakras and the four lower bodies)

I accept this done right now with full power!
I AM this done right now with full power!
I AM, I AM, I AM God-life expressing perfection all ways at all times.
This which I call forth for myself I call forth for every man, woman and child on this planet!

To Acquire Beauty, Study the Sacred Scriptures

Cordovero says that the way to acquire beauty, the attribute of *Tiferet,* is to study the Torah. To me, this includes studying the teachings of the saints, ascended masters and mystics of all time.

Cordovero warns that we will not attain beauty if we entertain spiritual pride. If we exalt ourselves above the poor, the ignorant, those whose minds are weak or those who are learning from us, we will block the flow of God's beauty into the world. But if we are pleasantly disposed toward others, teaching them as much as they can absorb, "Beauty will pour its flow into the pupils according to their capacities."

You may not think of yourself as a teacher, but we all play this role more often than we imagine—whether we are teaching our co-workers a new task, instructing a child or sharing a word of wisdom with someone we chance to meet.

Cordovero goes on to say that when we debate about spiritual teachings, we must do so for the sake of heaven and not for our own secular gain.

To Acquire Endurance and Majesty, Support Students of the Sacred Scriptures

To acquire endurance and majesty, the qualities Cordovero attributes to *Netzah* and *Hod,* he says we should supply students of the Torah (i.e., the world's sacred scriptures) with all they need to continue their studies. This may involve giving them money or doing other good deeds to help them. Do not disparage their learning, he says, but encourage them in their work.

Do all that you can, whether little or much; for everything you do to honor and strengthen the Torah and to arouse people's hearts to the Torah (and the pure teachings of the world's major religions) is firmly rooted in the *sefirot Netzah* and *Hod.* Cordovero also advises those who study the Torah to be prepared to learn from all people.

To Acquire Foundation, Guard against Speech That Evokes Sinful Thoughts

To acquire the attribute of *Yesod,* which is foundation, Cordovero advises us to guard against speech that gives rise to sexual or sinful thoughts. "Needless to say, [one] should not speak obscenities, but he should take care not to utter even clean words if they give rise to sexual thoughts," writes Cordovero. "The main precaution is to guard oneself from sexual imaginings."

Cordovero acknowledges that there is a time and place for sexual activities within the holy circle of marriage. Another Kabbalistic text affirms that sexual union, under the right circumstances, is sacred:

Sexual union is holy and pure, when performed in the right way, at the right time, and with the right intention. . . .

When sexual union is for the sake of heaven, there is nothing as holy or pure. The union of man and woman, when it is right, is the secret of civilization. Thereby, one becomes a partner with God in the act of Creation. This is the secret meaning of the saying of the sages: "When a man unites with his wife in holiness, the divine presence *[Shekhinah]* is between them.". . .

. . .When a man and a woman unite, and their thought joins the beyond, that thought draws down the upper light.[18]

As I noted in chapter 3, Kabbalists considered the sexual union of those who are married to be a celebration of the divine union of *Tiferet* and *Shekhinah*.

While many spiritual teachers, like Cordovero, believe that sexual activity in balance and in the right context is healthy, they also teach that becoming preoccupied with sex can slow down our spiritual growth. This is because the energy we exchange through sexual union is the same energy we use to climb the Tree of Life and reunite with God. When we dissipate this energy through excessive sexual thoughts or practices, we do not have as much spiritual fire to propel us upward. We can regain and conserve that fire through our devotions, prayers and spiritual practice.

To Acquire Sovereignty, Do Not Take Pride in Your Belongings

Cordovero says that the way to acquire sovereignty (or kingdom), the attribute of *Malkhut/Shekhinah*, is to never take pride in your belongings but always to behave like a beggar. Even if you are wealthy, you can train yourself to behave in this way, he says, by reminding yourself that none of your possessions are "attached" to you and that you require the mercies of heaven at all times.

Your family and your belongings are not what will carry you

back to God, says Cordovero. "What can. . .[a man's] wife and children do for him when he is judged before the Creator or when his soul departs? Can they accompany him beyond the grave? Of what use are they to him from the entrance of the grave and onwards?" Our ascent to God is indeed a solo flight.

Cordovero teaches that we can also acquire sovereignty if we fear the Lord, perform marital duties in a spirit of holiness, and behave in such a way that *Shekhinah,* the Divine Presence of God, will always cleave to us. He says *Shekhinah* will unite with us when we develop the qualities of the *sefirot,* study the Torah and follow its precepts.

Another way to acquire the quality of sovereignty, he says, is to "divorce" yourself from your home to study the Torah. Aryeh Kaplan says that Cordovero practiced a form of meditation known as divorce. Kaplan writes:

> No mere theorist, [Cordovero] was. . .actively engaged in Kabbalah meditation, through a method known as *Gerushin* or "Divorce." We know very little of this method. . . .Most probably it consisted of meditating on a given scripture, or perhaps repeating it over and over like a mantra until one could relate to it on a high meditative state. One would then gain deep insight into it, without having to analyze it logically.
>
> The word "Divorce" in this context most probably meant divorce from the physical, even though it also obviously had the connotation of separation and seclusion from inhabited places.[19]

Undoubtedly, those who practiced this technique also "divorced" themselves from their wives by remaining celibate for periods of time so they could devote all of their energy to their meditations.

Forgetting the Self

In Kabbalah and other spiritual traditions, the mystic's goal of embodying the virtues of God is sometimes called "forgetting the self." Forgetting the self means forgetting about the lesser self, the human ego. It means emptying yourself to make room for God.

Forgetting the self is the ultimate expression of humility. The eighteenth-century Hasid Issachar Ber of Zlotshov says that humility is the goal of all spiritual practices:

> The essence of the worship of God and of all the *mitzvot* [commandments] is to attain the state of humility, namely, . . .to understand that all one's physical and mental powers and one's essential being are dependent on the divine elements within. One is simply a channel for the divine attributes. One attains such humility through the awe of God's vastness, through realizing that "there is no place empty of Him."[20]

The Hasidic leader Dov Baer taught, "Think of yourself as *ayin* [nothingness] and forget yourself totally. . . .If you think of yourself as something, then God cannot clothe himself in you, for God is infinite. No vessel can contain God, unless you think of yourself as *ayin*."[21]

Another Hasidic writer uses similar language to describe the inspired preacher:

> One who preaches for the sake of heaven must consider that the intellect and the sermon are not his; rather he is as dead as a trampled corpse, and all is from God, may His name be blessed. . . .God is putting into his mind the words and the moral message that he is delivering to the congregation; so each word should feel like burning fire and he should feel compelled to let them all out. Otherwise, he is like a prophet who suppresses his prophecy.[22]

The same principle of allowing oneself to be a channel for the divine applies to those who pray. Daniel Matt says the Hasidim teach that "the mystic's only active role is the decision to pray and the effort to maintain the clarity essential for conveying divine energy."[23] The mystic allows himself to be the instrument, and God does the rest. In one Hasidic work we read:

> One who merits this level [of being an instrument for the con-
> veyance of divine energy] is nothing but a channel through
> whom are conducted words from on high. This person merely
> opens his mouth. . . . The essential condition for prayer is that
> one be clean from all dross, so that the voice from above not
> be corporealized in his voice. Everyone can merit this level. . . .
> Their voice is the voice of the Shekhinah, as it were; they are
> simply vessels.[24]

"In such a state," explains Matt, "the subject and the object
of prayer are one and the same. One 'worships God with God.'
God becomes like a high priest, serving Himself through human prayer."[25] Dov Baer sums it all up when he says, "Whatever one does, God is doing it."[26]

Other mystics of the world's religions speak about forgetting
the self. Taoists, for example, use the phrase "forgetting the self"
or "losing the self" to describe the process of losing the sense
of a self that is separate from the Tao, from Ultimate Reality.
They say "losing the self" does not mean obliterating your identity; it means not letting your lesser self get in the way of the Tao.

The Sufi poet Rūmī describes the process of forgetting
the self as the abandonment of the lesser self. Self-abandon-
ment, he says, is a prerequisite to the mystic ascent to God:

> Ere it is annihilated, no single soul
> Finds admittance to the divine hall of audience.
> What is 'ascension' to heaven?
> Annihilation of self;
> Self-abandonment is the creed and religion of lovers.[27]

Jesus also experienced the same process of forgetting the
self and becoming a vessel for God, for he said:

> My Father worketh hitherto, and I work. . . .
>   The Son can do nothing of himself, but what he seeth the
> Father do. . . .
>   I can of mine own self do nothing. . . . I seek not mine own

will, but the will of the Father which hath sent me. . . .

Believest thou not that I am in the Father, and the Father in me? The words that I speak unto you I speak not of myself: but the Father that dwelleth in me, he doeth the works.[28]

Jesus taught the fourteenth-century saint Catherine of Siena that the secret of developing a mystical and intimate relationship with God was, again, forgetting the self—becoming, as Dov Baer says, "nothingness." One day Jesus appeared to Catherine as she was praying and said:

> Do you know, daughter, who you are and who I am? If you knew these two things, you would be blessed. You are that which is not; I am He who is. If you have this knowledge in your soul, the enemy can never deceive you; you will escape all his snares; you will never consent to anything contrary to my commandments; and without difficulty you will acquire every grace, every truth, every light.[29]

"With that lesson Catherine became fundamentally learned," writes her biographer Igino Giordani. "She was founded upon a rock; there were no more shadows. *I, nothing; God, All. I, nonbeing; God, Being.*"[30]

Forgetting one's self through supreme humility is the essence of the mystic's path. It is what allowed the ancient prophets to be infused with tremendous power as they delivered the messages of God in the "Spirit of the LORD." It is what empowered mystics like Catherine of Siena to change the course of the Church and leaders like Gandhi to change the course of history. And it is what can empower you to change the world.

Ralph Waldo Emerson, whom author Thomas Moore rightly calls "one of the great soul-doctors of our American history," describes this empowerment in terms of the unlimited power of God that literally surges through us. The spirit of mysticism and of Kabbalah breathes through this passage from his essay *Nature:*

[Spirit] does not act upon us from without, . . .but spiritually, or through ourselves: therefore, that spirit, that is, the Supreme Being, does not build up nature around us, but puts it forth through us, as the life of the tree puts forth new branches and leaves through the pores of the old. As a plant upon the earth, so a man rests upon the bosom of God; he is nourished by unfailing fountains and draws at his need inexhaustible power. Who can set bounds to the possibilities of man? . . . Man has access to the entire mind of the Creator, is himself the creator in the finite.[31]

Interpreted in Kabbalistic terms, Emerson is saying that we are nourished by the light of *Ein Sof* that flows through the unfailing fountains of the *sefirot*. And we can indeed draw inexhaustible power from them when we "forget" ourselves, when we empty ourselves and let God in.

The process of forgetting the self—of self-emptying and being filled with the attributes and energy of God—takes place step by step, day by day. At a certain point, you will find that God becomes so much a part of you that he is the one who is thinking, feeling, talking, working, loving, caring and comforting through you. That is when the path of the mystic reaches its highest and most practical expression, for when we are one with God we truly bring heaven to earth.

CHAPTER EIGHT

PRAYER AND THE POWER OF GOD'S NAMES

*The higher and lower worlds are blessed by the one who prays.
...He is loved from above and adored from below. His needs are
answered and all his heart's desires are fulfilled, because he is
loved by all the Spheres [sefirot]."*

JOSEPH GIKATILLA

"The greatest Kabbalists," writes
Gershom Scholem, "were all great masters of prayer."[1] Prayer,
along with the performance of good deeds, is central to the
Kabbalist's supreme mission of *tikkun*—the restoration of our
fractured world that must take place because of the breaking
of the vessels and the subsequent fall of Adam.

Thus, the Kabbalist prays with more than a desire for a
personal boon or a yearning to commune with God. He does
so with the conviction that his prayer will restore peace and

*The Jewish mystics teach that joy and enthusiasm are necessary
ingredients to spiritual progress and effective prayer. (David in the
Temple by Pieter Lastmann.)*

harmony to this world and to the heavenly realms. The Zohar says that prayer works on four levels to perform *tikkun*. It not only "builds up him who prays," but it also restores the physical world, the upper world with the heavenly hosts, and the world of the *sefirot*.[2]

Again we meet the principle that makes Kabbalah unique among the mystical paths of the world's religions: just as the harmony of our world depends on divine support, so the harmony of the divine world depends on our support.

Kabbalah portrays the relationship between the human and divine worlds not as one of mankind's dependence on God but as one of *mutual interdependence*. "Those who are below are always in need of help from above to complete what they have to do," writes Isaac Luria's disciple Hayim Vital. "The powers above also need the help of those below."[3]

God depends on us. Our actions, our devotion, our lifestyle can mend the fractures so that there will once again be a continuous union between Creator and creation.

Kavvanah: A Unique Marriage of Prayer and Meditation

While the Kabbalists used traditional Jewish prayers, they went beyond standard rituals by stressing the Kabbalistic significance of each word they recited or ritual they performed. They breathed new life into the traditional concept of *kavvanah*— the intention or spiritual concentration and awareness with which one performs religious duties.

"What is *kavvanah*?" asked Maimonides in the twelfth century. "One should empty one's mind of every thought and regard oneself as if one were standing in the presence of the *Shekhinah*."[4]

Kabbalah teaches that *kavvanah* allows us to engage in a mystical, inner work. *Kavvanah* creates a flow of blessings upon the one who prays, upon the world in which he lives and upon the upper worlds. In essence, the Jewish mystics teach that we get the best results from our spiritual practices when we do them with profound devotion and understanding.

One traditional prayer that takes on special meaning for Kabbalists is the *Shema,* the declaration of faith that is at the core of Jewish worship. The *Shema* is to be said twice a day, upon arising and before retiring. The first verse, *"Shema Yisrael: Adonai Elohenu, Adonai Ehad,"* means "Hear, O Israel: the LORD, our God, the LORD is One."[5]

Jesus underscored the significance of the *Shema.* God had given Moses 613 commandments, and the rabbis often discussed which was the greatest. When one of the scribes asked Jesus what was the greatest commandment, he replied by quoting the first two verses of the *Shema* and a command from Leviticus:

Traditional Jewish practices took on new meaning for Kabbalists as they focused on the Kabbalistic significance of each word they recited in prayer and each ritual they performed. By wedding prayer to special meditations, Kabbalists believed they could restore both the upper and lower worlds to their divine estate. (The Feast of the Rejoicing of the Law at the Synagogue in Leghorn, Italy, *by Solomon Alexander Hart.)*

Jesus answered him, "The first of all the commandments is, Hear, O Israel: The LORD, our God, the LORD is one.

"And thou shalt love the LORD thy God with all thy heart, and with all thy soul, and with all thy mind, and with all thy strength: this is the first commandment.

"And the second is like, namely this, Thou shalt love thy neighbour as thyself. [Lev. 19:18] There is none other commandment greater than these."[6]

In traditional Judaism, the *Shema* affirms the oneness of God and the monotheism of Judaism. The first and second sections of the *Shema* are taken from Moses' final advice to the Israelites on the eve of their entrance into the land of Canaan. The statement "the LORD is One" is intended to remind the Israelites not to worship other gods and idols because their God is the one, true God who is above all other gods.

The declaration that opens the *Shema* has no less meaning to us today. It reminds us that God alone—and not the lesser gods of material comfort, human personality or worldly honor—should be the object of our devotion.

Kabbalists take the *Shema's* declaration of monotheism to new heights. They see an inner meaning in the words of the *Shema* relating to the unity of the *sefirot*. They teach that when the *Shema* is said with *kavvanah*—that unique marriage of prayer and meditation—it restores the world of the *sefirot*. It also allows the upper and lower worlds to function in perfect harmony and unity and causes blessings to flow from *sefirah* to *sefirah* until they reach our physical world. The Zohar says that when a person recites the *Shema* properly, "the *Shekhinah* comes and settles upon his head and blesses him with an abundance of blessings."[7]

A Mystical Affirmation of Oneness

The words *Adonai Ehad* ("the LORD is One") in the *Shema* are not only an affirmation of the one God. When we say them with *kavvanah,* we can experience a profound sense of universal oneness. "The LORD is One" means that although there are many spiritual paths, they all lead to a single Source; and if we are all children of the one LORD, then we are all part of the same family. And if the LORD is One, there is nowhere he is not.

At the heart of Kabbalah, and of mysticism wherever it appears, lies a deep sense that we are already one with God and that God is everywhere—we just haven't taken the time to look for him. We are too caught up in the illusions that rise to the surface of life and hide the inner core of reality.

Moses Cordovero writes, "The essence of divinity is found in every single thing—nothing but It exists. . . . *Ein Sof* exists in each existent. Do not say, 'This is a stone and not God.' God forbid! Rather, all existence is God, and the stone is a thing pervaded by divinity."[8]

Speaking from the Christian perspective, Saint Symeon the New Theologian wrote: "You must understand that the Godhead is undivided. . . . And we shall all together become gods, intimately united with God. . . . For the One, when he has become many, remains One undivided, but every part is the whole Christ."[9]

Likewise, the nineteenth-century Hindu saint Ramakrishna taught this prayer affirming our oneness with God: "I am the machine, Thou [God] art the operator. I am the house, Thou art the householder. I speak as Thou makest me to speak. I act as Thou makest me to act."[10]

To truly realize that we are made in the image and likeness of God, that we are sparks of God, that we are a part of his very being is what we must strive for each time we recite the sacred declaration of our oneness with God and with each other: *"Shema Yisrael: Adonai Elohenu, Adonai Ehad."*

Prayer That Flows from a Joyous Heart

To the Jewish mystic, in addition to *kavvanah* there are two more ingredients necessary to spiritual progress and effective

prayer: joy and enthusiasm. "When you observe a commandment with joy," says the Baal Shem Tov, "there is reward without limit."[11] Luria teaches that it is healthy to rejoice when we
serve God and that depression prevents us from attaining
enlightenment. Vital wrote down the following teachings of
Luria on this subject:

> When a person prays, studies Torah, or observes a Command-
> ment, he must be happy and joyful. He must have more plea-
> sure than if he had reaped a great profit or had found a
> thousand gold coins. . . .
>
> The trait of sadness is a very bad quality, especially for one
> who wishes to attain wisdom and *Ruah HaKodesh* [the Holy
> Spirit]. There is nothing that can prevent enlightenment more
> than depression, even for those who are worthy. We find evi-
> dence for this from the verse, "And now bring a minstrel, and
> when the minstrel played, the hand of God came upon him"
> (2 Kings 3:15).[12]

Elijah de Vidas, a sixteenth-century Kabbalist, suggests
that we seclude ourselves for part of each day to meditate on
the "greatness of the Creator" and "recite several verses from
King David's Psalms, which tell of God's wonders and greatness."[13]

I have found that one of the best ways to generate joy is
to meditate on how much I have to be grateful for, not the least
of which is the boundless love and mercy of God. Try making
yourself a notebook and writing at the top of the first page,
"Hear, O Universe, I AM grateful!" Then once a day write
down something you are grateful for, whether it be the blessing of good health, the first daffodils of spring or the smile of
a little child. If you are ever tempted to become discouraged
or depressed, open that book and it will remind you that God
does indeed love you—because he has given you so much to
be grateful for.

The Power of the Names of God

Some Kabbalistic methods for achieving restoration focused on praying to and meditating on the names of God. Kabbalists associated a different name of God with each *sefirah* (see fig. 17, chapter 9). They believed that by meditating on the divine name associated with a *sefirah*, the energy flowing through that *sefirah* is activated.

They said that simply meditating on the divine names, however, will not produce results. This practice must be accompanied by good deeds. Joseph Gikatilla says that our good deeds stimulate God's blessings to descend until they reach *Malkhut,* the *sefirah* closest to the physical world. *Malkhut,* brimming with God's energy, is then able to mete out rewards to the righteous on earth. On the other hand, our negative actions are disastrous, for they block the flow of energy to this world, and thus God's children are left "hungry, thirsty, naked and totally deprived."[14]

Like many mystics of the world's religions, Kabbalists recognized the extraordinary power of the divine names. Thirteenth-century Kabbalist Rabbi Moses ben Simeon of Burgos says that "those prophets who concentrated intensely in deed and in thought. . .and whose pure thoughts cleaved to the Rock of the World with purity and great cleanliness. . .received an influx of the supernal inner emanation by virtue of the Divine names, to perform miraculous actions in physical things, working changes in nature."[15]

Rabbi Judah Albotini says that the use of God's names is so powerful that Moses saved Israel by invoking them. "With the power of the Divine Names, which [Moses] pronounced in his prayers," says Albotini, "he was able to turn back the anger and fury."[16] Gikatilla says Moses "learned the secret utterance of God's name from the ministering angels when he went up on High."[17]

The Kabbalists' techniques for meditating on the divine names often involved complex letter combinations of those names. The *Greater Hekhalot,* a text of *Merkabah* mysticism that dates back to the first century, speaks of letter combinations and names of God that can be repeated much like a mantra to bring the devotee into a mystical state.

Thirteenth-century Kabbalist Abraham Abulafia instructed his disciples to write, pronounce and meditate on the combinations that are formed when the letters of the names of God are combined with other letters. They were to do this along with certain body motions and breathing techniques.[18]

Abulafia says his teaching on the divine names is based on the tradition of the patriarchs and prophets. The statement in Genesis 12:8 that Abraham "called in the name of God" is traditionally interpreted to mean that Abraham prayed to or praised God. But Abulafia and his fellow Kabbalists claim that Abraham literally pronounced God's name and that he attained the highest mystical levels by doing so.

Some who practiced Abulafia's system had profound mystical experiences. One of Abulafia's students twice wrote that he saw light emanating from within himself. This anonymous student, whom some scholars believe to be Gikatilla, described his first mystical experience in his book *Sha'are Tzedeq:*

> The third night, after midnight, I nodded off a little, quill in hand and paper on my knees. Then I noticed that the candle was about to go out. I rose to put it right, as oftentimes happens to a person awake. Then I saw that the light continued. I was greatly astonished, as though, after close examination, I saw that it issued from myself. I said: "I do not believe it." I walked to and fro all through the house and, behold, the light is with me; I lay on a couch and covered myself up, and behold, the light is with me all the while.[19]

Other Kabbalists who used Abulafia's system had similar experiences. Isaac of Acco writes:

In the third watch, when I was half asleep, I saw the house in which I was sleeping full of a light which was very sweet and pleasant, for this light was not like the light which emanates from the sun, but was [bright] as the light of day, which is the light of dawn before the sun rises. And this light was before me for about three hours, and I hastened to open my eyes to see whether the dawn had broken or not, so that I might rise and pray, and I saw that it was yet night, and I returned to my sleep with joy.[20]

In the sixteenth century, Luria taught a system of meditation on God's names called *yihudim* (unifications). His exercises usually consisted of contemplating combinations of the letters of two or more names of God.

As we have seen, some Kabbalists not only meditated on the divine names but also recited them. Yet despite early traditions of pronouncing God's names, Kabbalists have been generally cautious about doing so. Some claim that the light that is drawn down when we say these names is tremendous and, in most cases, too much for us to handle.

According to Luria, only those who are free from sin dare pronounce the divine names and go unpunished by God. He says that early Kabbalists were able to recite the names of God because they could cleanse themselves from defilement with the ashes of the Red Heifer but that this cleansing is no longer possible.[21] Similarly, Moses Luzzatto says that repeating God's names mentally or verbally can be done only by a "holy individual," one who has "attained a high degree of closeness and attachment to God."[22]

Summarizing the view of most Kabbalists, Aryeh Kaplan writes: "The Name is. . .used primarily as a meditative device to bring the individual into certain states of consciousness, transporting him to the proper spiritual framework, whether for prophecy or to direct spiritual energy in other ways. . . .Since all the Divine Names are extremely potent. . . , one must be extremely careful not to use them except in the proper context and in the most serious manner."[23]

The warning of the Kabbalists has merit, for when we say a name of God we do tap into a tremendous source of power. But today God has provided us with a safe way to access the power of his divine names.

First, as an ongoing foundation for reciting the names of God, we should strive to live in accordance with the will of God and his laws. When we do transgress spiritual laws, we can return to center by confessing our transgressions and performing self-imposed penances for our misdeeds. Unconfessed sin compromises our relationship to our Higher Self. It also compromises our opportunity to access the power of God through the *sefirot* and the divine names.

Kabbalah, like many religious traditions, teaches that confession is an integral part of the spiritual path. Vital says that each evening, when we are lying in bed, we should confess to God every sin we have committed during the day, not omitting "a single sin or fine point that one transgressed."[24]

Second, we can prepare to recite the names of God by establishing a strong aura of spiritual protection around ourselves and by purifying our chakras. We can best accomplish spiritual protection and purification with an accelerated form of prayer known as the Science of the Spoken Word. When we practice this prayer technique under the sponsorship of the ascended masters, God is equipping us—and encouraging us—to use his names to call forth light where it is most needed on earth.

I will talk about this technique in chapter 10. But first, let us explore the meaning and purpose of the divine names that will facilitate our mystic ascent through the *sefirot*.

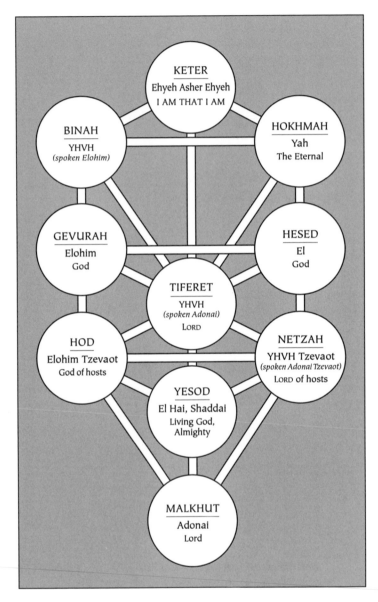

FIGURE 17. *The Names of God on the Tree of Life*

CHAPTER NINE

THE MYSTIC ASCENT

*One who wishes to attain what he desires from God should
concentrate on a particular Divine Name.... One must concentrate on the Name associated with the thing that he needs....
When a person prays, he must concentrate and ascend from
sefirah to sefirah, from desire to desire. He must continue in this
manner until in his heart he reaches the Source of the Highest
Will, which is called the Infinite (Ein Sof).*

JOSEPH GIKATILLA

What's in a name? A lot. Your
name is the key to your identity. If I know your name, I can make
contact with you. If I know a name of God or the name of a part
of God, I can make contact with God or with that part of God.

As we explore the ten divine names that unlock the power
of the *sefirot,* bear in mind that in the ancient world a name
was more than a label. It often indicated a person's character.
When someone's character was transformed, he was given a
new name. Thus, at turning points in their lives, Abram's name

Kabbalists associated a different name of God with each sefirah. *They
said that these names were keys to our ascent up the Tree of Life and
recorded profound mystical experiences after meditating on them.*

(meaning "the father is exalted") was changed to Abraham ("father of a multitude") and Jacob's name (meaning "supplanter") was changed to Israel ("he strives with God.")[1]

The names of God are also more than mere labels. Each one reflects a specific aspect of God's multifaceted character. More than that, each divine name concentrates a singular facet of God's power. And when you properly call upon that name, God releases the particular concentration of energy that is channeled through the corresponding *sefirah*.

The Divine Names as Keys to Entering the Gates of Light

Thirteenth-century Kabbalist Joseph Gikatilla unveils the mystical applications of God's names in his classic work *Sha'are Orah (Gates of Light)*, a work Luria later called the key to the mystical teachings. Gikatilla was a friend and colleague of Moses de León, the reputed author of the Zohar. Gikatilla himself was an influential Kabbalist and liturgical poet who gained a reputation as one who could work miracles.

In his introduction to *Gates of Light*, Gikatilla explains that each of God's names has a unique function and that each one "is like a key for all of [one's] needs, no matter what they are."[2] Eighteenth-century Kabbalist Moses Luzzatto echoes this theme. He affirms that God has distinct names that are connected with each *sefirah* and says that "when a particular name of God is uttered and used to call upon Him, it results in the emanation of an Influence associated with that Name."[3]

The Kabbalists who accessed the power of God's names treated their work as an exact science. In order for any equation to work, we need to "plug in" the correct components. In the same way, these Kabbalists knew that in order to get the results we want from our prayers and meditations, we have to plug in the correct name of God. For this reason Gikatilla advises us to become expert in the "purpose" of each divine name so that when we need to request something from God we can "concentrate on the Name designated to handle that question."[4]

How do we become experts in the "purpose" of each name of God? Gikatilla says we first have to understand the meaning of each name as revealed in the scriptures. He says that is why God promised in Psalm 91, "I will keep him safe, for he knows my name. When he calls on me I will answer him." "The verse does not promise safety by merely mentioning His Name," writes Gikatilla, "but by *knowing* His Name."[5]

Kabbalists believe that the names of God reveal the hidden meaning of scripture. They relate each name of God in the Bible to a different *sefirah,* and whenever a name of God is used in a certain verse of scripture, they read that verse as a story about one of the *sefirah.* Gikatilla uses this type of analysis in *Gates of Light.*

In this chapter, we will explore the mysteries of the divine names, including some of Gikatilla's insights into the significance and purpose of each name. Gikatilla examines the names of God corresponding to the *sefirot* in ascending order, starting with the last *sefirah, Malkhut,* and moving to the first, *Keter.* He does not explain why he takes this approach, but Moshe Idel, in his introduction to *Gates of Light,* concludes that it is because Gikatilla advocated a mystical ascent, or return, through the *sefirot.*[6]

Malkhut—Adonai

Our ascent up the Tree of Life begins with the lowest *sefirah, Malkhut.* The name of God associated with *Malkhut* is *Adonai. Adonai* is the plural form of *Adon* ("Lord"), which was used in ordinary speech as a title of respect when addressing a superior. When applied to God, *Adonai* is a title of honor that denotes God's absolute lordship. Although *Adonai* literally means "my Lords," it is translated as "Lord."

Gikatilla says that *Adonai* is the name of God that is "closest to all created things."[7] *Adonai* is "the great provider of Creation" who "governs all creatures, gives life and death, bequeaths and enriches, brings low and exalts, makes sick and heals."[8] He also says that the wise draw their wisdom from *Adonai.*

SEFIRAH	NAME OF GOD	NAME SIGNIFIES
MALKHUT (Kingdom)	ADONAI (Lord)	Absolute lordship
YESOD (Foundation)	EL HAI (Living God)	The Living God
	SHADDAI (Almighty)	Power, strength, stability
HOD (Splendor/Majesty)	ELOHIM TZEVAOT (God of hosts)	Supreme commander over heavenly and earthly forces
NETZAH (Victory)	YHVH TZEVAOT, spoken Adonai Tzevaot (LORD of hosts)	
TIFERET (Beauty/Compassion)	YHVH, spoken Adonai (LORD)	The Passionate, He who speaks, I cause to be. The essence of God.
GEVURAH (Justice/Judgment)	ELOHIM (God)	The Strong One, Mighty One, Foremost One. God over all other gods. Ruler over the affairs of men and nature.
HESED (Love/Mercy)	EL (God)	Might, authority, transcendence
BINAH (Understanding)	YHVH, spoken Elohim	Redemption, freedom, salvation
HOKHMAH (Wisdom)	YAH (The Eternal)	Eternal existence
KETER (Crown)	EHYEH ASHER EHYEH (I AM THAT I AM)	I will reveal myself in the outworking of events.

FIGURE 18. *The Sefirot and the Names of God*

ROLE OR ACTION

The great provider. Governs all creatures. Gives life and death and heals. Through this name one enters the presence of God.

Source of eternal life. Gives mercy to those who intend to mend their ways. Here the penitent repents of misdeeds and is consoled.

Sustains all creatures, prevents tribulation in the world.

Source of prophecies, visions, wonders and miracles. Wages and wins the Lord's wars. Saves the lovers of God. Consoles mourners and those in pain. Rescinds judgments and grants favors to the guilty depending on their repentance. Receives petitions of those who ask for children.

The greatest and holiest name. Embodies all of God's names in the Torah. Teaches the essence of the Creator. Sustains and enriches all that exists. Protects from evil. Gives happiness, strength, joy and vitality.

Dispenses justice and judgment. Brings death or life, annihilates or sustains, wounds or heals. Wages war against foes.

Absolute mercy, compassion, forgiveness. Mitigates punishment. Can save even the unworthy.

Acts as a Supernal Mother. Connects and blesses all the *sefirot.* Gives freedom and many kinds of salvation.

Alludes to the realm of mercy, where there is no sadness or misery. Compassionately forgives and compensates for inadequacy. Source of miracles, wonders, limitless supply. Facilitates ascent, redemption and the return to the original divine design.

Absolute mercy and compassion. Fills the world with rejoicing, friendship and peace.

Yesod—El Hai and Shaddai

The names of God that Kabbalists associate with *Yesod* are *El Hai* ("Living God") and *Shaddai* ("Almighty"). The patriarchs knew God by the name *El Shaddai,* meaning "God Almighty."[9] When God appeared to Abraham to announce that he would make his covenant with him, he said, "I am *El Shaddai;* walk before me, and be thou perfect."[10]

Scholars say the literal meaning of *Shaddai* is uncertain. It may be derived from the word for "mountain," "deal violently with" or "to be strong and powerful." Thus, *El Shaddai* may mean the God of the Mountain or it may be a title suggesting power, strength and stability.

Gikatilla says that *El Shaddai* is known as "the Fount of living waters" because it sustains all creatures. *El Shaddai* is also "responsible for the prevention of tribulation."[11]

Gikatilla relates the name *El Hai* to eternal life and repentance.

> The person who wants to reach eternal life should cleave to *El Hai*....
>
> ...*[El Hai]* stands ready to be merciful and do the bidding of all who ask when the person intends to mend and improve his ways....
>
> [The] Shrine which is called *El Hai* has a place which is called the Gates of Tears, and God Himself opens these gates three times a day. For the penitent, these are the gates where they take consolation and repent their evil deeds. For when the penitent prays, cries and lets tears fall in his prayers, his prayer and his cries enter the Gates of Tears.[12]

Hod—Elohim Tzevaot
Netzah—YHVH Tzevaot

Elohim Tzevaot ("God of hosts") is the divine name associated with *Hod.* The divine name associated with *Netzah* is *YHVH Tzevaot* ("LORD of hosts"), which Jews vocalize as *Adonai Tzevaot* because they are forbidden to pronounce *YHVH.*

Tzevaot means "hosts" or "armies." It is sometimes written in English as *Sabaoth*.

When *Tzevaot* is attached to either *Elohim* or *YHVH*, it depicts God as the supreme commander over all heavenly and earthly forces—the God who is transcendent, exalted and omnipotent. In the Old Testament, *YHVH Tzevaot* is the divine warrior and leader of the armies of Israel and is linked with the judgment of Israel and her neighboring nations.

When David faced Goliath, he said with confidence in the power of his God, "Thou comest to me with a sword, and with a spear, and with a shield: but I come to thee in the name of the LORD of hosts *[YHVH Tzevaot]*, the God of the armies of Israel, whom thou hast defied."[13]

Thus Gikatilla says that war and miracles are the domain

The names of God associated with the sefirot Hod *and* Netzah (Elohim Tzevaot *and* YHVH Tzevaot) *signify the omnipotent God who leads heavenly and earthly armies to save the lovers of God.* (The Apparition of the Army in the Heavens *by Gustave Doré.)*

of *YHVH Tzevaot* and *Elohim Tzevaot*. These two divine names also deal with thanksgiving and rescinding judgments, he says. Those who are guilty may be granted favors through those names. Gikatilla writes:

> It is in these two attributes that messengers are appointed to cancel the decrees upon man, whether it be death or other forms of punishment....
>
> ...In the Shrines of *Netzah* and *Hod* which are called *YHVH Tzevaot,* there is an angel who is in charge of all the legal decisions which go forth from the heavenly court to all the children of the world, and there are two scribes under his supervision, prior to the pronouncement of these decrees to the world. This appointee has the power to rescind the decree or repair it, all of which depends on the force of the repentance of the one upon whom the decree was levied.[14]

YHVH Tzevaot and *Elohim Tzevaot* also dispense consolation to mourners and those in pain, says Gikatilla. They dispense vengeance on "those who are unfit" to be before God.[15] He says that those who desire to have children can also direct their thoughts to *Hod* and *Netzah* when they pray to God.

Elohim Tzevaot is the name of God used frequently by the prophets, and Gikatilla says that the prophets draw their prophecies from both *Netzah* and *Hod*. "There are places in these Shrines [of *Netzah* and *Hod*]," he says, "from which all masters of wisdom nurse their ability to enter and achieve the intrinsic hidden heavenly truths, and gain access to visions, prophecy and dreams."[16]

Tiferet—YHVH (Adonai)

The name of God that Kabbalists associate with *Tiferet* is designated in Hebrew by the consonants *YHVH (yod, heh, vav, heh)*. These four letters are known as the Tetragrammaton, the Greek word meaning "four letters."

YHVH is considered to be the greatest name of God—the

Thirteenth-century Kabbalist Joseph Gikatilla says that the sefirot
Hod *and* Netzah *and the names of God associated with them are the
source of prophecies, visions, wonders and miracles. (*Baruch Writing
Jeremiah's Prophecies *by Gustave Doré.)*

name from which all other names spring. It is also the name
of God most frequently used in the Old Testament. English
versions of the Old Testament generally translate *YHVH* as
"Lord" (with the ORD in small capital letters) or as "Jehovah,"
although Jehovah is an erroneous pronunciation of *YHVH*.[17]

While some biblical accounts indicate that *YHVH* was
known during the time of the patriarchs,[18] it gained special
meaning for the Israelites at the time of Moses. The passage
from the Book of Exodus in which God speaks to Moses about
his name *YHVH* is one of the most cryptic in the Old Testament.

The scene is Mount Sinai, where Moses is tending his father-
in-law's flock. God calls to Moses out of the midst of the bush
that burns but is not consumed and promises that he will
deliver the Israelites from their Egyptian taskmasters. He tells

Moses that he is sending him to Pharaoh, for he has chosen Moses to bring the Israelites out of Egypt. Moses says, "Who am I, that I should go to Pharaoh?" But God assures Moses that he will be with him. Then Moses says to God:

"Behold, when I come unto the children of Israel and shall say unto them, 'The God of your fathers hath sent me unto you,' and they shall say to me, 'What is his name?' what shall I say unto them?"

And God *[Elohim]* said unto Moses, "I AM THAT I AM" *[Ehyeh Asher Ehyeh]*. And he said, "Thus shalt thou say unto the children of Israel: 'I AM *[Ehyeh]* hath sent me unto you.'"

And God said moreover unto Moses, "Thus shalt thou say unto the children of Israel, 'The LORD *[YHVH]*, the God of your fathers, the God of Abraham, the God of Isaac, and the God of Jacob, hath sent me unto you': this is my name for ever, and this is my memorial unto all generations."[19]

The last phrase has also been translated as "By this name I shall be invoked for all generations to come"[20] and "This is how I am to be addressed for generations to come."[21] Although these translations indicate that God intended us to invoke him by his name *YHVH,* no one is sure how *YHVH* should be pronounced or even what it means.

Scholars have proposed many different interpretations. Some say *YHVH* is derived from the Arabic word for "passion," thus giving the meaning "he who acts passionately," or "the Passionate." Others say it comes from the verb "to speak" and therefore means "he who speaks," which emphasizes *YHVH's* revelatory role.

Other commentators say that *YHVH* is connected with the Hebrew word for "to be," or "I am." In this sense, the root "I am" can be taken to mean either "I am here, ready to help" or, in its causative form, "I cause to be"—that is, "I create; I cause to be what happens; I am the God who shapes history." In his renowned *Guide for the Perplexed,* Maimonides says that while other names of God are derived from terms signifying God's actions, the name *YHVH* indicates "simple existence."[22]

YHVH is traditionally called *Shem HaMeforash,* literally "the name as clearly pronounced," "the articulated name" or "the explicit name." However, according to Jewish tradition, the name *YHVH* was so sacred that only the priests knew how to pronounce it. Eventually, during the period after the exile in Babylon, its pronunciation was lost.

Some sources tell us that the rabbis guarded the correct

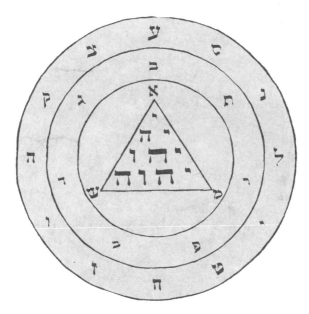

In the center of this diagram from the mystical text the Sefer Yetzirah, *the letters of the Tetragrammaton* (YHVH) *are arranged in the form of the Pythagorean tetractys. The tetractys is a dotted triangle whose four rows (1 + 2 + 3 + 4) add up to ten, a sacred number symbolizing the universe. This diagram places the three "mother letters" of the Hebrew alphabet (representing air, water and fire) at the corners of the triangle. The remaining nineteen Hebrew letters are placed within the outer circles to correspond to the seven planets and the twelve signs of the zodiac. According to the* Sefer Yetzirah, *the Hebrew alphabet symbolizes the universe.*

pronunciation of *YHVH* because the people had misused it or because they feared that the people would eventually do so. Maimonides, for instance, says that *YHVH* was "no longer uttered in the sanctuary on account of the corruption of the people."[23] He claims that "the greatness of this name and the prohibition against pronouncing it are due to its being indicative of the essence of [God]."[24] In other words, the name *YHVH* has such awesome power because it embodies the pure, undiluted, undifferentiated essence of God.

Based on references to the pronunciation of *YHVH* preserved in the writings of the church fathers Theodoret and Origen, scholars believe it was probably originally pronounced as *Yahweh* (YAH-weh or YAH-way) or *Yahveh* (YAH-veh or YAH-vay). But Jews, including Kabbalists, still consider the name *YHVH* to be too sacred to pronounce. When praying they substitute *Adonai* in its place.

In *Gates of Light,* Gikatilla says that the real reason it is customary to say *Adonai* in place of *YHVH* is that *Adonai* (the divine name associated with *Malkhut*) is the storehouse for

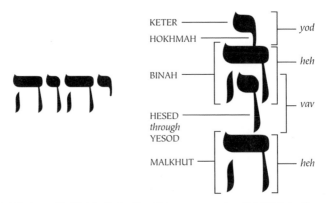

FIGURE 19. *To Kabbalists, the Tetragrammaton (YHVH) is the greatest name of God—the name from which all other names of God spring. They said that those who meditate on and cleave to this name will be filled with happiness, strength, joy and vitality. Kabbalists arranged the letters of the Tetragrammaton to symbolize the* sefirot, Adam Kadmon *and man in the likeness of God (right).*

the treasures of God, the palace where *YHVH* dwells, and the opening through which one enters to reach God.[25]

Gikatilla tells us that *YHVH* is the source of all the holy names of God in the Bible. This sacred name is like a tree trunk and all the other names are like branches or offshoots of it. Gikatilla describes *YHVH* as the core and pillar of the Tree of Life and says that there isn't anything in the world that doesn't rely on or isn't enriched with the name *YHVH*.[26]

For Kabbalists, the name *YHVH* is a key to the mystic ascent, and they formulated several meditations based on the symbolism of its letters. Isaac of Acco teaches that the secret to cleaving to God and being protected from evil is to meditate on *YHVH* by seeing those letters in one's mind's eye while keeping one's heart focused on *Ein Sof*.[27] Another Kabbalist taught that those who meditate on and cleave to the name *YHVH* are filled with happiness, strength, joy and vitality.[28]

To the Kabbalist, the Tetragrammaton, *YHVH,* represents the different aspects of the *sefirot. Yod* stands for the father (active) principle and represents *Keter* and *Hokhmah. Heh* stands for the mother (passive/receptive) principle and represents *Binah.* The union of father and mother produces *vav,* the Son. *Vav* also stands for six *sefirot, Hesed* through *Yesod.* The final *heh* represents *Malkhut,* known as the daughter, bride or lower mother. (fig. 19)

Kabbalists also saw a special relationship between the letters of the Tetragrammaton and the human body. They arranged the Hebrew letters vertically, one under the other, to form the figure of *Adam Kadmon* and of man in the likeness of his Creator. (fig. 19) *Yod* forms the head, *heh* the shoulders and arms, *vav* the trunk, and the final *heh* the legs.

Gevurah—Elohim

Elohim is the name of God that Kabbalists associate with *Gevurah.* In the Old Testament, *Elohim* is the generic term for the

Deity. It is a plural word, but when used as a name for God it is singular in meaning. For example, in the opening chapter of Genesis we read: "And God *[Elohim]* said: 'Let *us* make man in *our* image, after *our* likeness.' "[29] Some commentators say that *Elohim* is thus roughly equivalent to Godhead and that it suggests a heavenly council or circle of heavenly beings —a "divine plurality in unity."

Scholars say *Elohim* may be derived from one of several root words, including those meaning "powerful," "strong" or "foremost," giving *Elohim* the meaning "the Strong One," "the Mighty One" or "the Foremost One." Those roots all indicate that the name *Elohim* expresses the fullness of God's powers and describes a God who presides over all other gods.

Elohim and *YHVH* are the two chief names of God used in the Old Testament. *YHVH* is used in situations that refer to God's covenant with his people and is the name that shows God's personal, redemptive nature. *Elohim* refers to God in his role as Creator and Governor of the universe who rules the affairs of men and controls nature. Puzzled over why *Elohim* was used in certain passages of the Old Testament and *YHVH* in others, rabbis concluded that *Elohim* stands for the attribute of justice and *YHVH* stands for the attribute of mercy.

Gikatilla affirms that *Elohim* represents justice and judgment. *Elohim* "takes revenge against the wicked who rebel against *YHVH*," he says. "It has the ability to judge, exact punishment, and to overcome everyone. For there is nothing that can stand in its path."[30]

Gikatilla advises us never to be brazen in the face of the judgments of *Elohim:*

> If a plague, a disease or death comes to an individual, he should not be brazen before the Heavenly Court and *Elohim,* which is the place of true justice.
>
> He should not speak blasphemously, saying, "Elohim decided all this in heaven, and because of Him all this trouble

has descended upon me," lest a man open his mouth without thinking, as Job's wife said to him: "Do you still keep your integrity? Blaspheme *Elohim* and die." (Job 2:9)

One should rather answer as Job did: "Should we only receive the good from *Elohim* and not accept the evil?" (Job 2:10)...This is the belief of Israel: to receive the judgments of *Elohim* with joy and enjoy His afflictions, His rebuke, and His judgments and to thank Him for all, and bless His Name. ...One should not be upset when afflicted and unleash harsh words from one's mouth.[31]

There is great wisdom in these words, for we never know when a hardship or challenge that comes our way is our opportunity to balance negative karma for an unjust act we performed in this life or a past life. That is one reason we are still on earth today—we have to pay off all our accounts and to comfort those whom we have burdened. We are learning to love and serve those to whom we owe a karmic debt so that both they and we are free to accelerate on our respective spiritual paths.

Elohim is not only the dispenser of divine punishment but also the giver of life. Gikatilla writes:

Elohim is known to some Kabbalists as the essence of the consuming fire,...but this attribute may do exactly the opposite with the same simple force. This power can bring death or life on the one hand; it can, however, annihilate or sustain, make ill or heal, and all this is contained within one attribute with one pattern. It is from this power that all messengers from above must have permission to complete the judgments that have been decreed on humanity: for life or death, to destroy or sustain, to wound or to heal, all are contained in this attribute.[32]

Hesed—El

The name of God associated with *Hesed* is *El*, the Hebrew word translated as "God." *El* was the common name for a god in ancient Near Eastern cultures. It may come from a root meaning "to be strong" or "power," connoting not only might but authority and transcendence.

In the Old Testament, the term *El* is often combined with adjectives, resulting in names like *El Elyon* (the Most High God), *El Hai* (the Living God), *El Shaddai* (God Almighty) and *El Olam* (God Everlasting). *El* occurs by itself frequently in the Book of Job and other biblical poetry. We can see the importance of this name in ancient Israel by the fact that the name *Israel* (meaning "he strives with God") is a compound that includes the divine name *El*.

El, says Gikatilla, is "absolute mercy" that descends to save us. "In times of trouble the saints and the pious would hasten to pray and direct their thoughts to the attribute *El*," thus saving the world from "many kinds of tribulation."[33] Gikatilla says that *El* saves those who have been sentenced from their punishment. If God decrees that the world's peoples are to be slaughtered, but one righteous person directs his thoughts to *El*, then *El* will come forth with his mercy.

Even when a person's sins have tilted the scales against him, *El* enumerates all the merits and good he has done—"even a pleasant conversation he has brought up"—in order to mitigate his punishment so he will not suffer too intensely. El calculates a person's deeds very carefully, including his smallest actions, and then gives "generous rewards for whatever good he has done."[34]

Binah—YHVH (Elohim)

The name of God associated with *Binah* is *YHVH*, vocalized as *Elohim*. As I said earlier, Kabbalah teaches that the names of God are keys to understanding the secret meaning of the Bible. Since *Elohim* appears in the first three words of Genesis, Kabbalists say this passage reveals something about *Binah*.

According to the Zohar, those opening words of the Old Testament, *"Bereshit bara Elohim"* ("In the beginning God created"), are not about the creation of the world but about the creation of *Binah*. The Zohar says *"Bereshit bara Elohim"* really means: By means of the Beginning [a code name for *Hokhmah*], the hidden emanator *[Ein Sof* or *Keter]* created *Elohim* [a code name for *Binah*].

Gikatilla says that *Binah,* the Supernal Mother, merits the whole name *YHVH* because she delivers blessing to all the *sefirot. Binah* is also "the essence of redemption, freedom and many other kinds of salvation."[35]

In his section on *Binah,* Gikatilla again stresses that the activity of the *sefirot* is largely dependent on our actions. When we fulfill the law and perform good deeds, *Binah* brings blessing and favor to all the *sefirot.* This in turn causes *Malkhut/ Shekhinah* to dwell among us and to bestow God's blessings upon us. But if we are disobedient, *Binah* removes herself and God's light ceases to flow to the earth.

Hokhmah—Yah

The name of God associated with *Hokhmah* is *Yah.* Saadia Gaon, a tenth-century Jewish scholar, translates *Yah* as "the Eternal."[36] Maimonides says that the name *Yah* implies "eternal existence."[37]

Yah is an abbreviation of *YHVH* that is made up of the Hebrew letters *yod* and *heh,* and some scholars believe that *Yah* may be an older form of *YHVH. Yah* was combined with proper names, as in the name Isaiah, which means "*Yah* or *Yahu* is salvation."[38]

According to the Zohar, "All is included in *[Yah]:* those that are above and those that are below. In it the six hundred and thirteen commandments of the Torah, which are the essence of the supernal and terrestrial mysteries, are included— the essence of the Masculine world above and of the Feminine world below."[39] Leo Schaya interprets this to mean that "when this name is invoked sincerely, then it is as though one were carrying out all the commandments of the Jewish religion."[40]

In the Bible, *Yah* is found chiefly in poetry, where it is often used in the phrase *Hallelujah (Hallelu-yah),* meaning "praise *Yah.*" For instance, the final verse of the last Psalm proclaims,

"Let every thing that hath breath praise *Yah* [the LORD]! *Hallelujah* [Praise ye the LORD]!"[41]

"This name *[Yah]* compassionately forgives and compensates for the inadequacy of man in relation to the divine will," writes Schaya. "That is why the psalmist and 'prophet of *Yah*' cried out: 'In my anguish I called upon *Yah; Yah* heard my prayer and set me in a large place' (Ps. 118:5). . . . *Yah* is also the name for the return to the 'beginning,' to the perfect original of all things."[42]

Gikatilla says that *Yah* alludes to "the realm of mercy which is the essence of the three upper Spheres." The realm of mercy is a place where "there is no sadness, no misery, and no division; there is only glory, beauty and grace." "There is still some judgment in the Name *Yah,*" he writes, "but it is done gently and not through a legal verdict," which is the domain of *Gevurah* and the lower *sefirot.*[43]

The realm of mercy is the key to miracles and wonders, writes Gikatilla. Just as the world is renewed from the realm of mercy, so the righteous who direct their prayers to that realm can "renew signs and wonders in the world with their prayers, thereby changing the world's natural routine."[44]

Kabbalists also call *Hokhmah* "*Ratzon,*" or "Will." All the miracles and wonders performed in the time of the prophets and the Talmudic sages were possible "because their prayers could reach the source of *Ratzon,*" says Gikatilla. "The one whose prayer reaches the source of *Ratzon* may have limitless supply of all his needs. . . . He who has the key in his hand can get from that room anything he wishes."[45]

Keter—Ehyeh Asher Ehyeh

The name of God associated with *Keter* (Crown) is *Ehyeh* ("I AM") or *Ehyeh Asher Ehyeh* ("I AM THAT I AM"). *Ehyeh Asher Ehyeh* has also been translated as "I am who I am," "I am what I am" or "I will be what I will be." To me *Ehyeh Asher Ehyeh* means: "I AM Being. I will reveal myself in the unfolding of events. For you cannot know me as pure Being; you can only know me as I make myself known to you through my actions."

Gikatilla says that *Keter* encompasses different kinds of mercy and compassion. God used the names "I AM" and "I AM THAT I AM" when he spoke to Moses out of the burning bush and gave him the commission to lead the Israelites to the promised land (see pp. 209–10). Gikatilla says that the people were not fit for redemption at that time, but God's bountiful mercy saved them.

Gikatilla emphasizes that supplication and prayer, coupled with performing God's commandments, "can open the gates of mercy and rip apart stern decrees and push aside a vast array of tribulation and punishment."[46] When *Malkhut* receives the blessings that come from *Ehyeh,* "all heavenly and earthly creatures of the world are filled with rejoicing and tranquility, and the world will be filled with peace and friendship."[47]

Ehyeh Asher Ehyeh (I AM THAT I AM) is more than a sacred name. It is an empowerment. It is a scientific formula. When you recite that name with faith and love, God releases his energy as a stupendous waterfall of light to heal mind, heart and soul.

To me "I AM THAT I AM" means simply but profoundly "as above, so below." God is affirming, "I am here below that which I AM above." When *you* say, "I AM THAT I AM," you are affirming that God is where you are. In effect, you are saying: "As God is in heaven, so God is on earth within me. Right where I stand, God is. I am that 'I AM.' "

The names of God as Gikatilla describes them are keys for your mystic ascent up the Tree of Life, each one capable of opening another gate of light and another dimension of God's vast consciousness. "We have given you ten keys for connecting [the *sefirot*]," writes Gikatilla at the conclusion of *Gates of Light.* "With them you can open many gates, sealed with many locks."[48]

Now that we have the keys in hand, let's explore how the creative power of sound can enhance our work with God's names.

CHAPTER TEN

THE CREATIVE POWER OF SOUND

When Moses said, "Give ear, ye heavens, and I will speak,"
all worlds were shaken. A voice came forth and said, "Moses,
why dost thou shake the world, being but a mortal?"
He replied, "Because I will call on the name of the Lord."

THE ZOHAR

Recent scientific advances point to what sages knew thousands of years ago: sound holds the key to the mysteries of the universe. Sound can create matter and change matter. And it can create spiritual and material changes in our lives.

We know that sound can be a dramatic, destructive force— a high-pitched note can shatter a wineglass, a sonic boom can crack plaster, a gunshot can set off an avalanche. But sound is

Like other spiritual traditions, Kabbalah recognizes the incredible
power of sound through spoken prayer. Kabbalists even claimed that
Moses saved Israel by pronouncing the names of God in his prayers.
(Moses, Aaron and Hur during the Battle against Amalek by Julius
Schnorr.)

also a constructive force, as doctors and health practitioners are discovering every day. Ultrasound (high-pitched sound waves) is used for everything from cleaning wounds to diagnosing tumors to pulverizing kidney stones. Someday it may even be used to inject drugs into the body, making needles obsolete.

Scientists are now researching sound's impact on the brain. Certain kinds of classical music, by composers like Bach, Mozart and Beethoven, have a range of positive effects, including temporarily raising IQ, expanding memory and speeding up learning. Alternative medical practitioners are experimenting with using specific tones to heal the organs. Some researchers have documented that prayer heals the body. One study with a group of Benedictine monks showed that their Gregorian chants literally energized their bodies.

Spoken prayer is at the heart of the world's religions East and West, whether as the Jewish Shema and Amidah, the Christian Our Father, the Muslim Shahadah, the Hindu Gayatri or the Buddhist Om Mani Padme Hum.

The Zohar emphasizes that prayer is not effective unless it is spoken aloud:

> Whatever a man thinks or whatever he meditates in his heart cannot be realized in fact until he enunciates it with his lips. . . .And the word that he enunciates cleaves the air and goes up and flies through the world. And a sound is produced from it.
>
> The winged creatures take this sound up to the king, and it enters his ears. . . .Therefore, every prayer and petition that man wishes to lay before the Holy One, blessed be He, must be enunciated in words by the lips, because if he does not enunciate them his prayer is no prayer, and his petition is no petition.[1]

Aryeh Kaplan points out that "in later Kabbalistic schools, it appears that biblical verses or selections from the Talmud or Zohar would be used as mantras." For example, in the famed Palestinian community of Safed, Kabbalists would repeat a verse from the Bible like a mantra. Joseph Caro and his followers recited over and over certain sections of the Mishnah, the oldest portion of the Talmud. Isaac Luria may have used a similar technique with the Zohar. Kaplan says that the meditators would gain deep insights into the meaning of these sacred works by repeating their words this way.[2]

The Science of the Spoken Word

The prayer technique known today as the Science of the Spoken Word is a method of accessing the power of God that combines prayers, mantras, affirmations and visualizations with what are called "dynamic decrees." Like prayers, decrees are spoken petitions to God. But more than that, they are a command for the will of God to be manifest.

When we decree, we are scientifically commanding God's light to enter our world for alchemical change. We are directing God to send his light and his angels into action for personal and world transformation.

Prayer, meditation and decrees are all ways of connecting with God and your own Higher Self, and there is a time and place to practice each type of devotion. But no matter what spiritual path you follow, you can benefit from adding decrees to your devotions because decrees are the most powerful and effective of all applications to God.

When you decree, you are entering into a partnership with God. As the LORD said to Job, "Thou shalt make thy prayer unto him [the Almighty], and he shall hear thee. . . . Thou shalt also *decree a thing*, and it shall be established unto thee." And Isaiah tells us, "Thus saith the LORD, the Holy One of Israel, and his Maker, 'Ask me of things to come concerning my sons, and concerning the work of my hands *command ye me.*'"[3]

God is in effect telling us, "Call to me. I will answer. Command my energies flowing through the *sefirot* and through you and I will channel them into a constructive purpose. I will enter your world and work my works through you."

Many wonder: "Is it really necessary to *ask* God to help us? Isn't he omniscient? Doesn't he already know our problems and how to take care of them?"

According to God's laws, he and his heavenly representatives may not intervene in human affairs unless we specifically ask them to. For when God created us, he gave us free will; and he respects that free will. You can think of earth as a laboratory where God has given us the freedom to experiment and to evolve. If he hadn't given us free will and let us experience the good and bad results of our actions, we wouldn't be able to learn from—and grow from—the lessons of life.

When we wed the creative power of sound to a spiritual lifestyle that integrates the attributes of the *sefirot,* we have a winning combination. Together, these practices give us an exponential ability to accelerate *tikkun*—the restoration of our life and the world to their original divine design.

There are many different ways to apply the Science of the Spoken Word to personal and planetary needs.[4] In this chapter, we will discuss two kinds of decrees that can prepare us to recite the names of God.

Archangel Michael,
Guardian of Our Spiritual Practice

The first step in preparing to invoke the names of God is to call for Archangel Michael's protection. Archangel Michael is the most revered of angels in Jewish, Christian and Islamic scriptures and tradition. In the Old Testament Archangel Michael figures as the guardian of Israel. He appeared to Joshua as he prepared to lead the Israelites into battle at Jericho and revealed himself as "captain of the hosts of the Lord."

In one of the Dead Sea Scrolls, Michael is the "mighty, ministering angel" through whom God promises to "send perpetual help" to the sons of light. In Catholic tradition, he is

Archangel Michael is the most revered angel in Jewish, Christian and Islamic scriptures. He and numberless angels under his command guard us from every kind of physical and spiritual danger.

the patron and protector of the Church. In Muslim lore, he is Mika'il, the angel of nature who provides both food and knowledge to man.

Archangel Michael has numberless angels at his command whose job is to protect the children of God from physical and spiritual dangers. He is the guardian angel who oversees our spiritual practice.

Following are two simple decrees to Archangel Michael that you can recite at the beginning of your spiritual devotions. You can give them every morning for the protection of yourself and loved ones, and you can give them at night for protection while your soul travels out of your body during sleep.

In addition, throughout the day whenever you feel the need to reinforce God's protection around yourself or around those who may be suffering, stop and summon this all-powerful Archangel by reciting these decrees. You will get the best results from your decrees if you accompany them with specific visualizations. Some suggested visualizations are given here.

Visualization while giving decrees to Archangel Michael:

Visualize Archangel Michael as a majestic angel, arrayed in shining armour and wearing a brilliant sapphire blue cape. See him standing before you, then behind you, then to your left, to your right, beneath, above and in the center of your form. See him accompanied by untold numbers of angels who will protect and escort you wherever you go.

Imagine Archangel Michael wielding a sword of blue flame to deliver you from all negative conditions that work against your soul's progress on the spiritual path. You can also imagine yourself wearing a helmet and armour of blue steel that will prevent any physical or spiritual danger from reaching your body or mind.

Preamble to the decrees:

In the name of the beloved mighty victorious Presence of God, I AM in me, and my very own beloved Holy Christ Self, I call to Archangel Michael and his angels. I command you to _____

_____ [insert your personal prayer] _____ .

I ask that my prayers be multiplied for the consolation of all souls who are in distress.

I thank you and I accept it done this hour in full power, according to the will of God.

Decrees:

Traveling Protection

Lord* Michael before, Lord Michael behind,
Lord Michael to the right, Lord Michael to the left,
Lord Michael above, Lord Michael below,
Lord Michael, Lord Michael wherever I go!

I AM his Love protecting here!
I AM his Love protecting here!
I AM his Love protecting here!

(give decree three or nine times)

Guard, Guard, Guard Us!

Guard, guard, guard us!
By the lightning of thy love!
Guard, guard, guard us!
By thy Great Self above!
Guard, guard, guard us!
By thy secret power of light!
Guard, guard, guard us!
By thy great and glorious might!
And seal us safe forever
In thy diamond heart of light!

(give decree three or nine times)

To be given once at the close of decrees:
And in full faith I consciously accept this manifest,
manifest, manifest! right here and now with full power,
eternally sustained, all-powerfully active, ever expanding
and world enfolding until all are wholly ascended in the
light and free! Beloved I AM! Beloved I AM! Beloved I AM!

Lord is used here as a term of honor and does not connote equivalence to the God-head.

Purifying and Energizing Your Chakras

The second step in preparing to recite the names of God is to purify your chakras. Your chakras are the spiritual centers located along your spinal column. They are invisible to the physical eye, yet your very life and spiritual progress depend on their vitality (see p. 89).

As I said in chapter 4, the chakras are centers for receiving and distributing the energy of God that flows to and from you each day. Each chakra has a unique function and frequency, denoted by a symbolic number of petals. As the light of the Divine Mother (the Kundalini) rises from the base of the spine and activates the chakras one by one, each chakra begins to spin. The chakra opens its petals, signifying the unfoldment of latent spiritual powers.[5]

Unfortunately, our negative interactions with one another throughout this life and our past lives have caused karmic debris to accumulate around our chakras. This debris is like the soggy leaves that clog up a drain after a rain. In order for the water to run through the drain, you need to clear away the leaves. Likewise, in order for God's light to flow through your chakras, you need to clear the effluvia that clings to them.

Let me take an analogy from the ancient Oriental art of Feng Shui. According to the principles of Feng Shui, clutter and the arrangement of your environment determine how energy will flow through your surroundings. How that energy flows will powerfully affect your health, your wealth, your relationships and the very course of your life. In the same way, karmic clutter in your body, mind and emotions can cause the energy within and around you to stagnate.

We all have varying degrees of karmic clutter that has calcified around our chakras. As a result, we don't feel as free, light, happy, vibrant and spiritual as we could. When our chakras are clogged, we can feel sluggish, pessimistic or sick without even knowing why. When they are clear, we feel positive, energetic, joyful and generous.

Since our chakras are sending-and-receiving stations capable of broadcasting God's light to the world, we have a responsibility to purify them before invoking God's light. I've watched thousands of people successfully clear their chakras by using a unique spiritual energy in their prayers known as the violet flame.

In chapter 4, I talked about the seven rays of spiritual light, each one having a specific color, frequency and quality. When you invoke any one of the rays in the name of God, it manifests as a "flame." (You could compare this to a ray of sunlight that passes through a magnifying glass and creates a flame.) Thus, metaphysical teachers speak about the seven spiritual flames, such as the blue flame or the yellow flame. The violet flame is the seventh of these flames.

When invoked in prayer, each of the spiritual flames creates a specific positive action. The violet flame creates an action of transmutation. To *transmute* is to alter in form, appearance or nature, especially to change something into a higher form.

The term *transmutation* was used by alchemists who attempted to transmute base metals into gold, separating the "subtle" from the "gross" by means of heat. For ancient and medieval alchemists, the real purpose of alchemical transmutation was spiritual transformation. That is precisely what the violet flame does for us. When we diligently invoke it through heartfelt prayer, the violet flame consumes the "gross" elements of our negative karma and activates the "subtle," spiritual part of us that is native to our soul.

The violet flame can literally consume the debris around our chakras. Using the violet flame is like soaking your chakras in a chemical solution that dissolves, layer by layer, the negative karmic substance that has been trapped there for perhaps thousands of years.

The buildup of misqualified energy around our chakras can blunt the effectiveness of our prayers. If our chakras are

230 The Creative Power of Sound

clogged, the light of *Ein Sof* we invoke in our prayers will become tainted as it flows through us. As the light passes through, it then takes on our negatives.

This is why it is so important to clear our chakras and the passageways that connect them before we invoke the names of God. When properly applied, the violet flame clears the channels of the chakras so there is a pure flow of *Ein Sof's* energy through the *sefirot* to our physical and spiritual bodies.

Chakra Affirmations and Visualizations

You can use the following violet-flame chakra affirmations to purify and energize your chakras. Some suggested visualizations you can give accompanying the decree are given here.

Visualizations:

Visualize violet flames enveloping and cleansing your chakras. In your mind's eye, see the flames dissolve the debris that has collected around them.

Now turn your attention to each individual chakra with these visualizations, starting with the base chakra:

I now visualize my base-of-the-spine chakra, four-petaled, pure white, sending the energy of *Malkhut/Shekhinah* and God's light for the sealing of the sacred fire of the Divine Mother in the soul and base chakra of every child of light.

I now visualize my seat-of-the-soul chakra, six-petaled, violet-purple-pink, sending the energy of *Yesod* and God's violet flame for freedom, forgiveness, justice and world transmutation.

I now visualize my solar-plexus chakra, ten-petaled, purple and gold with ruby flecks, sending the energy of *Netzah* and *Hod* and the light of God's peace and brotherhood to harmonize all life.

I now visualize my heart chakra, twelve-petaled, a vibrant rose pink, sending the energy of *Tiferet* and the light of God's love to all sentient life.

I now visualize my throat chakra, sixteen-petaled, an electric sapphire blue, sending the energy of *Hesed* and *Gevurah* and the light of God's will to all nations and peoples.

I now visualize my third-eye chakra, ninety-six-petaled, an intense emerald green, sending the energy of *Hokhmah* and *Binah* and the light of God's vision and truth for healing.

I now visualize my crown chakra, thousand-petaled, a brilliant yellow fire, sending the energy of *Keter* and the light of God's wisdom, enlightenment and illumined action to dispel all darkness.

Now close your eyes and visualize your seven chakras lined up (as shown on p. 89). See the center of each chakra as a fiery sun of white light. Then see, surrounding the white center, the petals of each chakra in the vibrant, electric, intense color of that chakra.

As you give the violet-flame chakra affirmations below, sustain in your mind's eye the thoughtform of seven powerful white rays of light shooting out from the center of each chakra. Once you have visualized these rays with intensity, see each white ray wrapped in a cylinder the color of the chakra.

Chakra Affirmations

In the name I AM THAT I AM, I decree:

> I AM a being of violet fire!
> I AM the purity God desires!*

> My base chakra is a fount of violet fire,
> My base chakra is the purity God desires!

> I AM a being of violet fire!
> I AM the purity God desires!

*Give each two-line affirmation three times before going on to the next affirmation.

My soul chakra is a sphere of violet fire,
My soul is the purity God desires!

I AM a being of violet fire!
I AM the purity God desires!

My solar plexus is a sun of violet fire,
My solar plexus is the purity God desires!

I AM a being of violet fire!
I AM the purity God desires!

My heart is a chakra of violet fire,
My heart is the purity God desires!

I AM a being of violet fire!
I AM the purity God desires!

My throat chakra is a wheel of violet fire,
My throat chakra is the purity God desires!

I AM a being of violet fire!
I AM the purity God desires!

My third eye is a center of violet fire,
My third eye is the purity God desires!

I AM a being of violet fire!
I AM the purity God desires!

My crown chakra is a lotus of violet fire,
My crown chakra is the purity God desires!

I AM a being of violet fire!
I AM the purity God desires!

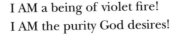

Relying on Prayer

Having given this basic ritual of protection and purification with decrees to Archangel Michael and the violet flame, we are ready to ascend the Tree of Life of the *sefirot* by invoking God's names in prayer.

The mystical side of Kabbalah does not preclude the practical side of prayer. God wants us to petition him to fill our physical, mental, emotional and spiritual needs, as long as the fulfillment of our requests will help us serve him and grow spiritually.

As cited in the last chapter, Joseph Gikatilla tells us that each of God's names is like a key for all our needs, no matter what they are. The Zohar itself encourages us to pray for the fulfillment of our needs and says that the righteous rely on their prayers and supplications rather than on their own merits to fill those needs.

The Zohar even gives a formula for making requests to God: We should begin by praising God and then present our petitions to him. When petitioning God, it prescribes, we should "state in precise terms" what we require so that there is "no possibility of misunderstanding."[6] God wants our prayers to be specific.

Kabbalists stress that our prayers are not directed to the *sefirot* but through them, so to speak. We are not worshiping the *sefirot,* for they are not gods or goddesses. You can think of the *sefirot* as the chakras of the cosmos. They are step-down transformers for the light of *Ein Sof,* vessels that channel God's bounty to humanity. In answer to our prayers, *Ein Sof's* energy moves through the *sefirot* to effect change.

Kabbalists also stress that our prayers should not always focus exclusively on one *sefirah* to the exclusion of the others. Rather, our prayers are meant to enhance the unity of the *sefirot* so that there is a harmonious flow of energy from *Ein Sof* through the channels of the *sefirot* to our world.

The following prayers reflect Kabbalah's teachings on the names of God and the virtues of the *sefirot*. You can give them as a daily ritual from beginning to end. Or if you want to rectify an imbalance within yourself or ask God to solve a particularly knotty problem, you can give selected prayers. For example, if you want to concentrate on opening your heart to give more love, recite the prayer invoking *YHVH* and *Tiferet's* attribute of beauty and compassion. If you are concerned about a certain injustice taking place, give the prayer to *Elohim*.

At the end of each prayer, there is an invitation to add your specific needs or make petitions on behalf of loved ones, your neighborhood, community, nation or the world. Remember, the more specific your prayer, the more specific the response from God. (The Hebrew letters for the name of God invoked in each prayer appear to the left of the title. The pronunciations of these names can be found in the guide following this chapter.)

Now I invite you to experience the empowerment of the divine names as you give the prayers that follow with profound devotion and gratitude. "O magnify the LORD with me, and let us exalt his name together!"[7]

Ascending the Tree of Life through the Names of God

"Because he hath set his love upon me, therefore will I deliver him: I will set him on high, because he hath known my name. "He shall call upon me, and I will answer him: I will be with him in trouble; I will deliver him and honour him."

PSALM 91:14, 15

We begin with a beautiful prayer taught by the sixteenth-century rabbi Joseph Tzayach. It is unique among Kabbalistic prayers because it includes both the names of the *sefirot* and the names of God associated with them.

> *Ehyeh Asher Ehyeh,* Crown me *(Keter).*
> *Yah,* grant me Wisdom *(Hokhmah).*
> *Elohim Haim,* grant me Understanding *(Binah).*
> *El,* with the right hand of His Love,
>   make me great *(Hesed).*
> *Elohim,* from the Terror of His Judgment,
>   protect me *(Gevurah).*
> *YHVH* (Adonai),* with His mercy, grant me
>   Beauty *(Tiferet).*
> *Adonai Tzevaot,* watch me Forever *(Netzah).*
> *Elohim Tzevaot,* grant me beatitude
>   from His Splendor *(Hod).*
> *El Hai,* make his covenant my Foundation *(Yesod).*
> *Adonai,* open my lips and my mouth will speak
>   of Your praise *(Malkhut).*[8]

*Depending on which *sefirah* the name *YHVH* is being associated with, the name *"Adonai"* or *"Elohim"* is said in place of *"YHVH."* Throughout these prayers, the pronunciation is noted in parentheses after *YHVH.*

אדני   Prayer to Adonai
                      (Malkhut/Kingdom,
                      Shekhinah/Divine Presence)

"I will praise thee, O *Adonai,* among the people: I will sing unto thee among the nations."

"I will declare thy name unto my brethren; in the midst of the congregation will I praise thee. . . .For the kingdom *[Malkhut]* is *Adonai's,* and he is the governor among the nations."[9]

Adonai, great provider and governor of all creatures, you who are closest to all created things, fill me with vigor and strength. Heal me of the maladies of body, mind and soul. Heal those less fortunate than I, especially those who suffer from life-threatening diseases that would cut short their lives.

O *Adonai,* bring me closer to God every day. Bestow your wisdom upon me, that I may act wisely in all matters you have placed under my care.

Adonai, well of living waters, eclipse the enemy of pride. I affirm, O God, that you are the source of my talents. In gratitude and love, I offer these to the benefit of God and man. May I serve thee all the days of my life.

Ein Sof, direct your light through *Malkhut* that the kingdom of God—the consciousness of God—may be made manifest in me, in all your children and in the world.

I offer all my devotions and my good deeds to unite the Blessed Holy One and his *Shekhinah. Shekhinah,* Feminine Presence of God, take up thy abode within me!

[Here offer personal prayers to *Adonai.*]

אֵל חַי
שַׁדַּי

**Prayer to El Hai
and Shaddai**
(Yesod/Foundation)

"My soul thirsteth for God, *El Hai*." "The Spirit of God hath made me, and the breath of *Shaddai* hath given me life."

"Yea, *Shaddai* shall be my defense. . .For then shalt I have my delight in *Shaddai* and shalt lift up my face unto God. I shall make my prayer unto him, and he shall hear me. . . .I shall also decree a thing, and it shall be established unto me: and the light shall shine upon my ways."

"The blessing of the LORD, it maketh rich, and he addeth no sorrow with it. . . . As the whirlwind passeth, so is the wicked no more: but the righteous is an everlasting foundation *[Yesod]*."[10]

El Shaddai, God Almighty, fount of living waters who sustains all creatures, release abundance to all your children—especially those who hunger and thirst for thee.

El Hai, the Living God, I ask you to forgive me for all misdeeds I have ever committed in this life and past lives. Each time that I fall, comfort me that I might have the courage to rise again and the strength to face and conquer the evil urge. *Shaddai,* give me the willpower and fortitude to right every wrong.

El Hai and *Shaddai,* help me to overcome all lusts of the flesh and turn my thoughts to thee. Let no harsh or discordant words issue from me. "Let the words of my mouth and the meditation of my heart be acceptable in thy sight, O LORD, my strength and my redeemer."[11]

Ein Sof, direct your light through *Yesod* to transform tribulation into joy, poverty into the abundant life, and barrenness into fruitfulness.

[Here offer personal prayers to *El Hai* and *Shaddai.*]

אלהים צבאות
יהוה צבאות

Prayer to Elohim Tzevaot
and YHVH Tzevaot
*(Hod/Splendor and Majesty,
Netzah/Victory)*

"Turn us again, *Elohim Tzevaot*, and cause thy face to shine; and we shall be saved."

"The LORD God is a sun and shield: the LORD will give grace and glory: no good thing will he withhold from them that walk uprightly. *YHVH (Adonai) Tzevaot*, blessed is the man that trusteth in thee."

"*YHVH (Adonai) Tzevaot* is with us; the God of Jacob is our refuge."

"Every day will I bless thee, and I will praise thy name for ever and ever. . . .I will speak of the glorious honour of thy majesty *[Hod]* and of thy wondrous works."

"O sing unto the LORD a new song, for he hath done marvellous things: his right hand and his holy arm hath gotten him the victory *[Netzah]*."[12]

Elohim Tzevaot, God of hosts, and *YHVH (Adonai) Tzevaot*, LORD of hosts, you who are the supreme commander over all heavenly and earthly forces, render impotent the evildoers in the earth. Perform your miracles to avert war—between brother and brother, nation and nation—wherever it would rear its ugly head.

Ein Sof, direct your light through *Hod* and *Netzah* to mitigate or forestall the judgments God has decreed against mankind that we may yet prove that we can work together to bring peace to this planet.

I know that world peace starts with me. Therefore, I ask you to help me establish and sustain peace in my heart. Give me the will to master all forces of anti-victory and anti-peace that would assail me and my life's work, from within or without.

Elohim Tzevaot and *YHVH (Adonai) Tzevaot,* reveal to me your heavenly truths, prophecies and visions and their correct interpretation. Infuse me with the stamina, endurance and enthusiasm to fulfill my purpose in life.

Console all those who mourn or are in pain. Bestow children upon those whom you choose to bear children, and help them to be good parents.

Protect all devotees of the pure stream of the world's religions who uphold your majesty and who labor for your victory.

[Here offer personal prayers to *Elohim Tzevaot* and *YHVH (Adonai) Tzevaot.*]

יהוה   Prayer to YHVH
(Tiferet/Beauty and Compassion)

"Praise ye the LORD *[YHVH]* from the heavens: praise him in the heights. Praise ye him, all his angels: praise ye him, all his hosts."

"Let the beauty *[Tiferet]* of the LORD our God be upon us, and establish thou the work of our hands upon us; yea, the work of our hands establish thou it."

I would cleave to you, *YHVH (Adonai)*. Grant me happiness, health and holiness. Grant me the strength to move the mountains of my pride and the boulders of my hardness of heart. Let your joy and élan dance in my soul. Infuse the works of my heart, head and hand with your inexhaustible energy.

Let the Heart of Hearts of *Tiferet* come into my heart. You have promised: "I am the LORD that healeth thee."[13] Heal my heart! Open my heart and dissolve all fear of failure and fear of rejection that keep me from giving and receiving love.

Forgive me, *YHVH (Adonai)*, my fretfulness when I ought to have trusted thee implicitly. Protect my family and all children of the world from the influence of evil.

Show me how I may actively be your compassion in action, and give me the opportunity to nurture the divine spark in all.

Lead me to the highest truth in all circumstances, and give me the courage to stand up for that truth. Eradicate prejudice, envy and jealousy. And help me to teach others—by my words and by my example— how to love God.

Ein Sof, direct your light through *Tiferet* for the restoration of harmony and wholeness in the community of nations.

Let the symmetry of truth prevail over all injustice. And let the energy of *Tiferet* cultivate nobility, honor and truth in the leadership of the nations.

"From the end of the earth will I cry unto thee, when my heart is overwhelmed. Lead me to the rock that is higher than I—the rock of my Higher Self. For thou hast been a shelter for me, and a strong tower from the enemy."[14]

[Here offer personal prayers to *YHVH (Adonai).*]

אלהים Prayer to Elohim
(Gevurah/Justice and Judgment)

"*Elohim* is our refuge and strength, a very present help in trouble."

"In *Elohim* I have put my trust; I will not fear what flesh can do unto me." For thou, O LORD, hath said, "I AM thy shield and thy exceeding great reward."

"[The Almighty] is excellent in power and in judgment and in plenty of justice *[Gevurah]:* he will not afflict."

"I will sing of mercy and judgment *[Gevurah];* unto thee, O LORD, will I sing. I will behave myself wisely in a perfect way. O when wilt thou come unto me? I will walk within my house with a perfect heart. I will set no wicked thing before mine eyes."

O *Elohim,* Mighty One, who dispenses justice and judgment, bind and cast out the evil urge within me. Help me to bear my karmic burdens with equanimity and zeal, for I know that "whom the Lord loveth, he chasteneth."[15]

Ein Sof, direct your light through *Gevurah* to dispense judgment upon the fallen angels who poison the children of God and whose time has come for judgment. *Elohim,* let your divine justice take dominion over the following injustices: _____

_____ .

Elohim, I ask you to balance within me the qualities of *Gevurah* (judgment and power) and *Hesed* (love) so that I might overcome all abuses of power—including aggression, anger, arrogance, argumentation, accusation, agitation, aggravation, irritation, condemnation and criticism—that I express toward myself or others. Help me overcome worldly ambition or passivity that has taken root within me.

Give me the discrimination to set wise boundaries that I might conserve my energies to serve humanity.

O *Elohim,* free all nature spirits of fire, air, water and earth, who are bowed down by environmental pollution. Restore all life to its original pristine estate.

[Here offer personal prayers to *Elohim.*]

אֵל   **Prayer to El**
(Hesed/Love and Mercy)

"As for *El*, his way is perfect. . . .He is a buckler to all those that trust in him." "He that trusteth in the Lord, mercy *[Hesed]* shall compass him about."

"Thou, O Lord, art a God full of compassion, and gracious, longsuffering and plenteous in mercy *[Hesed]* and truth."

"They shall prosper that love thee."

"His banner over me was love *[Hesed]*. . . .His left hand *[Gevurah]* is under my head, and his right hand *[Hesed]* doth embrace me."[16]

El, the King who dwells on the throne of mercy, in this time of trouble and strife among the nations, shower us with your mercy.

Sages and seers of ancient and modern times have prophesied the coming years as a crossroads—a time of tremendous progress or a time of war, turmoil and even cataclysm. *El*, whose light descends to save even the unworthy, mitigate the potential for calamity, that we might save this earth as a platform for soul evolution.

Restore each of my relationships—with family, loved ones, friends and co-workers—to the level of the heart. As you give forgiveness unending, *El*, help me to let go of the past and forgive all who have wronged me.

Comfort all whom I have ever wronged, and help me to forgive myself. Bring me into contact with those to whom I owe a debt of love, and give me the opportunity to rescue the sparks of light, the souls, who are part of my soul family.

Ein Sof, direct your light through *Hesed* as an unguent to quicken the hearts of all mankind to care for those who suffer—especially the elderly, those who are dying and those in hospitals.

Cultivate in me your living flame of divine love that I might be the embodiment of your loving-kindness. I offer myself through sacrifice, surrender, selflessness and service to assist those experiencing deep inner pain.

[Here offer personal prayers to *El.*]

יְהוָה   Prayer to YHVH
(Binah/Understanding)

"Let my cry come near before thee, O *YHVH**
(Elohim)*: give me understanding according to thy
word."

"My mouth shall speak of wisdom, and the meditation of my heart shall be of understanding *[Binah]*."

"The entrance of thy words giveth light; it giveth
understanding *[Binah]* unto the simple."

"Great is our Lord and of great power; his understanding *[Binah]* is infinite."[17]

YHVH (Elohim), increase my understanding and
intelligence, my insight and discernment. Help me
develop the feminine side of my nature. For I would
be an agent of *Binah* in the earth, succoring souls who
are oblivious to their spiritual potential. Cast out all
mediocrity and superficiality.

I surrender unto you all doubt and worry, for
I know that you will never leave me bereft. *YHVH (Elohim),* help me to see how I have limited myself by my
false concepts about myself and others, and show me
the shining vision of my soul's purity. Grant me the
faith and courage to see and rectify every flaw in my
character.

Ein Sof, direct your light through *Binah,* the Supernal Mother, to bless all youth. Free them from peer
pressure and substance abuse.

Guide our ascent up the Tree of Life until we reestablish within ourselves the perfect pattern of *Adam
Kadmon* and return to you.

[Here offer personal prayers to *YHVH (Elohim).*]

---

*YHVH is vocalized as "Elohim" when referring to Binah.

‏יָהּ‎   Prayer to Yah
(Hokhmah/Wisdom)

"The LORD is my strength and song, and is become my salvation. . . . *Yah* hath chastened me sore, but he hath not given me over unto death. Open to me the gates of righteousness; I will go into them and I will praise *Yah!*"

"O LORD, how manifold are thy works! In wisdom *[Hokhmah]* hast thou made them all; the earth is full of thy riches."[18]

Yah, the Eternal One who resides in the realm of mercy, where there is no misery, send your light to alleviate all suffering everywhere on earth.

I now confess to you the following acts of unkindness and transgressions of spiritual law that I have committed in thought, word and deed: —————— ——————————————— . Forgive my shortcomings and compensate for my inadequacies until I have imbibed and become the fullness of your wisdom.

Ein Sof, let your lightning flash illumine me. Pour into me the energy of *Hokhmah* as creative genius and insight. Flash forth your invincibility! Let truth be revealed!

I appeal to you, *Yah,* the source of wonders and limitless supply, to bring miracles to my doorstep, especially in the following matters that are close to my heart: ——————————————————— .

Ein Sof, direct your light through *Hokhmah*—who contains the blueprint for the whole creation—to restore all souls to their original design. O *Yah,* in this dark night of soul testing, be unto me as the beacon of the lighthouse, guiding me to distant shores. For it is to my God that I would ascend.

[Here insert your personal prayer to *Yah.*]

אהיה
אשר אהיה

Prayer to Ehyeh Asher Ehyeh
(Keter/Crown)

"In that day shall the LORD of hosts be for a crown *[Keter]* of glory and for a diadem of beauty unto the residue of his people."

"Thou shalt also be a crown *[Keter]* of glory in the hand of the LORD, and a royal diadem in the hand of thy God."

"Bless the LORD, O my soul, and forget not all his benefits, who forgiveth all thine iniquities, who healeth all thy diseases, who redeemeth thy life from destruction, who crowneth thee with loving-kindness and tender mercies."[19]

Ehyeh Asher Ehyeh, I AM THAT I AM, let the gates of the realm of mercy be opened!

Rescue me from pride, arrogance and egotism. Instill in me *Keter's* thirteen attributes of mercy and the chief attribute of humility, which is the cornerstone of the spiritual path.

With my head, let me be humble and praise the good in all. With my mind, let me think the thoughts of God. With my forehead, let me soothe all with goodwill.

Let my ears be open only to hear good. Let my eyes be alert to the suffering of others. Let me transform all anger into the peace of resolution. Let me face all with a joyful and friendly countenance. Let me speak well of everyone.

Let the Divine Will become my will: Thou the All; I the nothing.

Beloved I AM Presence, the personal presence of I AM THAT I AM within me, walk and talk with me every hour of every day. Seal your white light around me. Guide each of my steps that I might not stray off course in fulfilling my unique mission in life.

Ein Sof, direct your light through *Keter* to fill the world with rejoicing and friendship and to establish an era of peace.

Ehyeh Asher Ehyeh, infill me with your Holy Spirit. Let me transcend myself many times over until I am wholly filled with thy presence.

[Here insert your personal prayer to *Ehyeh Asher Ehyeh.*]

I AM Light

To seal your prayer ritual, give the following decree affirming "I AM Light." As you give it, visualize yourself enfolded in the white light of God that descends from your I AM Presence, as depicted in the Chart of Your Divine Self (see p. 78). As one thirteenth-century Kabbalist advised, "imagine you are light":

> Whatever one implants firmly in the mind becomes the essential thing. So if you pray and offer a blessing to God, or if you wish your intention to be true, imagine you are light. All around you—in every corner and on every side—is light. Turn to your right, and you will find shining light; to your left, splendor, a radiant light. Between them, up above, the light of the Presence. Surrounding that, the light of life. Above it all, a crown of light—crowning the aspirations of thought, illumining the paths of imagination, spreading the radiance of vision. This light is unfathomable and endless.[20]

"I AM" is capitalized in the "I AM Light" decree because each time you say, "I AM...," you are really affirming, "God in me is...." And whatever you affirm following the words "I AM" will become a reality, for the light of God flowing through you will obey that command.

I AM light, glowing light,
Radiating light, intensified light.
God consumes my darkness,
Transmuting it into light.

This day I AM a focus of the Central Sun.*
Flowing through me is a crystal river,
A living fountain of light
That can never be qualified
By human thought and feeling.
I AM an outpost of the divine.
Such darkness as has used me is swallowed up
By the mighty river of light which I AM.

I AM, I AM, I AM light;
I live, I live, I live in light.
I AM light's fullest dimension;
I AM light's purest intention.
I AM light, light, light
Flooding the world everywhere I move,
Blessing, strengthening and conveying
The purpose of the kingdom of heaven.

This decree reflects the aim of Kabbalists and the mystics of every religion: to become an "outpost of the divine"—an instrument of God. For Kabbalah teaches that we are a replica of the divine—that the *sefirot,* the emanations of God, are mirrored in our own bodies and souls.

As we have seen, Kabbalah provides a map for exploring the mysterious inner workings of God and the soul. At the same time, it unfolds a practical path of spirituality. It shows us how to make the attributes of the *sefirot* our own and how to integrate them into our daily life. It teaches us how to bring light into the world by calling on the names of God.

But ultimately, Kabbalah gives us keys to the most sacred adventure of all—union with God. May your ongoing practice of the techniques offered in this book bring you closer to that goal.

---

*Ein Sof

Pronunciation Guide

Key

ah	father
air	care
ay	ray, rain
ee	teeming
eh	yet
g	God
h	heart
ie	pie, light
kh	as in German *buch* or Scots English *loch.* Place tongue in position for sounding the letter *k,* but release the breath in a stream.
oh	so
oo	toot
or	or
uh	but

Pronunciation of Terms

Note: capitalized syllables indicate stressed syllables

Adam Kadmon	ah-DAHM kahd-MOHN
Adonai	ah-doh-NIE*
Adonai Ehad	ah-doh-NIE ekh-AHD
Adonai Elohenu	ah-don-NIE ehl-oh-HAY-noo
Adonai Tzevaot	ah-doh-NIE tsvah-OHT
Binah	been-AH
Da'at	dah-aht
devekut	dveh-KOOT
Din	deen

*Ashkenazic Jews sometimes pronounce as ah-doh-NOY

Ehyeh Asher Ehyeh	eh-heh-YEH ah-SHAIR eh-heh-YEH
Ein Sof	ayn sohf
Ein Sof Or	ayn sohf or
El	ehl
El Hai	ehl <u>kh</u>ie
Elohim	ehl-oh-HEEM
Elohim Haim	ehl-oh-HEEM hah-YEEM
Elohim Tzevaot	ehl-oh-HEEM tsvah-OHT
Gevurah	gvoo-RAH
Hesed	<u>kh</u>eh-sehd
Hod	hohd
Hokhmah	<u>khokh</u>-MAH
Kabbalah	kah-bah-LAH, kah-BAH-lah
kavvanah	kah-vah-NAH
kelippot	klee-POHT
Keter	KEH-tehr
Malkhut	mahl-<u>KH</u>OOT
Merkabah	mair-kah-BAH, mer-KAH-bah
	or mair-kah-VAH, mer-KAH-vah
mitzvot	mits-VOHT
Nefesh	neh-fehsh
Neshamah	nehsh-ah-MAH
Netzah	neht-zah<u>kh</u>
ruah	roo-ah<u>kh</u>
Ruah HaKodesh	roo-ah<u>kh</u> hah-KOD-dehsh
Safed	tzfaht
sefirah	spheer-AH
sefirot	spheer-OHT
Shaddai	shah-DIE
Shekhinah	sheh-<u>kh</u>ee-NAH
Shema	Sheh-MAH
Tiferet	teef-AIR-eht
tikkun	tee-KOON
tzimtzum	tseem-TSOOM
Yah	yah
Yesod	yeh-SOHD
Yesod Olam	yeh-SOHD oh-LAHM
Yisrael	Yihs-rah-EHL

Notes

Introduction

Opening quotation: Merkabah Shelemah 1a, 4b.

1. According to Professor Daniel Matt, the restriction that only married men over the age of 40 were allowed to study Kabbalah originated in Islamic tradition, which warned scholars not to study philosophy until they were ready. The injunction spread to Jewish philosophy and made its way to Kabbalah. Matt says the restriction is a warning that students of Kabbalah should be grounded in an occupation and the practical life, perhaps to be married or to have a trade, before exploring its inner truths. (Telephone interview with Daniel Matt, professor at the Center for Judaic Studies, Graduate Theological Union, Berkeley, California, 22 October 1993.)

2. Quoted in Abraham Azulai, *Or ha-Hammah*. See Gershom Scholem, *Kabbalah* (1974; reprint, New York: New American Library, Meridian, 1978), p. 68; David Biale, "Jewish Mysticism in the Sixteenth Century," in Paul E. Szarmach, ed., *An Introduction to the Medieval Mystics of Europe* (Albany, N.Y.: State University of New York Press, 1984), p. 315.

CHAPTER 1 *The Big Bang and Jewish Mysticism*

Opening quotation: Zohar 1:15a; 2:68b.

1. Rae Corelli, Marci McDonald, and Hilary Mackenzie, "Looking at God," *Maclean's*, 4 May 1992, p. 38.

2. Ibid., p. 39.

3. Zohar 1:15a, quoted in Arthur Green, "The Zohar: Jewish Mysticism in Medieval Spain," in Szarmach, *Introduction to the Medieval Mystics*, p. 116.

4. Zohar 1:15a, in Isaiah Tishby and Fischel Lachower, comps., *The Wisdom of the Zohar: An Anthology of Texts,* 3 vols., trans. David Goldstein (1989; reprint, New York: Oxford University Press for the Littman Library of Jewish Civilization, 1991), 1:310 (hereafter cited as Tishby, *Wisdom of the Zohar*).

5. Zohar 2:68b, quoted in Green, "The Zohar," pp. 117–18.

6. Creation Hymn, Rig-Veda 10.129.1–4. Translation from Ralph T. H. Griffith, *Hymns of the Rgveda,* rev. ed., 2 vols. (New Delhi: Munshiram Manoharlal Publishers, 1987), 2:621–22; and Jai Guru Dev, *Rig Veda: Tenth Mandala,* p. 236.

7. Gen. 1:1–5. All Bible verses are from the King James Version unless otherwise indicated.

8. David Sheinkin, *Path of the Kabbalah,* ed. Edward Hoffman (New York: Paragon House, 1986), pp. 25–27.

9. Ezek. 1:4–6.

10. Ezek. 1:22. (Jerusalem Bible)

11. Exod. 3.

12. I Enoch 14:8–25.

13. Songs of the Sabbath Sacrifice (4Q405 20–21–22.ii.8 [4QShir-Shab^f]), in Florentino Garcia Martinez, *The Dead Sea Scrolls Translated: The Qumran Texts in English* (Leiden: E. J. Brill, 1994), p. 429.

14. See discussion of Jesus and Paul as mystics in the Merkabah tradition in Elizabeth Clare Prophet with Erin L. Prophet, *Reincarnation: The Missing Link in Christianity* (Corwin Springs, Mont.: Summit University Press, 1997), chapters 22, 23. See also Gershom G. Scholem, *Jewish Gnosticism, Merkabah Mysticism, and Talmudic Tradition,* 2d ed. (New York: Jewish Theological Seminary of America, 1965), pp. 14–19; C. R. A. Morray-Jones, "Paradise Revisited (2 Cor. 12:1–12): The Jewish Mystical Background of Paul's Apostolate: Part 1: The Jewish Sources," *Harvard Theological Review* 86:2 (1993), pp. 177–217; and "Part 2: Paul's Heavenly Ascent and Its Significance," *Harvard Theological Review* 86:3 (1993), pp. 265–92; Ithamar Gruenwald, *Apocalyptic and Merkavah Mysticism* (Leiden: Brill, 1980), pp. 62–69; Neil S. Fujita, *A Crack*

in the Jar: What Ancient Jewish Documents Tell Us about the New Testament (New York: Paulist Press, 1986), pp. 174–76.

15. Scholem, *Kabbalah,* p. 16.

16. Hai Gaon, quoted in David S. Ariel, *The Mystic Quest: An Introduction to Jewish Mysticism* (Northvale, N.J.: Jason Aronson, 1988), p. 22.

17. *Merkabah* hymn, trans. Judah Goldin, in Scholem, *Jewish Gnosticism, Merkabah Mysticism, and Talmudic Tradition,* pp. 21–22.

18. Telephone interview with Rabbi Devorah Jacobson, 2 June 1992.

19. Scholem, *Kabbalah,* p. 373.

20. Ariel, *The Mystic Quest,* pp. 42–43.

21. Ibid., p. 42.

22. Ibid., p. 49.

23. P. Alexander, "3 (Hebrew Apocalypse of) Enoch," in James H. Charlesworth, ed., *The Old Testament Pseudepigrapha,* 2 vols. (Garden City, N.Y.: Doubleday and Company, 1983–85), 1:234.

24. Gershom Scholem, *Origins of the Kabbalah,* ed. R. J. Zwi Werblowsky, trans. Allan Arkush (Princeton, N.J.: Princeton University Press, 1987), p. 3.

25. Scholem, *Kabbalah,* pp. 4, 5.

26. Green, "The Zohar," p. 102.

27. Green, "The Zohar," p. 100.

28. Tishby, *Wisdom of the Zohar* 1:230.

29. Green, "The Zohar," p. 115.

30. Ibid., p. 113.

31. Daniel Chanan Matt, trans., *Zohar: The Book of Enlightenment* (Ramsey, N.J.: Paulist Press, 1983), pp. xv, 5; Scholem, *Kabbalah,* pp. 27, 29.

32. Gershom Scholem, ed., *Zohar: The Book of Splendor* (1949; reprint, New York: Schocken Books, 1963), p. 7.

33. Perle Epstein, *Kabbalah: The Way of the Jewish Mystic* (Garden City, N.Y.: Doubleday and Company, 1978), p. 10.

34. Lawrence Fine, "The Contemplative Practice of Yihudim in Lurianic Kabbalah," in Arthur Green, ed., *Jewish Spirituality:*

From the Sixteenth-Century Revival to the Present, vol. 14 of *World Spirituality: An Encyclopedic History of the Religious Quest* (New York: Crossroad Publishing Company, 1987), p. 71.

CHAPTER 2   *The Inner Faces of God*

Opening quotation: Sefer Yetzirah 1:4.

1. *Ma'arekhet ha-'Elohut,* quoted in Matt, *Zohar,* p. 33.

2. Zohar 1:21a, quoted in Charles Poncé, *Kabbalah: An Introduction and Illumination for the World Today* (1973; reprint, Wheaton, Ill.: Theosophical Publishing House with the assistance of the Kern Foundation, 1978), p. 239.

3. *The Way of Lao Tzu (Tao-te ching),* chap. 1, trans. Wing-tsit Chan (Indianapolis, Ind.: Bobbs-Merrill Co., 1963), p. 97.

4. Lao-tzu, *Te-tao ching,* chaps. 21, 41, trans. Robert G. Henricks (New York: Random House, Ballantine Books, 1989), pp. 73, 9.

5. Kena Upanishad, quoted in S. N. Dasgupta, *Hindu Mysticism* (Delhi: Motilal Banarsidass, 1927), p. 49.

6. Pseudo-Dionysius, *The Mystical Theology,* quoted in Harvey Egan, *An Anthology of Christian Mysticism* (Collegeville, Minn.: Liturgical Press, Pueblo Book, 1991), pp. 102–3.

7. Tishby, *Wisdom of the Zohar* 1:233.

8. Biale, "Jewish Mysticism in the Sixteenth Century," in Szarmach, *Introduction to the Medieval Mystics,* p. 320.

9. Aryeh Kaplan, trans., *The Bahir* (1979; reprint, York Beach, Maine: Samuel Weiser, 1989), p. 170.

10. Poncé, *Kabbalah,* p. 38.

11. Z'ev ben Shimon Halevi, *Kabbalah: Tradition of Hidden Knowledge* (New York: Thames and Hudson, 1980), p. 32.

12. Sefer Yetzirah 1:4–7. Translation by W. Wynn Westcott, *Sepher Yetzirah: The Book of Formation,* 3d ed., rev. (1893; reprint, New York: Samuel Weiser, 1980), pp. 15, 16; and Westcott, *Sepher Yetzirah* (New York: Occult Research Press, n.d.), quoted in Poncé, *Kabbalah,* p. 106.

13. Moses C. Luzzatto, *General Principles of the Kabbalah,* trans. Research Centre of Kabbalah (New York: Press of the

Research Centre of Kabbalah, 1970), p. 3.

14. Poncé, *Kabbalah,* pp. 103, 15.

15. Matt, *Zohar,* p. 21.

16. Zohar 3:70a. Translation from Matt, *Zohar,* p. 20; and Tishby, *Wisdom of the Zohar* 2:482.

17. Zohar 3:288a, quoted in Tishby, *Wisdom of the Zohar* 1:240.

18. Scholem, *Kabbalah,* p. 102.

19. Luzzatto, *General Principles of the Kabbalah,* p. 13.

20. Matt, *Zohar,* p. 20.

21. Luzzatto, *General Principles of the Kabbalah,* pp. 10–11.

22. *Tradition of Wisdom from the Sages of Mata Mehasya,* quoted in Ariel, *The Mystic Quest,* p. 77.

23. The following description of the emanation of the *sefirot* is taken from the Zohar 1:15a, 65a; 2:68b.

24. Tishby, *Wisdom of the Zohar* 1:277.

25. Zohar 2:68b, quoted in Green, "The Zohar," pp. 117–18.

26. Zohar 3:65a, in Tishby, *Wisdom of the Zohar* 1:344.

27. Tishby, *Wisdom of the Zohar* 1:282.

28. Rev. 22:1, 2.

CHAPTER 3 *The Tree of Life: The Sefirot Unveiled*

Opening quotation: Bahir 119.

1. Luzzatto, *General Principles of the Kabbalah,* p. 4.

2. Poncé, *Kabbalah,* p. 111.

3. Phil. 2:5.

4. *Tradition of Wisdom from the Sages of Mata Mehasya,* quoted in Ariel, *The Mystic Quest,* p. 77.

5. Zohar 1:65a, in Tishby, *Wisdom of the Zohar* 1:324.

6. Green, "The Zohar," p. 116.

7. Ibid., p. 115.

8. Zohar 3:65a–b, in Tishby, *Wisdom of the Zohar* 1:345, 346.

9. Hymn to *Keter* in *Prayer of Nehunyah ben ha-Kanah,* quoted in Ariel, *The Mystic Quest,* p. 74.

10. Matt, *Zohar,* pp. 34, 209.
11. Zohar 1:246b, in Tishby, *Wisdom of the Zohar* 1:326.
12. Zohar 1:2a, in Tishby, *Wisdom of the Zohar* 1:331.
13. Green, "The Zohar," p. 116.
14. Halevi, *Kabbalah,* p. 6.
15. Z'ev ben Shimon Halevi, *An Introduction to the Cabala: Tree of Life* (New York: Samuel Weiser, 1972), p. 37.
16. Sefer Yetzirah 3:3, in Westcott, *Sepher Yetzirah,* 3d ed., rev., p. 20.
17. Halevi, *Kabbalah,* p. 6.
18. Matt, *Zohar,* pp. 34, 36.
19. Poncé, *Kabbalah,* p. 126.
20. Halevi, *Introduction to the Cabala,* p. 41.
21. Halevi, *Kabbalah,* p. 7.
22. Matt, *Zohar,* p. 36.
23. Zohar 2:105a, quoted in Matt, *Zohar,* p. 19.
24. Zohar 3:191b, quoted in Matt, *Zohar,* p. 19.
25. Matt, *Zohar,* p. 20.
26. Zohar 2:11b, in Matt, *Zohar,* p. 100.
27. Matt, *Zohar,* p. 237.
28. Zohar 1:147a–148b, in Matt, *Zohar,* p. 79.
29. Matt, *Zohar,* p. 229.
30. Zohar 3:149a, quoted in Matt, *Zohar,* pp. 18–19.
31. John 1:9.
32. John 1:14.
33. Col. 2:9.
34. Acts 10:34, 35.
35. Job 19:26.
36. Some scholars and commentators believe that Job was a legendary figure. They say that the author of the Book of Job used an ancient folktale about Job as the framework for his narrative about an innocent sufferer. In the second century, Rabbi Resh Laqish expressed the view that Job never existed

and that the biblical story was a parable. Other commentators say that the Book of Job may be based on an ancient figure named Job who was associated with righteous men of the past, including Noah (see Ezek. 14:14, 20).

Commentators also disagree on the meaning of Job's statement "yet in my flesh shall I see God" (Job 19:26). Job 19:23–27, especially verse 26, is notoriously difficult to translate and ancient versions of this verse all differ. The Hebrew preposition *min* in verse 26 has different meanings and therefore the verse can be correctly translated "from my flesh" or "in my flesh" as well as "without my flesh." Most commentators who accept the translation "from my flesh" or "in my flesh" presume that Job expects to be in a flesh body when he sees God. However, they debate whether Job expects to see God while he is still alive on earth or after death, when he will have a resurrected, corporeal body. Those who comment on the translation "without my flesh I shall see God" speculate that Job may be expecting to see God "without" his flesh body, i.e., as a disembodied spirit.

The Zohar says Job 19:26 refers to the covenant of the circumcision. Tishby writes: "Through circumcision the divine name is marked as it were in the flesh of every Jewish boy. . . . Secrets of the divine mystery are revealed through the holy seal, which is the sign of the covenant of circumcision. [Zohar 1:94a says:] 'It is taught: Whenever a man is marked with the sacred mark of this sign he can see from it the Holy One, blessed be He; from it literally. . . . And it is written concerning this "And from my flesh shall I see God" (Job 19:26). This is the perfection of all: "from my flesh" literally—from this actual sign'" (*Wisdom of the Zohar* 3:1364).

37. Ps. 1:1–3.

38. Matt. 13:31, 32.

39. *karma* [Sanskrit, "deed"]: a mental or physical act; the consequence of a virtuous or evil deed of the body, speech or mind; the sum of the consequences of all deeds or actions of an individual in this and previous lives; the universal law of cause and effect. A group of individuals, such as a nation, may also create a common karma.

40. Gal. 6:5, 7.

41. Phil. 2:12.

42. Gershom Scholem, *On the Kabbalah and Its Symbolism*, trans. Ralph Manheim (New York: Schocken Books, 1969), p. 117.

43. Phil. 3:14.

44. John 14:6.

45. John 15:4, 5.

46. John 14:12.

47. Matt. 5:48.

48. Gal. 4:19; 2:20.

49. I Cor. 2:16.

50. Phil. 2:5.

51. Sentences of Sextus 394/395, 376a, in James M. Robinson, ed., *The Nag Hammadi Library in English*, 3d ed., rev. (San Francisco: Harper and Row, 1988), pp. 508, 507.

52. Apocryphon of James 2.29–33; 6.19–20, in Robinson, *Nag Hammadi Library in English*, pp. 31, 32.

53. Gospel of Philip 67.26–27; 61.29–31, in Robinson, *Nag Hammadi Library in English*, pp. 150, 147.

54. Gospel of Thomas, sayings 13, 108. Translation from Robinson, *Nag Hammadi Library in English*, pp. 127, 137; and Marvin W. Meyer, trans., *The Secret Teachings of Jesus: Four Gnostic Gospels* (1984; reprint, New York: Random House, Vintage Books, 1986), p. 37.

55. Kisari Mohan Ganguli, trans., *The Mahabharata of Krishna-Dwaipayana Vyasa*, 12 vol. (New Delhi: Munshiram Manoharlal, 1970), 4:109, 108.

56. Chu-hsi, quoted in J. C. Cooper, *Taoism: The Way of the Mystic*, rev. ed. (Wellingborough, Northamptonshire, England: Aquarian Press, Crucible, 1990), p. 126.

57. Arya Maitreya and Aryasanga, *Uttaratantra, or Ratnagotravibhaga: The Sublime Science of the Great Vehicle to Salvation*, trans. E. Obermiller (1931; reprint, Talent, Oreg.: Canon Publications, 1984), p. 157.

58. Saicho, quoted in Vandana, *Nama Japa (The Prayer of the*

Name) (Bombay: Bharatiya Vidya Bhavan, 1984), p. 274.

59. Halevi, *Kabbalah*, p. 7; *Introduction to the Cabala*, pp. 42–43.

60. Matt, *Zohar*, p. 36.

61. Ibid.

62. Gershom Scholem, *On the Mystical Shape of the Godhead: Basic Concepts in the Kabbalah*, trans. Joachim Neugroschel, ed. Jonathan Chipman (New York: Schocken Books, 1991), p. 175.

63. Scholem, *Kabbalah*, p. 110.

64. Zohar 2:51a, in Tishby, *Wisdom of the Zohar* 1:399.

65. Scholem, *Kabbalah and Its Symbolism*, p. 105.

66. Tikkune Zohar.

67. Scholem, *Kabbalah and Its Symbolism*, p. 107.

68. Zohar 3:297b, quoted in Tishby, *Wisdom of the Zohar* 1:382.

69. Zohar 3:114a.

70. Zohar 3:115b, in Tishby, *Wisdom of the Zohar* 1:422.

71. Scholem, *Mystical Shape of the Godhead*, pp. 159, 185.

72. Zohar 1:182a, in Tishby, *Wisdom of the Zohar* 1:410.

73. Zohar 3:42b, in Tishby, *Wisdom of the Zohar* 1:412.

74. Joseph Gikatilla, *Gates of Light (Shaare Orah)*, quoted in Matt, *Zohar*, p. 216.

75. Zohar 1:67a, quoted in Tishby, *Wisdom of the Zohar* 1:425.

76. Zohar 3:197a. Translation from Harry Sperling, Maurice Simon, and Paul P. Levertoff, *The Zohar*, 5 vol. (London: Soncino Press, 1934), 5:283; and Tisbhy, *Wisdom of the Zohar* 1:425.

77. Scholem, *Mystical Shape of the Godhead*, p. 192. See also Tishby, *Wisdom of the Zohar* 3:1160; Scholem, *Kabbalah and Its Symbolism*, pp. 108–9; Isaac Luria, *The Gate of the Holy Spirit*, quoted in Aryeh Kaplan, *Meditation and Kabbalah* (1982; reprint, York Beach, Maine: Samuel Weiser, 1985), p. 230.

78. Scholem, *Kabbalah and Its Symbolism*, p. 109.

79. Zohar 2:11b, in Matt, *Zohar*, p. 100.

80. Moses Cordovero, quoted in Matt, *Zohar*, pp. 236–37.

81. Gershom G. Scholem, *Major Trends in Jewish Mysticism* (1954; reprint, New York: Schocken Books, 1961), p. 235.

82. Raya Mehemna, quoted in Tishby, *Wisdom of the Zohar* 3:1159.

83. Matt, *Zohar*, p. 37.

84. Zohar 2:51a; 1:7b, in Tishby, *Wisdom of the Zohar* 1:398, 399–400.

85. Tishby, *Wisdom of the Zohar* 1:400 n. 113.

86. Rev. 12:1.

87. Job 22:21.

88. Matt. 7:13, 14.

89. Matt. 25:21, 23; Luke 19:17.

90. Scholem, *Kabbalah*, p. 107.

91. Ibid.

92. Halevi, *Kabbalah*, p. 6.

93. Epstein, *Kabbalah*, p. 24.

94. Sefer Yetzirah 1.6, in Westcott, *Sepher Yetzirah*, 3d ed., rev., p. 16.

95. Halevi, *Kabbalah*, pp. 5, 6.

96. Halevi, *Introduction to the Cabala*, p. 32.

97. Ibid., pp. 33–34.

CHAPTER 4   *A Portrait of the God Within*

Opening quotation: Zohar 2:20a, *Midrash ha-Ne'elam.*

1. Zohar 1:38a, quoted in Tishby, *Wisdom of the Zohar* 1:273.

2. See Schaya, *Universal Meaning of the Kabbalah*, pp. 34–35, 116–19; Halevi, *Introduction to the Cabala*, pp. 35–50; Halevi, *Kabbalah*, pp. 6–7, 50; Aryeh Kaplan, *Innerspace: Introduction to Kabbalah, Meditation and Prophecy*, ed. Abraham Sutton (Jerusalem: Moznaim Publishing, 1990), pp. 52–54, 61–68.

3. Schaya, *Universal Meaning of the Kabbalah*, p. 35.

4. Kaplan, *Innerspace*, p. 62.

5. Ibid., p. 64.

6. Scholem, *Mystical Shape of the Godhead*, p. 39.

7. Exod. 33:20, 23.

8. See Halevi, *Kabbalah,* p. 12.

9. Hayim Vital, *Sefer Etz Hayyim* 12a, quoted in Ariel, *The Mystic Quest,* pp. 169–70.

10. Matt, *Zohar,* p. 34.

11. The ascended masters are the saints and sages of East and West who once lived on earth, fulfilled their reason for being and reunited with God. Today they serve as teachers of mankind from the realms of Spirit, guiding all devotees of God. Among those who have become ascended masters are Abraham, Moses, Jesus, Gautama Buddha, Krishna, Kuan Yin, Mary and Saint Francis.

12. Zohar 1:21a, quoted in Poncé, *Kabbalah,* p. 239.

13. James 1:12.

14. Matt. 6:19, 20; Luke 12:33.

15. Zohar 1:164a.

16. See chapter 5, pp. 141–45.

17. Ezek. 1:26–28.

18. Jer. 23:5, 6; 33:15, 16.

19. Luke 1:80; 2:40.

20. Saint Germain, "A Trilogy On the Threefold Flame of Life," in *Saint Germain On Alchemy* (Livingston, Mont.: Summit University Press, 1985), p. 350.

21. I Cor. 3:16, 17; 6:19, 20; II Cor. 6:16.

22. Epstein, *Kabbalah,* p. 61.

23. Telephone interview with Rabbi Yonassan Gershom, 12 May 1992.

24. Tishby, *Wisdom of the Zohar* 1:272.

25. Z'ev ben Shimon Halevi, *The Way of Kabbalah* (New York: Samuel Weiser, 1976), p. 142.

CHAPTER 5   *Mysteries of the Soul*

Opening quotation: From a hymn by Nahmanides.

1. Moses de León, *Sefer ha-Nefesh ha-Hakhamah,* quoted in Tishby, *Wisdom of the Zohar* 2:683.

2. Ibid., pp. 681, 680.

3. Zohar 2:75b–76a, quoted in Tishby, *Wisdom of the Zohar* 2:680.

4. Scholem, *Kabbalah,* p. 156.

5. The predominant view of the Zohar is that the *nefesh, ruah* and *neshamah* correlate to *Malkhut, Tiferet* and *Binah* respectively. However, a few passages in the Zohar say that these three parts of the soul are images of *Tiferet, Gevurah* and *Hesed* respectively. Other Kabbalists associate the *nefesh* with *Binah,* the *ruah* with *Keter,* and the *neshamah* with *Hokhmah.* (See Tishby, *Wisdom of the Zohar* 2:687–88, 692.)

6. Sidney Spencer, *Mysticism in World Religion* (1963; reprint, Gloucester, Mass.: Peter Smith, 1971), p. 194.

7. Scholem, *Kabbalah,* p. 155.

8. Scholem, *Major Trends in Jewish Mysticism,* p. 241.

9. Zohar 1:62a, in Sperling, Simon, and Levertoff, *The Zohar* 1:203.

10. Zohar 3:70b, in Sperling, Simon, and Levertoff, *The Zohar* 5:67.

11. Zohar 1:83b. Translation from Sperling, Simon, and Levertoff, *The Zohar* 1:278; and Tishby, *Wisdom of the Zohar* 2:732.

12. Tishby, *Wisdom of the Zohar* 2:683.

13. Zohar 1:83b, in Sperling, Simon, and Levertoff, *The Zohar* 1:278–79.

14. Scholem, *Kabbalah,* p. 161.

15. Ibid., p. 157.

16. I Cor. 3:16.

17. II Pet. 1:3, 4.

18. Meister Eckhart, quoted in Spencer, *Mysticism in World Religion,* p. 245.

19. *Meister Eckhart: Sermons and Treatises,* trans. and ed. M. O'C. Walshe (Longmead, Shaftesbury, Dorset: Element Books, 1987), 3:107.

20. Meister Eckhart, quoted in Joseph James, comp., *The Way of Mysticism* (New York: Harper and Brothers Publishers, n.d.), p. 64.

21. *Ratnagotravibhāga* 1.28, in Edward Conze et al., eds., *Buddhist Texts through the Ages* (1954; reprint, New York: Harper and Row, Harper Torchbooks, 1964), p. 181.

22. Ezek. 18:4, 20.

23. Rev. 21:7, 8.

24. Mark L. Prophet and Elizabeth Clare Prophet, *Climb the Highest Mountain,* 2d ed. (Livingston, Mont.: Summit University Press, 1972), pp. 8–9.

25. Mark L. Prophet and Elizabeth Clare Prophet, *The Lost Teachings of Jesus 1* (Livingston, Mont.: Summit University Press, 1986), pocketbook edition, pp. 56–57.

26. Scholem, *Kabbalah,* p. 152.

27. *tannaim* (sing. *tanna*): literally "teachers"; the name for over two hundred rabbis who contributed to the Mishnah, a collection of Jewish laws and the rabbis' commentaries on them, compiled around A.D. 200.

    amoraim (sing. *amora*): literally "speakers," "interpreters"; the title given to Palestinian and Babylonian rabbis who interpreted the Mishnah from A.D. 200 to 500. The Mishnah and the commentary of the *amoraim* compose the Talmud, the authoritative body of written Jewish tradition.

    Rabbi Simeon bar Yohai, second century: eminent *tanna* who is traditionally believed to have written the Zohar.

    Rabbi Akiva (or Akiba), c. 50–c. 135: the most prominent *tanna* and Jewish leader of his time. He championed the Jewish patriot Bar Kokhba and his revolt against the Romans. The Romans subsequently martyred Akiva for breaking an ordinance forbidding the teaching of the Jewish law. A *Merkabah* mystic, Rabbi Akiva wrote some of the most important *Merkabah* literature.

    Rabbi Eliezer the Great (or Eliezer ben Hyrcanus), first–second centuries: teacher of Rabbi Akiva and one of the most important *tannaim.*

28. Hayim Vital, quoted in Perle Besserman, comp. and ed., *The Way of the Jewish Mystics* (Boston: Shambhala, 1994), pp. 160–61; and Meir Benayahu, *Sefer Toldot ha-'Ari,* quoted in

Moshe Idel, *Kabbalah: New Perspectives* (New Haven, Conn.: Yale University Press, 1988), p. 92.

29. Idel, *Kabbalah*, p. 93.

30. Ibid.

31. Shem Tov ibn Gaon, quoted in Idel, *Kabbalah*, p. 93.

32. Hayim Vital, *Sefer ha-Hezyonot,* quoted in Idel, *Kabbalah,* p. 93.

33. Tishby, *Wisdom of the Zohar* 2:818 n. 22.

34. Ibid. 2:818 n. 23.

35. Zohar 1:83a. Translation from Tishby, *Wisdom of the Zohar* 2:818; and Sperling, Simon, and Levertoff, *The Zohar* 1:277.

36. Eph. 6:10, 11, 14–18.

37. Tishby, *Wisdom of the Zohar* 2:819 n. 32.

38. Zohar 1:83a. Translation from Sperling, Simon, and Levertoff, *The Zohar* 1:277; and Tishby, *Wisdom of the Zohar* 2:819.

39. Zohar 1:85b. Translation from Sperling, Simon, and Levertoff, *The Zohar* 1:285–86; Tishby, *Wisdom of the Zohar* 3:1381–82; and Ariel, *The Mystic Quest,* p. 131.

40. Plato, *Symposium,* 191, 192, trans. B. Jowett.

41. Ibid., pp. 192–93.

42. For more information about twin flames and soul mates, see the following Summit University Press publications: Elizabeth Clare Prophet, *Soul Mates and Twin Flames: The Spiritual Dimension of Love and Relationships,* paperback, #4465; *Twin Flames in Love II,* 3-audiocassette album, #A82155; condensed in 1-audiocassette album *Twin Flames and Soul Mates: A New Look at Love, Karma and Relationships,* #S86005; and *The Union of Twin Flames,* 1 videocassette, #HL88031.

43. Scholem, *Major Trends in Jewish Mysticism,* pp. 233, 123.

44. Scholem, *Kabbalah,* pp. 174–75; Idel, *Kabbalah,* pp. 49–50.

45. Nahmanides, *Commentary to the Torah,* Deut. 11:22, quoted in Tishby, *Wisdom of the Zohar* 3:986.

46. Scholem, *Kabbalah,* p. 175.

47. Maimonides, *Yad, Yesodey HaTorah* 7:1, quoted in Aryeh Kaplan, *Meditation and the Bible* (1978; reprint, York Beach,

Maine: Samuel Weiser, 1988), p. 22.

48. Moses Luzzatto, *Derekh HaShem,* quoted in Kaplan, *Meditation and the Bible,* p. 23.

49. Ibid., pp. 23–24.

50. *Tana DeBei Eliahu* 9, quoted in Kaplan, *Meditation and the Bible,* p. 21.

51. Joel 2:28, 29. Kaplan, *Meditation and the Bible,* p. 21.

52. Idel, *Kabbalah,* p. 59.

53. Scholem, *Major Trends in Jewish Mysticism,* pp. 122–23.

54. Idel, *Kabbalah,* pp. 59–60.

55. Isaac of Acco, *'Ozar Hayyim.* Translation from Idel, *Kabbalah,* p. 67; and Daniel C. Matt, "*Ayin:* The Concept of Nothingness in Jewish Mysticism," in Robert K. C. Forman, *The Problem of Pure Consciousness* (New York: Oxford University Press, 1990), p. 136.

56. Isaac of Acco, *'Ozar Hayyim,* quoted in Idel, *Kabbalah,* p. 48.

57. Menahem Nahum of Chernobyl, *Me'or 'Eynaim,* quoted in Idel, *Kabbalah,* p. 66.

58. Zohar 2:11b; 1:91a, in Tishby, *Wisdom of the Zohar* 3:995, 2:742–43.

59. Tishby, *Wisdom of the Zohar* 2:743 n. 178.

60. Zohar 1:99b, in Sperling, Simon, and Levertoff, *The Zohar* 1:324.

61. Zohar 1:99b–100a, in Sperling, Simon, and Levertoff, *The Zohar* 1:324–25.

62. Tishby, *Wisdom of the Zohar* 2:683.

63. *Zohar Hadash, Bereshit* 18b (*Midrash ha-Ne'elam*), quoted in Tishby, *Wisdom of the Zohar* 2:683.

64. Spencer, *Mysticism in World Religion,* p. 194.

65. Scholem, *Kabbalah,* p. 161.

66. Rev. 2:11; 20:6, 11–15; 21:7, 8. See p. 120.

67. Idel, *Kabbalah,* p. 64.

68. *Sha'arey Zedek,* quoted in Idel, *Kabbalah,* p. 63.

69. Idel, *Kabbalah,* p. 63.

CHAPTER 6 *The Origin of Evil*

Opening quotation: Rabbi Joseph Gikatilla, *Sod ha-Nahash u-Mishpato (The Mystery of the Serpent and Its Sentence)*.

1. Green, "The Zohar," p. 125.

2. Zohar 3:41b, quoted in Tishby, *Wisdom of the Zohar* 2:450.

3. Zohar 2:242b, in Tishby, *Wisdom of the Zohar* 2:475.

4. Zohar 1:243b, in Tishby, *Wisdom of the Zohar* 2:499. For a discussion of the Zohar's use of the imagery of the snake to represent evil, see Tishby, 2:467–70.

5. See Elizabeth Clare Prophet, *Fallen Angels and the Origins of Evil* (Corwin Springs, Mont.: Summit University Press, 2000). Contains the entire Book of Enoch and all the other Enoch texts plus an introduction on why church fathers suppressed the real story of the fallen angels.

6. Matt. 7:1; Luke 6:37.

7. John 3:17.

8. William Shakespeare, *The Merchant of Venice,* act 4, sc. 1, lines 183–96.

9. Shakespeare, *The Merchant of Venice,* act 4, sc. 1, lines 197–99.

10. Zohar 1:171a, in Tishby, *Wisdom of the Zohar* 3:1146.

11. Baal Shem Tov, quoted in Besserman, *Way of the Jewish Mystics,* pp. 144–45.

12. Jer. 6:14; 8:11; Ezek. 13:10.

13. Zohar 1:190a, in Matt, *Zohar,* p. 85.

14. Zohar 1:208b–209a, quoted in Tishby, *Wisdom of the Zohar* 2:456.

15. Zohar 3:43a. Translation from Sperling, Simon, and Levertoff, *The Zohar* 5:5; and Tishby, *Wisdom of the Zohar* 2:789.

16. Zohar 1:103b, in Tishby, *Wisdom of the Zohar* 1:400.

17. Zohar 2:163a, in Tishby, *Wisdom of the Zohar* 2:806.

18. Matt, *Zohar,* p. 220.

19. Zohar 1:83a. Translation from Tishby, *Wisdom of the Zohar* 2:457; and Sperling, Simon, and Levertoff, *The Zohar* 1:276.

20. Matt, *Zohar,* p. 220.

21. Tishby, *Wisdom of the Zohar* 2:457, 458.
22. Zohar 2:267b–268a, in Tishby, *Wisdom of the Zohar* 2:803–4.
23. Tishby, *Wisdom of the Zohar* 2:452.
24. Ibid.
25. Zohar 2:238b, quoted in Tishby, *Wisdom of the Zohar* 2:452.
26. Scholem, *Kabbalah and Its Symbolism,* p. 108.
27. Scholem, *Kabbalah,* p. 153.
28. Ibid., p. 154.
29. Zohar 3:135a–b, in Tishby, *Wisdom of the Zohar* 1:332.
30. Tishby, *Wisdom of the Zohar* 2:458.
31. Ibid. See also Zohar 3:135a–b, in Tishby, *Wisdom of the Zohar* 1:332–33.
32. Tishby, *Wisdom of the Zohar* 1:332 n. 252.
33. Scholem, *Kabbalah,* p. 131.
34. Scholem, *Major Trends in Jewish Mysticism,* p. 263.
35. Scholem, *Kabbalah and Its Symbolism,* p. 112.
36. Biale, "Jewish Mysticism in the Sixteenth Century," p. 324.
37. Ibid., p. 325.
38. Scholem, *Kabbalah and Its Symbolism,* p. 115.
39. Scholem, *Kabbalah,* pp. 162, 163.
40. Scholem, *Kabbalah and Its Symbolism,* p. 115.
41. Scholem, *Mystical Shape of the Godhead,* p. 234.
42. Gershom Scholem, *The Messianic Idea in Judaism and Other Essays on Jewish Spirituality* (New York: Schocken Books, 1971), p. 187.
43. Louis Jacobs, "The Uplifting of Sparks in Later Jewish Mysticism," in Green, *Jewish Spirituality,* p. 106.
44. Hillel Zeitlin, *Ha-Hasidut,* quoted in Scholem, *The Messianic Idea in Judaism,* p. 190.
45. Ephraim of Sedylkov, *Degel Mahane Efrayim,* quoted in Scholem, *The Messianic Idea in Judaism,* p. 189.
46. Baal Shem Tov, quoted in Scholem, *Mystical Shape of the Godhead,* p. 250.

47. *Toldot Ya'akov Yosef.* Translation from Scholem, *Mystical Shape of the Godhead,* p. 246; and *The Messianic Idea in Judaism,* p. 189.

48. Jacobs, "Uplifting of Sparks in Later Jewish Mysticism," pp. 116, 124.

49. Levi Isaac of Berdichev, *Qedushat Levi,* quoted in Daniel C. Matt, *The Essential Kabbalah: The Heart of Jewish Mysticism* (New York: HarperCollins Publishers, HarperSanFrancisco, 1995), p. 151.

50. Jacob Joseph of Polonnoye, *Ketoneth Passim,* quoted in Scholem, *Mystical Shape of the Godhead,* p. 248.

51. Scholem, *Kabbalah and Its Symbolism,* pp. 116, 117.

52. Ibid., p. 116.

CHAPTER 7   *The Practical Path of the Mystic*

Opening quotation: Moses Luzzatto, *Mesillat Yesharin.*

1. Shlomel of Moravia, quoted in Epstein, *Kabbalah,* p. 11.

2. Epstein, *Kabbalah,* pp. 12–13, 11.

3. Moses Cordovero, *The Palm Tree of Deborah,* trans. Louis Jacobs (New York: Sepher-Hermon Press, 1960), p. 69.

4. Cordovero, quoted in Scholem, *Major Trends in Jewish Mysticism,* p. 279.

5. Lev. 19:18.

6. Cordovero, *The Palm Tree of Deborah,* p. 52.

7. John Donne, *Devotions upon Emergent Occasions* 17.

8. Cordovero, *The Palm Tree of Deborah,* p. 46. All subsequent quotations from *The Palm Tree of Deborah* used in this chapter are taken from this edition.

9. Prov. 15:1.

10. Thomas Cleary, *The Tao of Politics Lessons of the Masters of Huainan* (Boston: Shambhala Publications, 1990), p. 68.

11. Mary Baker Eddy, "Taking Offense," in *Prose Works Other than Science and Health with Key to the Scriptures* (Boston: The First Church of Christ, Scientist, 1925), pp. 223–24.

12. John 21:22.

13. Luke 13:1–5.

14. Matt. 6:14, 15.

15. Matt. 18:21, 22. Revised Standard Version, hereafter cited as RSV.
16. Rom. 12:19 RSV; Rom. 12:19, 20, 21.
17. Prov. 3:11, 12.
18. *Iggeret ha-Qodesh,* quoted in Matt, *The Essential Kabbalah,* pp. 155, 156.
19. Kaplan, *Meditation and Kabbalah,* p. 170.
20. Issachar Ber of Zlotshov, *Mevasser Zedek,* quoted in Matt, *"Ayin,"* p. 139. The reference to "There is no place empty of Him" is from *Tiqqunei Zohar* 57.
21. Dov Baer, *Maggid Devarav le-Ya'aqov,* quoted in Matt, *Essential Kabbalah,* p. 71.
22. D. Benjamin ben Aaron of Zalozce, *Torei Zahav,* quoted in Matt., *"Ayin,"* pp. 141–42.
23. Matt, *"Ayin,"* p. 142.
24. Uziel Meizlish, *Tif'eret 'Uzzi'el,* quoted in Matt, *"Ayin,"* p. 142.
25. Avraham Hayyim of Zlotshov, *Orah la-Hayyim,* quoted in Matt, *"Ayin,"* p. 142.
26. Dov Baer, *Maggid Devarav le-Ya'aqov,* quoted in Matt, *"Ayin,"* p. 143.
27. Jalaluddin Rumi, *Mathnawi,* prologue.
28. John 5:17, 19, 30; 14:10.
29. Igino Giordani, *Saint Catherine of Siena—Doctor of the Church,* trans. Thomas J. Tobin (Boston: Daughters of St. Paul, 1975), p. 35.
30. Ibid., p. 36.
31. Ralph Waldo Emerson, *Nature,* in *Selected Essays, Lectures, and Poems,* ed. Robert D. Richardson, Jr. (New York: Bantam Books, 1990), pp. 48–49.

CHAPTER 8 *Prayer and the Power of God's Names*

Opening quotation: Joseph Gikatilla, *Gates of Light (Sha'are Orah).*
1. Scholem, *Kabbalah,* p. 176.
2. Zohar 2:215b, in Sperling, Simon, and Levertoff, *The Zohar* 4:232.

3. Hayim Vital, quoted in *Panu Derekh—Prepare the Way,* no. 5 (Dec. '94/Jan. '95): 34.

4. Maimonides, *Mishneh Torah, Hilkhot Tefillah* 4:15–16, quoted in Tishby, *Wisdom of the Zohar* 3:944.

5. Where the name *Adonai* occurs in the first verse of the *Shema,* the Hebrew is literally *YHVH,* the sacred name of God that consists of the Hebrew letters *yod he vav he. YHVH* is known as the Tetragrammaton. Jews pronounce *YHVH* as *Adonai,* meaning "Lord," because they are forbidden to pronounce *YHVH* aloud (see pp. 211–12).

   The first verse of the *Shema* literally says, *"YHVH, our God, YHVH, one."* This can be translated in several ways: "the LORD, our God, the LORD is one," "the LORD our God is one LORD," "the LORD is our God, the LORD is one," or "the LORD is our God, the LORD alone." The full text of the *Shema* is Deut. 6:4–9; 11:13–21 and Num. 15:37–41.

6. Mark 12:29–31 KJV and RSV.

7. Zohar 2:161a, quoted in Tishby, *Wisdom of the Zohar* 3:961.

8. Moses Cordovero, quoted in Daniel C. Matt, *God and the Big Bang: Discovering Harmony between Science and Spirituality* (Woodstock, Vt.: Jewish Lights Publishing, 1996), p. 39.

9. Symeon the New Theologian, "Hymns of Divine Love," no. 15, quoted in Martin Buber, *Ecstatic Confessions,* ed. Paul Mendes-Flohr, trans. Esther Cameron (New York: Harper and Row, 1985), pp. 38, 39.

10. Swami Prabhavananda, trans., *Narada's Way of Divine Love (Narada Bhakti Sutras)* (Madras, India: Sri Ramakrishna Math, 1971), p. 107.

11. The Baal Shem Tov, quoted in Besserman, *The Way of the Jewish Mystics,* p. 184.

12. Hayim Vital, *Shaar Ruach HaKodesh (Gate of the Holy Spirit),* quoted in Kaplan, *Meditation and Kabbalah,* p. 226.

13. Elijah de Vidas, quoted in Besserman, *The Way of the Jewish Mystics,* p. 93.

14. Joseph Gikatilla, *Gates of Light (Sha'are Orah),* trans. Avi Weinstein (New York: HarperCollins Publishers, 1994), p. 37.

15. Moses ben Simeon of Burgos, *Perus Sem- ben M"B Otiyot,* quoted in Moshe Idel, *The Mystical Experience in Abraham Abulafia,* trans, Jonathan Chipman (Albany, N.Y.: State University of New York Press, 1988), p. 19.

16. Judah Albotini, *Sulam HaAliyah (Ladder of Ascent)* 9, quoted in Kaplan, *Meditation and Kabbalah,* p. 113.

17. Gikatilla, *Gates of Light,* p. 4.

18. See Idel, *The Mystical Experience in Abraham Abulafia;* and "Abraham Abulafia and the Doctrine of Prophetic Kabbalism," in Scholem, *Major Trends in Jewish Mysticism,* pp. 119–55 for more information on Abulafia.

19. *Sha'are Tzedeq,* quoted in Idel, *The Mystical Experience in Abraham Abulafia,* p. 79.

20. Isaac of Acco, *Ozar Hayyim,* quoted in Idel, *The Mystical Experience in Abraham Abulafia,* p. 81.

21. In Numbers 19, the LORD instructs Moses and Aaron that the ashes of the heifer (a heifer is a young cow) should be used as "a purification for sin." Anyone who had come into contact with a dead body had to be purified with these ashes before he was allowed to enter the sanctuary. Likewise, says Luria, those who wish to recite the divine names must be purified in this manner. However, the sacrifice of the heifer could be done only in the Temple at Jerusalem, which was destroyed in A.D. 70., and by the fifth century the remaining ashes from the heifer sacrifice had been used up. Thus, Vital says Luria taught him, "We are all defiled by the dead, and we do not have the ashes of the [Red] Heifer, which is the only means of removing this defilement. . . .We are therefore no longer permitted to make use of [that is, pronounce] these Holy Names" (Kaplan, *Meditation and Kabbalah,* p. 231).

22. Moses Luzzatto, *Derekh HaShem,* quoted in Kaplan, *Meditation and the Bible,* p. 86.

23. Kaplan, *Meditation and the Bible,* p. 78.

24. Vital, *Shaar Ruach HaKodesh (Gate of the Holy Spirit),* quoted in Kaplan, *Meditation and Kabbalah,* p. 230.

CHAPTER 9 *The Mystic Ascent*

Opening quotation: Joseph Gikatilla, *Gates of Light (Sha'are Orah)*.

1. Gen. 17:5; 32:28.

2. Gikatilla, *Gates of Light*, quoted in Kaplan, *Meditation and Kabbalah*, p. 128.

3. Luzzatto, *Derekh HaShem*, quoted in Kaplan, *Meditation and the Bible*, p. 85.

4. Gikatilla, *Gates of Light*, p. 14.

5. Ibid., p. 5.

6. Moshe Idel, "Historical Introduction," in Gikatilla, *Gates of Light*, pp. xxvii–xxviii.

7. Gikatilla, *Gates of Light*, quoted in Kaplan, *Meditation and Kabbalah*, p. 128.

8. Gikatilla, *Gates of Light*, p. 120.

9. Exod. 6:3.

10. Gen. 17:1.

11. Gikatilla, *Gates of Light*, p. 58.

12. Ibid., pp. 56, 65, 109.

13. I Sam. 17:45.

14. Gikatilla, *Gates of Light*, pp. 123, 141.

15. Ibid., p. 142.

16. Ibid.

17. In order to avoid pronouncing *YHVH*, the Jews wrote the vowels of *Adonai* underneath the word *YHVH*. Christian theologians of the Middle Ages mistakenly combined the vowels of *Adonai* with the consonants *YHVH* to create the hybrid Jehovah (YeHoVaH).

18. Gen. 4:26; 12:8.

19. Exod. 3:13–15.

20. Exod. 3:15 Jerusalem Bible.

21. Bernhard W. Anderson, *Understanding the Old Testament*, 3d ed. (Englewood Cliffs, N.J.: Prentice-Hall, 1975), p . 53.

22. Moses Maimonides, *The Guide of the Perplexed*, trans. Shlomo

Pines (Chicago: University of Chicago Press, 1963), 1:156.

23. Maimonides, *The Guide of the Perplexed,* trans. M. Friedländer, 2d ed., rev. (New York: Dover Publications, 1956), p. 92.

24. Maimonides, *The Guide of the Perplexed,* trans. Pines, 1:148.

25. Gikatilla, *Gates of Light,* quoted in Kaplan, *Meditation and Kabbalah,* p. 129.

26. Gikatilla, *Gates of Light,* p. 147.

27. Idel, *The Mystical Experience in Abraham Abulafia,* p. 33.

28. Elijah de Vidas, quoted in Besserman, *The Way of the Jewish Mystics,* pp. 91, 93.

29. Gen. 1:26.

30. Gikatilla, *Gates of Light,* p. 262.

31. Ibid., pp. 256–57.

32. Ibid., p. 270.

33. Ibid., pp. 274, 272.

34. Ibid., p. 276.

35. Ibid., pp. 311–12.

36. Saadia Gaon, cited by Aryeh Kaplan in *Sefer Yetzirah: The Book of Creation* (York Beach, Maine: Samuel Weiser, 1990), p. 15.

37. Maimonides, *The Guide of the Perplexed,* trans. Friedländer, p. 95.

38. *Yahu* is another short form of *YHVH.*

39. Zohar 2:165b, in Sperling, Simon, and Levertoff, *The Zohar* 4:71.

40. Schaya, *Universal Meaning of the Kabbalah,* p. 158.

41. Ps. 150:6.

42. Schaya, *Universal Meaning of the Kabbalah,* pp. 158, 159.

43. Gikatilla, *Gates of Light,* pp. 325, 331.

44. Ibid., p. 333.

45. Ibid., p. 334.

46. Ibid., p. 355.

47. Ibid., p. 353.

48. Ibid., p. 370; and *Gates of Light,* quoted in Kaplan, *Meditation and Kabbalah,* p. 136.

CHAPTER 10 *The Creative Power of Sound*

Opening quotation: Zohar 3:287b.

1. Zohar 3:294a–294b, quoted in Tishby, *The Wisdom of the Zohar* 3:952.

2. Kaplan, *Jewish Meditation,* pp. 56–57.

3. Job 22:27, 28; Isa. 45:11.

4. See Mark L. Prophet and Elizabeth Clare Prophet, *The Science of the Spoken Word* (1974; reprint. Livingston, Mont.: Summit University Press, 1991); and Elizabeth Clare Prophet, *The Creative Power of Sound: Affirmations to Create, Heal and Transform* (Corwin Springs, Mont.: Summit University Press, 1997).

5. For further reading and exercises to activate and clear the chakras, see Kuthumi and Djwal Kul, *The Human Aura: How to Activate and Energize Your Aura and Chakras* (Livingston, Mont.: Summit University Press, 1996).

6. See Zohar 1:169a, in Sperling, Simon, and Levertoff, *The Zohar,* 2:148.

7. Ps. 34:3.

8. Kaplan, *Meditation and Kabbalah,* pp. 165–66.

9. Pss. 57:9; 22:22, 28.

10. Ps. 42:2; Job 33:4; Job 22:25–28; Prov. 10:22, 25.

11. Ps. 19:14.

12. Pss. 80:7; 84:11, 12; 46:11; 145:2, 5; 98:1.

13. Pss. 148:1, 2; 90:17; Exod. 15:26.

14. Ps. 61:2, 3.

15. Pss. 41:1; 56:4; Gen. 15:1; Job 37:23; Ps. 101:1–3; Heb. 12:6.

16. Pss. 18:30; 32:10; 86:15; 122:6; Song of Sol. 2:4, 6.

17. Pss. 119:169; 49:3; 119:130; 147:5.

18. Pss. 118:14, 18, 19; 104:24.

19. Isa. 28:5; 62:3; Ps. 103:2–4.

20. Matt. *God and the Big Bang,* p. 73.

BIBLIOGRAPHY

Texts

Cordovero, Moses. *The Palm Tree of Deborah.* Translated by Louis Jacobs. New York: Sepher-Hermon Press, 1960.

Gikatilla, Joseph. *Gates of Light (Sha'are Orah).* Translated by Avi Weinstein. San Francisco: HarperCollins Publishers, 1994.

Kaplan, Aryeh, trans. *The Bahir.* 1979. Reprint. York Beach, Maine: Samuel Weiser, 1989.

————. *Sefer Yetzirah: The Book of Creation.* York Beach, Maine: Samuel Weiser, 1990.

Maimonides, Moses. *The Guide of the Perplexed.* 2 vols. Translated by Shlomo Pines. Chicago: University of Chicago Press, 1963.

————. *The Guide of the Perplexed.* Translated by M. Friedländer. 2d ed., rev. New York: Dover Publications, 1956.

Matt, Daniel Chanan, trans. *Zohar: The Book of Enlightenment.* Ramsey, N.J.: Paulist Press, 1983.

Scholem, Gershom, ed. *Zohar: The Book of Splendor.* 1949. Reprint. New York: Schocken Books, 1963.

Sperling, Harry, Maurice Simon, and Paul P. Levertoff, trans. *The Zohar.* 5 vols. London: Soncino Press, 1934.

Tishby, Isaiah, and Fischel Lachower, comps. *The Wisdom of the Zohar: An Anthology of Texts.* 3 vols. Translated by David Goldstein. 1989. Reprint. New York: Oxford University Press for the Littman Library of Jewish Civilization, 1991.

Westcott, W. Wynn. *Sepher Yetzirah: The Book of Formation.* 3d ed., rev. 1893. Reprint. New York: Samuel Weiser, 1980.

Commentaries

Ariel, David S. *The Mystic Quest: An Introduction to Jewish Mysticism.* Northvale, N.J.: Jason Aronson, 1988.

Besserman, Perle, comp. and ed. *The Way of the Jewish Mystics.* Boston: Shambhala Publications, 1994.

Biale, David. "Jewish Mysticism in the Sixteenth Century." In *An Introduction to the Medieval Mystics of Europe.* Edited by Paul E. Szarmach. Albany, N.Y.: State University of New York Press, 1984.

Donin, Hayim. *To Pray as a Jew: A Guide to the Prayerbook and the Synagogue Service.* New York: Basic Books, 1980.

Epstein, Perle. *Kabbalah: The Way of the Jewish Mystic.* Garden City, N.Y.: Doubleday and Company, 1978.

Fine, Lawrence. "The Contemplative Practice of Yihudim in Lurianic Kabbalah." In *Jewish Spirituality: From the Sixteenth-Century Revival to the Present.* Edited by Arthur Green. Vol. 14 of *World Spirituality: An Encyclopedic History of the Religious Quest.* New York: Crossroad Publishing Company, 1987.

Green, Arthur. "The Zohar: Jewish Mysticism in Medieval Spain." In *An Introduction to the Medieval Mystics of Europe.* Edited by Paul E. Szarmach. Albany, N.Y.: State University of New York Press, 1984.

Gruenwald, Ithamar. *Apocalyptic and Merkavah Mysticism.* Leiden: E. J. Brill, 1980.

Halevi, Z'ev ben Shimon. *An Introduction to the Cabala: Tree of Life.* New York: Samuel Weiser, 1972.

————. *Kabbalah: Tradition of Hidden Knowledge.* New York: Thames and Hudson, 1980.

————. *The Way of Kabbalah.* New York: Samuel Weiser, 1976.

Idel, Moshe. *Kabbalah: New Perspectives.* New Haven: Yale University Press, 1988.

————. *The Mystical Experience in Abraham Abulafia.* Translated by Jonathan Chipman. Albany, N.Y.: State University of New York Press, 1988.

————. *Studies in Ecstatic Kabbalah* (Albany, N.Y.: State University of New York Press, 1988).

Kaplan, Aryeh. *Innerspace: Introduction to Kabbalah, Meditation and Prophecy.* Edited by Abraham Sutton. Jerusalem: Moznaim Publishing, 1990.

————. *Jewish Meditation: A Practical Guide.* New York: Schocken Books, 1985.

————. *Meditation and Kabbalah.* 1982. Reprint. York Beach, Maine: Samuel Weiser, 1985.

————. *Meditation and the Bible.* 1978. Reprint. York Beach, Maine: Samuel Weiser, 1988.

Luzzatto, Moses C. *General Principles of the Kabbalah.* Translated by the Research Centre of Kabbalah. New York: Press of the Research Centre of Kabbalah, 1970.

Matt, Daniel C. "*Ayin:* The Concept of Nothingness in Jewish Mysticism." In *The Problem of Pure Consciousness.* Edited by Robert K. C. Forman. New York: Oxford University Press, 1990.

————. *The Essential Kabbalah: The Heart of Jewish Mysticism.* HarperSanFrancisco, 1995.

————. *God and the Big Bang: Discovering Harmony between Science and Spirituality.* Woodstock, Vt.: Jewish Lights Publishing, 1996.

Morray-Jones, C. R. A. "Paradise Revisited (2 Cor 12:1–12): The Jewish Mystical Background of Paul's Apostolate: Part 1: The Jewish Sources," and "Part 2: Paul's Heavenly Ascent and Its Significance." *Harvard Theological Review* 86:2 and 3 (1993).

Poncé, Charles. *Kabbalah: An Introduction and Illumination for the World Today.* 1973. Reprint. Wheaton, Ill.: Theosophical Publishing House with the assistance of the Kern Foundation, 1978.

Prophet, Elizabeth Clare, with Erin L. Prophet. *Reincarnation: The Missing Link in Christianity.* (Corwin Springs, Mont.: Summit University Press, 1997).

Prophet, Mark L., and Elizabeth Clare Prophet. *The Science of the Spoken Word.* 1974. Reprint. Livingston, Mont.: Summit University Press, 1991.

Schaya, Leo. *The Universal Meaning of the Kabbalah.* Translated by Nancy Pearson. 1971. Reprint. Baltimore, Md.: Penguin Books, 1973.

Scholem, Gershom G. *Jewish Gnosticism, Merkabah Mysticism, and TalmudicTradition.* 2d ed. New York: Jewish Theological Seminary of America, 1965.

―――. *Kabbalah.* 1974. Reprint. New York: New American Library, Meridian, 1978.

―――. *Major Trends in Jewish Mysticism.* 1954. Reprint. New York: Schocken Books, 1961.

―――. *The Messianic Idea in Judaism: And Other Essays on Jewish Spirituality.* New York: Schocken Books, 1971.

―――. *On the Kabbalah and Its Symbolism.* Translated by Ralph Manheim. New York: Schocken Books, 1969.

―――. *On the Mystical Shape of the Godhead: Basic Concepts in the Kabbalah.* Translated by Joachim Neugroschel and edited by Jonathan Chipman. New York: Schocken Books, 1991.

―――. *Origins of the Kabbalah.* Edited by R. J. Zwi Werblowsky and translated by Allan Arkush. Princeton, N.J.: Princeton University Press, 1987.

Sheinkin, David. *Path of the Kabbalah.* Edited by Edward Hoffman. New York: Paragon House, 1986.

Spencer, Sidney. *Mysticism in World Religion.* 1963. Reprint. Gloucester, Mass.: Peter Smith, 1971.

ACKNOWLEDGMENTS

Excerpts from "*Ayin:* The Concept of Nothingness in Jewish Mysticism," by Daniel C. Matt. From *The Problem of Pure Consciousness,* edited by Robert K. C. Forman. Copyright © 1996 by Robert K. C. Forman. Reprinted by permission of Oxford University Press, Inc.

Excerpts from *The Essential Kabbalah: The Heart of Jewish Mysticism,* by Daniel C. Matt. Copyright © 1995 by Daniel C. Matt. Reprinted by permission of HarperCollins Publishers.

Excerpts from *Gates of Light (Sha'are Orah),* by Joseph Gikatilla, translated by Avi Weinstein. Copyright © 1994 by Avi Weinstein. Reprinted with the kind permission of Avi Weinstein.

Excerpts from *Kabbalah,* by Gershom Scholem. Copyright © 1974 by Keter Publishing House Ltd. Reprinted by permission.

Excerpts from *Kabbalah: New Perspectives,* by Moshe Idel. Copyright © 1988 by Yale University. Reprinted by permission of Yale University Press.

Excerpts from *Kabbalah: Tradition of Hidden Knowledge,* by Z'ev ben Shimon Halevi. Copyright © 1979 by Warren Kenton. Reprinted by permission of Thames and Hudson.

Excerpts from *Meditation and the Bible,* by Aryeh Kaplan. Copyright © 1978 by Aryeh Kaplan. Reprinted by permission of Samuel Weiser (York Beach, ME).

Excerpts from *Meditation and Kabbalah,* by Aryeh Kaplan. Copyright © 1982 by Aryeh Kaplan. Reprinted by permission of Samuel Weiser (York Beach, ME).

Excerpts from *Mysticism in World Religion,* by Sidney Spencer. Copyright © 1963 by Sidney Spencer. Reprinted by permission of Peter Smith Publisher (Gloucester, MA).

Excerpts from *On the Kabbalah and Its Symbolism,* by Gershom G. Scholem. English translation copyright © 1965 by Schocken Books, Inc. Reprinted by permission of Schocken Books, distributed by Pantheon Books, a division of Random House, Inc.

Excerpts from *The Palm Tree of Deborah,* by Moses Cordovero, translated by Louis Jacobs. Copyright © 1960 by Louis Jacobs. Reprinted with the kind permission of Louis Jacobs.

Excerpts from *The Wisdom of the Zohar,* edited by Fishel Lachower and Isaiah Tishby, translated by David Goldstein. Copyright © 1989. Reprinted by permission of the Littman Library of Jewish Civilization.

Excerpts from *Zohar: The Book of Enlightenment,* translated by Daniel Chanan Matt. Copyright © 1983 by Daniel Chanan Matt. Reprinted by permission of Paulist Press.

Excerpts from "The Zohar: Jewish Mysticism in Medieval Spain," by Arthur Green. From *An Introduction to the Medieval Mystics of Europe,* edited by Paul Szarmach. Copyright © 1984 by State University of New York. Reprinted by permission of State University of New York Press.

PICTURE CREDITS

frontispiece *The Name of God from Bible in Sefardi Hand,* 1385, by permission of the British Library, London.

xii *The Whirlwind: Ezekiel's Vision of the Cherubim and the Eyed Wheels* by William Blake, courtesy of the Museum of Fine Arts, Boston, purchased 1890.

12 *Chinese Torah scroll from the seventeenth century,* courtesy of the Library of the Jewish Theological Seminary of America.

25 *Abraham and Melchizedek* by Nicholas de Verdun, enamel plaque from altarpiece, Klosterneuberg, Austria, 12th century, Erich Lessing/Art Resource, N.Y.

63 *The Water and Moon Kuan-yin Bodhisattva,* Chinese sculpture, 11th–12th century, Northern Sung (960–1127) or Liao (907–1125) Dynasty, wood with paint, 95"x65" (241.3x165.1 cm), the Nelson-Atkins Museum of Art, Kansas City, Missouri (Purchase: Nelson Trust) 34–10.

63 *The Madonna of the Meadow* by Raphael, Kunsthistorisches Museum, Vienna, Austria, Foto Marburg/Art Resource, N.Y.

76 *Tzimtzum* and the Emanation of the *Sefirot* (figure 10), based on a drawing by James Russell, reprinted by permission.

141 *Israel in Egypt* (portion) by Sir Edward J. Poynter, Guildhall Art Gallery, London.

156 *Jeremiah at the Fall of Jerusalem* by Eduard Bendemann, Foto Marburg/Art Resource, N.Y.

157 *The Sorrowing Jews in Exile* by Eduard Bendemann, Rheinische Bildarchiv, Cologne.

160 *The Blessing over the Candles* by Isidor Kaufmann, 19th century, courtesy of the Library of the Jewish Theological Seminary of America.

188 *David in the Temple* by Pieter Lastmann, Dutch, 1583–1633, Herzog Anton Ulrich-Museums Braunschweig, Fotonachweis: Museumsfoto B. P. Keiser.

191 *The Feast of the Rejoicing of the Law at the Synagogue in Leghorn, Italy,* by Solomon Alexander Hart, 1850, oil on canvas. Gift of Mr. and Mrs. Oscar Gruss. Jewish Museum/Art Resource, N.Y.

211 The Tetragrammaton arranged in the form of the Pythagorean tetractys, reprinted by permission of James Russell.

FOR MORE INFORMATION

Summit University Press books are available
at fine bookstores everywhere. Our books have been
translated into more than 20 languages.

If you would like a free catalog of
Summit University Press books and other products,
please contact Summit University Press,
PO Box 5000, Corwin Springs, MT 59030-5000 USA.
1-800-245-5445 or 406-848-9500
Fax 1-800-221-8307 or 406-848-9555
E-mail: info@summituniversitypress.com
www.summituniversitypress.com

ELIZABETH CLARE PROPHET is a world-renowned author. She has written such classics of spiritual literature as *Soul Mates and Twin Flames, The Lost Years of Jesus, Fallen Angels and the Origins of Evil, Reincarnation: The Missing Link in Christianity* and her Pocket Guides to Practical Spirituality series.

She has pioneered techniques in practical spirituality, including the creative power of sound for personal growth and world transformation. Since the 1960s, Elizabeth Clare Prophet has conducted seminars and workshops around the world on spirituality, personal growth and the mystical paths of the world's religions. She has been featured on NBC's *Ancient Prophecies* and A&E's *The Unexplained* and has talked about her work on *Donahue, Larry King Live, Nightline, Sonya Live* and *CNN & Company.*

PATRICIA R. SPADARO and MURRAY L. STEINMAN are also coauthors with Elizabeth Clare Prophet of the best-selling *Saint Germain's Prophecy for the New Millennium.* Patricia has also coauthored *Your Seven Energy Centers* and *The Art of Practical Spirituality.* She has been featured on radio talk shows in over 150 markets and has also produced a 13-week radio series on practical spirituality. Murray, the founder of Time Strategies Consulting, is a communications specialist, public speaker and professional astrologer. He has appeared on many television and radio programs, including *Oprah* and *Donahue.*